Natasha A. Kelly, Olive Vassell (eds.)
Mapping Black Europe

Public and Applied History | Volume 7

Editorial

Public History is an interdisciplinary endeavour connecting history and society, research and practice. The issues of dealing with one's past, of conveying and popularizing history are key to our time but so far there have not been enough editorial platforms to discuss these issues and establish Public History in the context of memory cultures and heritage. This field thus not only includes research on how to teach history, but also more generally the work of museums and archives, any popular or performative forms of conveying history and memory in the media, in tourism etc. The edited series **Public and Applied History** aims to provide a forum for innovative research on the many facets of this field to create a collaborative Public History project within and beyond the realms of academia.

Natasha A. Kelly (PhD) is a bestselling author and editor of eight books. She is also a curator, artist, filmmaker, theater director and professor. Her film "Milli's Awakening" debuted at the 10th Berlin Biennale in 2018. Natasha is the founding director of Germany's first Institute for Black German Arts and Culture.

Olive Vassell is a journalist and professor who founded and headed the pioneering Black European news site, Euromight.com. In 2022, Olive launched the BBrit Project which focuses on People of African Descent in the UK. She heads the Digital Media program at the University of the District of Columbia in Washington, D.C.

Natasha A. Kelly, Olive Vassell (eds.)
Mapping Black Europe
Monuments, Markers, Memories

[transcript]

Funding: An electronic version of this book is freely available, thanks to the support of libraries working with Knowledge Unlatched. KU is a collaborative initiative designed to make high quality books Open Access for the public good. The Open Access ISBN for this book is 978-3-8394-5413-8. More information about the initiative and links to the Open Access version can be found at www.knowledgeunlatched.com.

Bibliographic information published by the Deutsche Nationalbibliothek
The Deutsche Nationalbibliothek lists this publication in the Deutsche Nationalbibliografie; detailed bibliographic data are available in the Internet at http://dnb.d-nb.de

This work is licensed under the Creative Commons Attribution-NonCommercial-NoDerivatives 4.0 (BY-NC-ND) which means that the text may be used for non-commercial purposes, provided credit is given to the author.
To create an adaptation, translation, or derivative of the original work and for commercial use, further permission is required and can be obtained by contacting rights@transcript-publishing.com
Creative Commons license terms for re-use do not apply to any content (such as graphs, figures, photos, excerpts, etc.) not original to the Open Access publication and further permission may be required from the rights holder. The obligation to research and clear permission lies solely with the party re-using the material.

First published in 2023 by transcript Verlag, Bielefeld
© Natasha A. Kelly, Olive Vassell (eds.)

Cover layout: Maria Arndt, Bielefeld
Cover illustration: Dreading the Map Nr 6, 2021. Artist: Sonia E. Barrett.
Photography: Damion Griffiths
Printed by: Majuskel Medienproduktion GmbH, Wetzlar
https://doi.org/10.14361/9783839454138
Print-ISBN 978-3-8376-5413-4
PDF-ISBN 978-3-8394-5413-8
ISSN of series: 2700-8193
eISSN of series: 2703-1357

Contents

Black Europe
Contesting, Conceptualizing, and Organizing
Natasha A. Kelly and Olive Vassell 7

Chapter 1
Black Berlin
Natasha A. Kelly 25

Chapter 2
Black Brussels
Sibo Rugwiza Kanobana 49

Chapter 3
Black London
Olive Vassell 69

Chapter 4
Black Luxembourg
Bernardino Tavares and Aleida Vieira 93

Chapter 5
Black Oslo
Michelle A. Tisdel 115

Chapter 6
Black Paris
Epée Hervé Dingong and Olive Vassell 137

Chapter 7
Black Rome
Kwanza Musi Dos Santos 159

Chapter 8
Black Warsaw
James Omolo and Natasha A. Kelly 179

Authors 195

Black Europe
Contesting, Conceptualizing, and Organizing

Natasha A. Kelly and Olive Vassell

Unless you were hiding in a cave or time-traveling back to the age of the Neanderthal, you would have witnessed the global impact of the Black Lives Matter (BLM) movement that shifted from the internet to the streets in the summer of 2020. Unlike most of the numerous deaths caused by the police, the case of African American George Floyd attracted attention and led to huge protests around the world. Stuck at home during the pandemic, we unwillingly became witnesses to the murder of this Black man, who was suffocated by a white police officer kneeling on his neck for more than nine minutes[1]. Continuously crying "I can't breathe" and calling for his mother, his last words were ignored by the perpetrator while being filmed via mobile phone and uploaded to the internet by African American teenager Darnella Frazier.[2]

As becomes clear in the contributions to this anthology, the BLM outcry did not pass over Europe without significant impact. Within a few days, demonstrators gathered simultaneously in scores of cities to pay tribute to Floyd. His public execution had retraumatized Black Europeans, igniting their experiences with racism and recalling violent memories of the many other victims of racism and police brutality in their own countries, as well as in the USA. Highlighting the rage against atrocities caused by systemic

---

1 George Floyd: What happened in the final moments of his life, July 16 2020 (https://www.bbc.com/news/world-us-canada-52861726)
2 Darnella Frazier (born 2003) was awarded a special journalism award by the Pulitzer Prize board for the courage she showed in recording the murder of George Floyd while walking with her cousin in Minneapolis on May 25, 2020. Her film spurred protests for racial justice around the world and was used as evidence in the trial that convicted police officer Derek Chauvin. (https://www.bbc.com/news/world-us-canada-57449229)

racism literally hiding in plain sight, statues of slave traders, colonizers, and white supremacists were torn down, raising questions of their validity in European societies today. With the letters BLM spray-painted on monuments and statues throughout Europe, marking them as colonial and unjust, Black Lives Matter called out white supremacy, ongoing coloniality, and racial injustice.

But BLM did not begin in 2020. The social justice movement was initially formed in response to the acquittal of former police officer George Zimmerman after killing the innocent Black teenager Trayvon Martin in the United States in 2012. It was set aflame by a Facebook post by Alicia Garza titled "A Love Letter to Black People," (Cobb 2016) in which she expressed her rage at the verdict and at the same time her love for the Black community, stating that we need to fight for a world where Black lives matter. Shortly after, fellow community organizer Patrisse Cullors established the hashtag #BlackLivesMatter, and Ayọ Tometi formerly known as Opal Tometi, created the website and social media platform that soon connected people across the country. However, the movement only gained international attention a year later with the police killings of two other Black men – Michael Brown and Eric Garner, whose last words, like George Floyd's, were "I can't breathe." At virtual speed, this sentence became a protest cry, chanted in choirs and written on banners during numerous demonstrations worldwide.

The BLM motto reached the German capital, for example, in 2014, when demonstrators used the hashtag for the first time to highlight the ongoing injustices against Black people. However, the first official Black Lives Matter (BLM) protest took place in Berlin in July 2016. Nearly nine years earlier demonstrations over the brutal death of Oury Jalloh, an asylum seeker from Sierra Leone who was burned in a police cell in the East German city of Dessau, did not attract as much public attention, despite the cruelty of the case. Participation in these early demonstrations against police brutality and systemic racism was not large enough for the national press and media to report on them. The public merely perceived them as being among the many demonstrations that take place in Berlin daily. It is important to mention that, to this day, justice has not been served in the case of Jalloh; this is why annual demonstrations continue to take place in Dessau on the anniversary of his murder, January 7.

More media attention was gained in 2016 after Black Lives Matter UK led a "national shutdown" in which activists in Birmingham, Manchester, London, and Nottingham simultaneously blocked roads, to raise awareness about how racism and climate change are interconnected. The protest also marked the fifth anniversary of the police shooting of 29-year-old father of six Mark Duggan, as well as highlighted deaths of Black people in police custody.[3]

In Paris, Adama Traoré, a Black Frenchman of Malian descent, died in custody after being apprehended and restrained by police in 2016. His death triggered riots and protests against police brutality in France, making him a major symbol for anti-police activism. A few days after the murder of Floyd, French authorities released a final report clearing the three officers involved in Traoré's death. This verdict set off renewed protests in Paris that connected both the Traoré and Floyd cases, which some perceived as having taken place in similar circumstances.

The magnitude of these events gave reason to open each of the following chapters in this anthology with a reflection on the influence of BLM in eight different European cities where the movement has brought to the fore the need to stress the Black populations' challenges and to recognize our contributions to the social, economic, and cultural domains of Black life in Europe today. We define and speak of Black people as People of African Descent (PAD) or African immigrants, not as "migrants." The latter is not a self-identification but an ascription by the white majority societies who uphold the power structures and constitute Europe as white by using this term.

It actually took until 2020 for a political momentum to unfold in which debates on structural racism were prioritized, despite numerous studies such as Being Black in the EU (BBE), conducted by the European Union Agency for Fundamental Rights (FRA) in 2018, which revealed that many PAD regularly experience fundamental rights violations (racial discrimination, racist hate crimes, racial profiling),[4] as well as the work done by the European Network Against Racism (ENAR), a pan-European agency combining racial equality

---

[3] Black Lives Matter: how the UK movement struggled to be heard in the 2010s, June 7, 2021 (https://theconversation.com/black-lives-matter-how-the-uk-movement-struggled-to-be-heard-in-the-2010s-161763)

[4] Being Black in the EU, Equality, non-discrimination and racism Legal migration and integration Racial and ethnic origin, November 28, 2018 (https://fra.europa.eu/en/publication/2018/being-black-eu)

advocacy with antiracist network building across Europe.⁵ For the first time in European history, issues of structural racism were freed of their taboo and light was shed on colonialism and enslavement from a Black European perspective. As a reaction to BLM, the European Commission implemented an antiracism action plan for 2020–25 and appointed the first Black female Commission coordinator for antiracism, Michaela Moua, a Finnish national of African origin.

Amplifying unheard Blacktivist voices from Europe, the timing of this anthology unintentionally coincides with the political BLM momentum. Ranging from Berlin to Brussels, from London to Luxembourg, Oslo, Paris, Rome, and Warsaw – well-known former colonial metropoles as well as cities rarely referenced in the decolonial debate – each chapter offers a counter-narrative to the violent memories of European histories. Allowing for a recollection from a Black perspective, the book's contributors are all Europeans of African descent, whether they were born in the countries they are writing about or have lived in them for a significant portion of their lives. Moreover, the BLM movement has increasingly impelled Black individuals themselves to critically share their own perception of the roles and places they occupy in the societies in which they live.

However, the initial idea to publish this book and create a Black-centered European network grew out of cooperation that began in 2010 between the editors Natasha A. Kelly and Olive Vassell for the latter's Black European online news site euromight.⁶ Out of this arose an awareness that there are few to no Black European voices that narrate Black European histories or highlight their routes to and roots in the continent, nor are there academic networks for Black Europeans in the context of which these histories could be researched and told. This led to the foundation of the Black European Academic Network (BEAN)⁷ long before BLM had gained prominence in Europe. Over the years, we incorporated other Black European contexts alongside London and Berlin and fostered opportunities for knowledge exchange and support by extending the histories that relate to Black lives, making the Black presence in other European cities visible, creating cohesion, and bridging divides.

---

5 Website of ENAR: https://www.enar-eu.org/about/
6 www.euromight.com
7 www.beaneu.com

The outcome of this collaboration is this groundbreaking publication that brings together the foundational work of the last decade. The project is intended to critique, inspire, and pave the way for a better understanding of Europe from a Black intellectual perspective and to foster opportunities for exchange between each of these communities, as well as between communities of varying ethnicities and between the communities and their dominant societies. In this sense, *Mapping Black Europe: Monument, Markers, Memories* is a tool of empowerment. In tracing Blackness in eight major European cities, it helps to connect, preserve, and curate the "unsung and unseen" contributions of Black Europeans. The goal is to take ownership of our social realities, to address issues of intolerance and discrimination, and to reveal stories of success and triumph.

Mapping as an Act of Contestation

The Black European experience is inextricably linked to the concept of Europe itself, which joined forces over 130 years ago when German chancellor Otto von Bismarck invited the European leaders, the rulers of the Ottoman Empire, and representatives from the USA to Berlin in 1884–5 to divide up Africa among themselves. Africans were not present, and Black European history was written in our absence. There are numerous traces of this history in the landscapes of European cities, whether they are locations marking the dominant culture's victimization of PAD, as in Berlin's and Rome's African Quarters, or whether Black people have claimed spaces themselves, as in the case of London's Windrush Square.

Through meticulous primary and secondary research, the authors of this anthology document the stories of these cities' realized or attempted involvement in colonization and enslavement and how these efforts enriched their coffers, even while they impoverished those they exploited. It is clear that European countries profited from colonization, whether they had their own colonies or not. This analysis reveals how the wealth garnered from colonialism is often hidden in plain sight, reflected in buildings, monuments, and other structures, as well as in the financial power of these societies as a whole.

But while this book catalogs some examples of Europe's horrendous acts, its purpose is to highlight the contributions of PAD to these cities. Marking Black contribution is fundamental to creating a society that reflects all its members. We, the editors, believe that the way in which a country celebrates its Black population and their experiences, which monuments are erected, and which organizations are funded indicate how questions of structural racism are dealt with, which political measures are in place, and which societal challenges are faced. As the Luxembourgish historian Fabio Spirinelli puts it, when discussing one kind of monument,

> statues are more than crafted stone or metal. They convey meanings, they carry symbols, they are meant to elicit feelings. They are erected not only for what they depict as such ... [they] honour and commemorate historic figures, deemed important by some people at the time [they] were erected – but not by all. (Spirinelli 2022)

This book makes history: for the first time, Black Europeans are collectively marking how our contributions to social and cultural life are reflected in sites of public memory, from monuments and statues to street names and city plaques, that can all be considered political representations of Black people in Europe. Looking at what our communities in Europe have in common and where they diverge allows us to reach beyond national borders and rewrite European history from a Black perspective. This is especially interesting when it comes to cultural phenomena such as language; this has been a challenge for this publication, as our authors have written in English, which is sometimes their second or even third language. Nonetheless, the editors and authors all have lived experiences in European cities, whose culture of remembrance they interrogate.

Thus, each chapter focuses on an individual city and highlights a particular experience, but, more importantly, allows for comparison and for a collective narrative to be formed across Europe. The writing reflects on current debates concerning contentious historical issues, judicial acts, or government programs that aim to strengthen specific historical interpretations and reshape others. At the same time, each chapter offers answers to the following questions: What is the state of Black memory in each European city? Which Black philosophical movements led to the rewriting of history? How is community activism involved? The answers to these questions are important milestones in the development of Black Europe and have a direct effect on the lives of PAD who have been permanent residents for centuries.

Spanning from the first wave of colonialism in the 15th century through the period of the Enlightenment to the second wave of colonialism in the 19th century, a sense of Europeanness was carried out into the world. First and foremost, Europe was associated with whiteness, becoming the center of the world and protected by the invisible membrane of its outer borders. This ideology led to the structuring of the globe from a Eurocentric perspective, a perspective inscribed in maps such as those used to discover what was already there. Maps told single stories from the perspective of the white map makers who reduced the sizes and proportions of the other continents they depicted to support their idea of European superiority. The result is a sense of humanity that has been denied to Black peoples in Europe and beyond.

Our decision to "map" Black Europe is based on the belief that mapping is an act of contestation. As author and academic Katherine McKittrick writes, "Black imaginations and mappings are evidence of the struggle over social space" (McKittrick 2006: 9). And, as the contributors of *Mapping Crisis: Participation, Datafication and Humanitarianism in the Age of Digital Mapping* state, rather than revealing the world, maps help to create it (Specht 2020). Furthermore, the practice

> generates questions that might otherwise go unasked, it reveals historical relations that might otherwise go unnoticed, and it undermines, or substantiates, stories upon which we build our own versions of the past. (White 2010)

The cover of our book is a detail of an image taken from a preliminary work that informed the installation titled *"Dreading the Map"* by Sonia E. Barrett in March 2021. The "map-lective," a group of Black and Brown women, created the work in the Map Room at the Royal Geographical Society (RGS) in London, a room celebrating key European mapmakers. They shredded and braided archival maps of Europe, Africa and the Caribbean to create a new map using community practices of care. This symbolic act of weaving Black culture into the fabric of Europe allowed for recognition of Black presence, counteracting Eurocentric domination. With its installation at the RGS, the artist collective took ownership of a location central to British imperialisation and colonisation, just like many of the interventions described in this book.[8]

---

8 www.map-lective.com

As a methodology, mapping allows individuals or groups to interpret objects or representations of objects from their own perspectives, thus validating their participants' own categorizations and understandings of an issue, person, or place. In Black London, for example, Black histories were readily available from both individual and organizational sources, while in Black Warsaw, key demographic information was almost non-existent. In this case, the Black Polish contributors drew on primary research that had been done by James Omolo for his 2017 book (*Strangers at the Gate: Black Poland*).

Methods of accessing information in each country differed according to the work that had already been done by the respective communities. This reflected their differing sizes, which ranged in population from the millions to less than ten thousand. Some numbers are approximate, as not every country counts its Black residents or publishes numbers that would allow for these figures to be readily accessed. In these cases, community organizations and members are doing the work themselves: for example, in France, the Representative Council of Black Associations (Conseil Representatif des Associations Noires or CRAN) has been at the forefront of this work, while in Germany, the Black community organization Each One Teach One and Citizens for Europe launched the "Afrozensus" online poll in 2020. According to its homepage, the census gives a comprehensive picture of how Black Germans assess their lives and of the expectations they have of society and politics today.[9]

Our focus on capital cities was informed, first, by the recognition that colonial history would take place in these large centers rather than in smaller towns; and, second, by the fact that cities with colonial heritage are often the locations of large Black populations. The city of Liverpool in the north of the UK, for example, is home to one of the oldest continuous Black communities in Europe, dating back over 300 years to when early Black residents came as sailors, soldiers, and enslaved persons. Liverpool was also one of the sites of Britain's most violent periods of racial upheaval in the 20th century. In 1919, stoked by social, economic, and political anxieties, white union workers and demobilized white servicemen attacked Black locals, killing a young Black man (Hunter 2018). The city is peppered with reminders of its enslavement history, with many streets and meeting places honoring prominent enslav-

---

9 https://afrozensus.de/

ers. These include Cunliffe Street, which is named after Foster Cunliffe, one of a number of Liverpool mayors who were involved in enslavement in the early 18th century (Tyrrell 2020). Following the BLM demonstrations, the city announced that it would install plaques on statues, buildings, monuments, and streets with connections to this period of domination and exploitation. A list of the first 20 was revealed in August 2020. Nonetheless, we do not want to ignore other areas, such as the small town of Bascharage on Luxembourg's border with Belgium, where these two countries' colonial alliance is visible in the statue of Nicolas Cito, which is described in Chapter 4.

Meanwhile, in Germany, several cities alongside its capital Berlin have been significantly marked by their involvement in colonialism. The north German cities of Hamburg and Bremen, for example, have major ports where colonial goods and African peoples were brought to the country. In the entire neighborhood around the port, buildings directly or indirectly financed by the triangular trade stand proud and are carefully maintained. Additionally, there is a sculpture in the small East German town of Halle that depicts a nearly naked African that is supposed to acknowledge the first Black professor at a German university and a philosopher of the Enlightenment, Anton Wilhelm Amo. The statue was not initially built for him but was re-commemorated to him in 1957 during East German ceremonies for the independence of Ghana, the country of his birth from where he was stolen. This depiction might be considered another commonality in white commemorations of Black Europeans who are rendered African and not European, although they were born and/or raised and spent the majority of their lives in Europe. Several Black communities have been criticizing this for decades. Looking back at Anton Wilhelm Amo, who wrote his dissertation titled "On the Rights of Blacks in Europe" as early as 1729, the quest for equal rights is not a new phenomenon but a continuing struggle.

Self-identification through Academic Activism

Using the hashtag #blacklivesmatter, a political momentum was sparked by communication technology. Like maps, it has developed rapidly over the years, becoming a tool to fight against white supremacy. Thanks to mobile cameras we were not only able to record the killing of George Floyd and enable it to go viral, but, nearly 30 years earlier in 1991, we also recorded the brutal police violence against African American Rodney King, the first video of its kind ever to be widely disseminated. It is not clear if the two cases would have attracted public as well as community attention and would have become global news if this had not been the case. Yet we would like to highlight that technology not only played a crucial role in the liberation of Black people but was also a tool in our damnation.

The latter can be explained by race, which itself became a form of technology, a weapon to suppress us (Coleman 2009). Over centuries, technology brought forth biological discourses that legitimized racism and inscribed it on several levels of society, especially in academia and science. Inventions included, for example, measuring tools for skulls and other body parts, while experiments were conducted to justify "medical apartheid" (Washington 2008). Moving away from this biologically determined understanding of race, the Black sociologist, journalist, educator, and activist W. E. B. Du Bois, among other African American academics, redefined race as a social category. With the question "How does it feel to be the problem?," which he posed in his 1903 seminal work *The Souls of Black Folk*, he showed that a biological understanding of race was relevant only to the extent that it had influenced the social realities of Black people and had affected our everyday lives and experiences worldwide. Based on this understanding, a racial turn took place in the USA at the dawn of the 20th century, which later led to social movements, including the institutionalization of Black knowledge production in the USA (Kelly 2016).

In Europe, however, instead of understanding race as a social category and implementing laws that move away from seeing race as biological, countries are leaning toward erasing race from their constitutions, as France did in 2018[10] or replacing it, as Germany continues to discuss, a debate that started long before the summer of 2020.[11] But although racism is politically and socially unacceptable according to both European and national laws, its existence cannot be denied. The events of the BLM movement in the summer of 2020 proved this, providing a sort of "wake-up call" and a sudden turning point, as mentioned above. Since then, it has become even more

---

10 'Race' out, gender equality in as France updates constitution, June 28, 2018 (https://www.france24.com/en/20180628-race-out-gender-equality-france-updates-constitution)

11 Experten mehrheitlich für Ersetzung des „Rasse"-Begriffs im Grundgesetz, June 21, 2021 (https://www.bundestag.de/dokumente/textarchiv/2021/kw25-pa-recht-rasse-847538)

important to rewrite European history from a Black perspective. For example, telling colonial history from the perspective of the colonized, not the colonizers, allows us to understand that, although the colonial governing era is over, colonialism still exists in knowledge and representation systems today. This paradigm shift is referred to as a postcolonial turn; it highlights what decolonial thinkers call "ongoing coloniality" (Maldonado-Torres 2007) that addresses the persistence and after-effects of colonial rule. By doing so, it offers an alternative perspective on the world and continues to question existing colonial power relations, in Europe, South America, and Africa alike.

W. E. B. Du Bois had already used the term "semi-colonialism" (Du Bois 1903) to make clear that all European countries profited from the capitalist system, whether they had colonies or not, as in the cases of Norway, Poland, and Luxembourg portrayed in this volume. Colonization was a pan-European project, and thus all European countries benefited from the suppression of Africa and her people. The overall goal was to stabilize the European economy by any means necessary and to control world trade and trading routes to the advantage of only a few. Thus, colonial influence varied from country to country, with Great Britain being the world's largest colonizer at its height in 1922, covering around a quarter of Earth's land surface and ruling over 458 million people.

However, it is also important to note that the concept of colonization is not only used in a European context in reference to the subjugation of Africa. Although Poland was "semi-colonial," as mentioned above, the East European country often refers to having been colonized by Russia, which did not target overseas areas but primarily focused on continental expansion into adjacent areas such as North and Central Asia. Furthermore, in the Norwegian context, the colonization of the traditional Sámi homeland must also be taken into consideration. There is ample scholarship and archival evidence to nuance and even refute claims of Norwegian colonial neutrality, as shown in Chapter 5.

Drawing on the early work of Pan-Africanists based in London, as we will see in Chapter 3, Du Bois was also influential in spreading ideas throughout Europe that are associated with concepts such as Afrocentricity or the Black Atlantic, all of which locate Africans and their descendants at the center of a history that was once denied to them by Europeans. After World War One, Black people came together to form a new intellectual movement that brought forth new forms of self-identification and led to the rise of Back

Internationalism and the Négritude movement, concepts that began with the Nardal sisters and other Black European women in Paris.

Still, Black European thought reaches farther back than the 20th century. Few people know that Blacks have been in Europe since Roman times (Fryer 1984), sometimes in significant numbers. In the 16th century, the Black Spanish university professor Juan Latino published works in numerous languages and became a professor of Latin and grammar at the University of Granada (PÄZ 2017), while scholars such as the Black German philosopher of the Enlightenment Anton Wilhelm Amo, mentioned above, had already produced Black knowledge in the early 18th century. Having the privilege to learn to read and write in five languages and later attend university, Amo became the first Black German professor to question white supremacy and fight for the rights of Black people in Europe. These contributions to Black knowledge production show that there has been a long tradition of academic activism in Europe for centuries.

In capitalizing Black, which is a linguistic act of sociopolitical resistance against white supremacy, the ongoing struggle is made visible. This self-identification reaches beyond the color black and farther than skin color itself. Instead, it is based on the understanding of race as a social category and, in this sense, refers to the racialized histories that are inscribed on the surface of our skin, making our bodies a "discourse terrain" (hooks 1994) for European history. Spelling white with a lowercase "w" reflects that it is not a self-identification but a category of analysis created by Black scholars to make the white European norm visible (Kelly 2016).

In this vein, the Black authors of this collection, be they Africans or their descendants, tell their individual narratives both in the context of national history and collectively as the Blackprint of Europe, which is associated with Black identities and gave reason to map our presence. Just as European countries are different (languages, cultures, etc.) while sharing a common history (colonization, enslavement, imperialism), Black Europeans are not a homogeneous group and therefore have different understandings of Blackness that are influenced by intersecting power structures constituted through nation, race, class, ability, religion, gender, and many other categories. Subject to Europe's global influence, they range from Africans to PAD from the Americas, the Caribbean, and Asia, as well as their offspring, who can be of single or mixed heritage. In line with this attestation, compositions such as Afro-German, Afro-Italian and so on are used. However, this is not a written rule for all countries, but is slowly becoming more and more common. But, as African American historian Allison Blakely observes, what Black communities in Europe – or Afro-Europe – share is an experience of routinely suffering personal indignities and adverse discrimination (Hines, Keaton, and Small 2009: 3).

Apart from a few institutions, Black Studies have not yet been fully institutionalized in Europe. In contrast to Eurocentricity, however, in producing knowledge from a Black perspective, it is not only academic works that are important but also the contributions of activists, artists, journalists, and authors who help shape Black European identities. More importantly, Black organizations are doing the work themselves to educate their communities. This is reflected in London with the beginnings of the Black Cultural Archives, where the gathering of material began after a racist arson attack that killed 13 Black teenagers, and in Berlin, where the young Black German Vera Heyer started a Black book collection that was continued after her sudden death and today is the basis of a community library that consists of around 7,000 pieces. Similar work is also being done in other cities not included in this book, such as the Black Archives in Amsterdam and numerous Black libraries in smaller German cities – these include the "Fasiathek," named after Fasia Jansen in Hamburg, and a library in Cologne dedicated to Theodor Wonja Michael, both of whom were prominent Black German activists and survivors of the Maafa (the Black Holocaust). The common goal is to create knowledge hubs where Black communities can access and learn our histories.

Community Organizing and Support

The Black communities highlighted in this book not only vary in size but also in the places where they are located within each of the capitals. Some are spread across a city, while others have increasingly been forced by gentrification to the periphery. London's Brixton and Paris's Chateau Rouge, for example, were once neighborhoods that PAD called home and that provided physical and emotional security, often in the face of hostile surroundings. Today, they are high-priced centers that no longer primarily house Black residents but still function as business hubs and sites of remembrance for the Black presence. The authors in this collection focus on some of the most prominent examples.

Black Berlin (Chapter 1) by Natasha A. Kelly reveals an active agenda of making Black contributions to society visible, despite the city's relatively small Black population. Significant action has centered around renaming streets and creating urban inscriptions as visual and linguistic devices, such as the May-Ayim-Ufer, dedicated to Afro-German poet May Ayim. These play a crucial role in social action and have the effect of social change. In Black Brussels (Chapter 2), Sibo R. Kanobana documents community organizations with strong Afro-Belgian affiliations who championed the renaming of a square in honor of Patrice Lumumba; this has become a place of Black experience near the Matonge neighborhood – an important area for the city's African community.

Meanwhile, Black London (Chapter 3), as noted by Olive Vassell, has seen an increasing number of memorials to PAD in recent years. A monument honoring African and Caribbean troops who fought for Britain in World Wars One and Two was unveiled in 2017. Both Black Luxembourg (Chapter 4), described by Bernardino Tavares and Aleida Vieira, and Black Oslo (Chapter 5), which is discussed by Michelle A. Tisdel, are characterized as capitals of nations that enjoyed "colonization without colonies" (Lüthi, Falkb and Purtschert 2016). Both cities contain buildings associated with colonial involvement. While in Luxembourg, no recognition of its Black population has been inscribed into the city landscape, the lived experiences of Black residents in the Norwegian capital have been marked, even if for tragic reasons: for example, a bust commemorates teenager Benjamin Hermansen, who was murdered by neo-Nazis in 2001.

Though well known as a place of respite for African Americans such as Josephine Baker and later James Baldwin, it is the contribution of Black French residents that is documented in Black Paris (Chapter 6), co-authored by Epée Hervé Dingong and Olive Vassell. Spurred by the efforts of a host of community organizations, a long history of activism dating back centuries is currently being marked. This includes the first statue of a Black woman, Solitude, an 18th-century heroine who won her freedom after the French Revolution. Chapter 7, by Kwanza Musi Dos Santos, looks at Black Rome through the lens of Italy's unsuccessful attempt to suppress Ethiopia, which was one of two African countries that was not colonized by Europe. The traces of that fiercely fought resistance are carved into Rome's landscape and represented by monuments such as the *Stele di Axum* (Axum obelisk), which was stolen from Ethiopia and brought to Rome by Benito Mussolini in 1937, during the Italian occupation of the East African nation.

Our final chapter, on Black Warsaw, is co-authored by James Omolo and Natasha A. Kelly and focuses on the history of Black Poles. One rarely thinks of Black people when considering Eastern Europe, which has a smaller Black population than other European countries. Black Poles had not been considered prominent heroes of national history until the summer of 2020, when Polish and international media picked up and covered the stories of Józef Sam Sandi and August Agboola "Ali" Browne, two Africans who played significant roles in the Warsaw Uprising. However, with racist and homophobic attacks openly happening in Poland, especially during Russia's invasion of Ukraine, which is taking place during the writing of this book, it is even more important to take a closer look at how Black European communities operate. Guided by small organizations, some of them newly established, their importance cannot be underestimated. Frequently functioning as lifelines and supporting a host of needs – from immigration issues and cultural connectivity to food and shelter – these organizations also often serve as the genesis of remembrance of Black European histories. They employ diverse tools to make their voices heard, often using strategies such as unmasking colonial continuities, like Luxembourg's Lëtz Rise Up and Richtung22's inventory of colonial buildings and sites.

When it comes to unearthing Black history, information lies between the gaps. Thus, we are dealing with a form of nothingness, the feeling of being in Europe but not of it. The work Black organizations have done and are doing is bridging these divides, discovering stories that in many cases have been either hidden or only partially revealed. Therefore, much information is sourced in the private sphere and the organizations are arranged in diverse ways, frequently centered on the country of origin, such as Warsaw's Foundation for Somalia, an active force in cultural and development work, and Rome's Association of Cameroonians.

Some have memberships that are overwhelmingly PAD, such as Brussels' Groupement des Femmes Africaines Inspirantes et Actives, while in others PAD form alliances with the white majority population, as in the Italian organization Rete Restiamo Umani, which changed a street name to *Via George Floyd and Bilal Ben Messaud* during the BLM protests. Many others wear multiple hats, focusing on intersectionality; these include the antiracist association QuestaèRoma (This is Rome). In London, it was a group of primarily Jamaican female medical professionals who first pushed for the contribution of famed nurse Mary Seacole to be recognized. Decades later, that effort would result in a pioneering statue in her honor, as shown in Chapter 3. In Paris, Blacktivists are presently championing the awarding of a plaque for Paulette, one of the Nardal sisters, to be placed in the Panthéon, an honor bestowed on the country's most revered citizens.

It must be said that Black communities have been challenging dominant societies for centuries, fighting social and political norms that seldom recognize them as citizens but as foreigners who are not here to stay. However, we see the strength of Black communities in Europe coming together to push Europe to fulfill its political, social, cultural, and historical responsibilities. Black Europeans are key to the present and future construction of a strong, diverse, and united Europe. In the frame of the International Decade for People of African Descent (2015–24), proclaimed by UN General Assembly Resolution 68/237, *Mapping Black Europe: Monuments, Markers, Memories*, provides an effective platform for the implementation of activities in the spirit of recognition, justice, and development.

With this publication we are bringing the voices of Black European academics, activists, and journalists together and creating a platform for connected research and study. By closing the knowledge gap we seek to provide readers with the capacities and skills needed to apply decolonial knowledge to a range of strategies for advancing community self-representation, intersectional justice, and human rights. These commitments are based on the understanding that the perspectives and lives of people throughout Black Europe are entangled in complex intersecting power relations, structures, and processes. It is within this context that we are proposing *Mapping Black Europe: Monuments, Markers, Memories* as a way to engage audiences around the importance of Black European narratives, and to lead in providing a systematic way of studying Black identities in Europe, including Black histories, Black cultures, and the mutual effects these have within society.

June 2022
Natasha A. Kelly and Olive Vassell

References

Cobb, Jelani (2016) *The Matter of Black Lives. A new kind of movement found its moment. What will its future be?*, The New Yorker; March 6, 2016 (https://www.newyorker.com/magazine/2016/03/14/where-is-black-lives-matter-headed)

Coleman, Beth (2009) "Race as Technology," *Camera Obscura*, 24 (1 (70)): 177–207, https://doi.org/10.1215/02705346-2008-018

Du Bois, W. E. B. (1903) *The Souls of Black Folk*. New York.

Fryer, Peter (1984) *Staying Power: The History of Black People in Britain*. London: Pluto.

Hines, Darlene, Trica Keaton, and Stephen Small (eds.) (2009) *Black Europe and the African Diaspora*. Urbana and Chicago: University of Illinois Press.

hooks, bell (1994) *Black Looks: Popkultur, Medien, Rassismus*. Berlin: Orlanda Verlag.

Hunter, Virgillio (2018) Britain's 1919 Race Riots, Black Past, November 28, 2018 (https://www.blackpast.org/global-african-history/events-global-african-history/britain-s-1919-race-riots/)

Kelly, Natasha A. (2016) *Afrokultur: Der Raum zwischen gestern und morgen*. Münster: Unrast Verlag.

Lüthi, Barbara, Francesca Falkb, and Patricia Purtschert (2016) "Colonialism without Colonies: Examining Blank Spaces in Colonial Studies," *National Identities*, 18 (1): 1–9, http://dx.doi.org/10.1080/14608944.2016.1107178

Maldonado-Torres, Nelson (2007) "On the Coloniality of Being," *Cultural Studies*, 21 (2–3): 240–70, https://doi.org/10.1080/09502380601162548

McKittrick, Katherine (2006) *Demonic Grounds: Black Women and the Cartographies of Struggle*. Minneapolis: University of Minnesota Press.

PÄZ (Pädagogisches Zentrum Aachen) (2017) *Legenden, die uns verborgen bleiben. Schwarzes Europa. Schwarze Jugendliche auf den Spuren ihrer Geschichte* [Legends who Remain Hidden from Us. Black Europe. Black Youths on the Traces of Their History]. Münster: edition assemblage.

Specht, Doug (ed.) (2020) *Mapping Crisis: Participation, Datafication and Humanitarianism in the Age of Digital Mapping*. London: University of London Press, Institute of Commonwealth Studies, https://www.jstor.org/stable/j.ctv14rms6g.9?seq=2

Spirinelli, Fabio (2022) *On the political uses of the past in Luxembourg*, C2DH, September 19, 2022 (https://www.c2dh.uni.lu/thinkering/political-uses-past-luxembourg)

Tyrrell, Nick (2020) Liverpool's streets that are named after slave traders, June 10, 2020 (https://www.liverpoolecho.co.uk/news/liverpool-news/nine-road-names-expose-liverpools-17590426)

Washington, Harriet A. (2008) *Medical Apartheid: The Dark History of Medical Experimentation on Black Americans from Colonial Times to the Present.* New York: Harlem Moon

White, Richard (2010) *What is Spatial History?* Stanford University Spatial History Lab (https://web.stanford.edu/group/spatialhistory/media/images/publication/what%20is%20spatial%20history%20pub%2020020110.pdf)

Chapter 1
Black Berlin

Natasha A. Kelly

Berlin is and always has been an activist city, in which the people have made their personal and collective viewpoints heard and have asserted numerous demands relating to social, political, cultural, and economic change. Public attention has also been drawn to the atrocities of racial profiling, police brutality, and institutional racism for many decades, commemorating Germany's Black victims of police killings: Kola Bankole (1994), Aamir Ageeb (1999), N'deye Mareame Sarr (2000), Michael Paul Nwabuisi (2001), Laye-Alama Condé (2005), Dominique Koumadio (2006), and Christy Schwundeck (2011) (Kelly 2021).

We should also remember Oury Jalloh, who was burned – probably after his death, as there were no signs of soot in his lungs – in a police cell in East German Dessau in 2005. To this day his case has still not been solved; instead, German authorities, courts, and politicians have been trying to cover up the truth for decades.[1] Since his death, demonstrators have been gathering in front of the police station in Dessau demanding justice every year on the date of his murder, January 7. And although these demonstrations attract several thousand protestors annually, the case has not gained the same attention of the white majority population or media as did the police murder of George Floyd in the USA in 2020.

Millions of Germans had witnessed Floyd's killing that not only went viral, but also was broadcast unfiltered on national TV at primetime. Locked at home during the global pandemic, it was impossible to ignore yet another Black man being murdered by the police. Consequently, another protest fol-

---

[1] Chronology in the Oury Jalloh case from January 7, 2005 to 2020 (https://initiativeouryjalloh.wordpress.com/2020/06/07/chronologie-im-fall-oury-jalloh-von-2005-bis-2020/)

lowed, under the hashtag Black Lives Matter, with Floyd's name being added to the list of victims of police homicides worldwide. In 2017, a working group of external experts had already been sent to Germany by the United Nations (UN) to gain knowledge about the human rights situation in the country. Their subsequent report highlighted racial profiling against People of African Descent (PAD) and stated that its repeated denial by German police and authorities fosters impunity.[2] Based on this report, Berlin became the first state in the country to pass an anti-discrimination law on June 4, 2020, shortly after Floyd's death; a conincidence in this case as the law was the result of combined community efforts over the years.

Hence, 2020 was not the first time BLM protesters had taken to the streets. The first demonstrations under this motto came to pass in Berlin in July 2016, after Philando Castile and Alton Sterling were shot dead by police officers in the USA. One year later, in June 2017, BLM Berlin founded the first BLM month,[3] which ended with a march in July. In 2020, however, these initial BLM demonstrators were joined by individuals from all walks of life as they gathered in front of the US embassy in Berlin on May 30, chanting "Black Lives Matter" at the top of their voices. Some days later, on June 6, 2020, a second protest followed that led more than 15,000 people to Berlin's historical Alexanderplatz.[4] From then onward, a wave of organized protests inundated the country with signs and slogans stating "Germany is not innocent," among other things.

On June 21, 2020 the state antidiscrimination law finally came into force, closing a legal gap and expanding the catalogue of discrimination characteristics to be protected, including social status and chronic illness, and extending the law to structurally related discrimination.[5] But this is not enough! Combating racism also includes knowing your history, as stated

---

[2] "Germany: UN rights panel highlights racial profiling against people of African descent", February 27, 2017 (https://news.un.org/en/story/2017/02/552282-germany-un-rights-panel-highlights-racial-profiling-against-people-african)

[3] Information on BLM month 2021: https://www.blacklivesmatterberlin.de/blm-month-2021/

[4] "George Floyd killing spurs fresh protests across Europe", June 6, 2020 (https://p.dw.com/p/3dLWS)

[5] Berlin state anti-discrimination law: https://www.berlin.de/sen/lads/recht/ladg/

on the homepage of BLM Berlin.⁶ Yet, our (hi)stories are structurally hidden or described as alien or inferior to the dominant culture, despite numerous community organizations, including BLM in recent years, poking their fingers in the wounds of German colonialism for decades. But with statues toppling all over Europe, the media's attention was eventually drawn to questions of ongoing coloniality, memory culture, and restitution, leading politicians to pick up in pace and shift these topics to the top of their agendas.

Despite (or because of) these slow steps of improvement, an anonymous memorial appeared on the legendary Oranienplatz, known as O-Platz, in Berlin-Kreuzberg at the end of September 2020. The square gained political significance after asylum seekers, most of them from African countries, erected a protest camp there from October 2012 to April 2014. The refugees had come from camps all over Germany in an act of civil disobedience to demonstrate against the Dublin III Regulation,⁷ insufficient shelters, and the so-called *Residenzpflicht*, which restricted freedom of movement, as well as to fight for the right to work and study in Germany. In the face of the rejection of most refugee applications, the camp was forcefully cleared in 2014, yet the groups remained active, raising awareness of their cause through their website and an information point that was established in the square during the resistance.

Today, the meter-high concrete stela is all that remains of the past struggle, linking it to present day protests. It is surrounded by a stainless steel base plate that reads: "In memory of the victims of racism and police violence." The anonymous monument builders had anticipated the #woistunserdenkmal (#whereisourmonument) initiative; the latter was established by several antiracist groups in the summer to publicly address racism and police violence. Among them were the Initiative in Memory of Oury Jalloh and KOP, the campaign for victims of police brutality; they had planned to meet on the September afternoon after the monument had been discovered.⁸

---

6 BLM Berlin Common Consensus: https://www.blacklivesmatterberlin.de/blmb-gemeinsamer-konsens/

7 The Dublin III Regulation refers to EU No 604/2013 of the European Parliament and determines where a refugee should apply for asylum and which country is responsible for the application: http://www.orac.ie/website/orac/oracwebsite.nsf/page/eudublinIIIregulation-main-en

8 "Da ist unser Denkmal - und es muss bleiben", September 8, 2021 (https://gruene-xhain.de/da-ist-unser-denkmal-und-es-muss-bleiben/)

A video on social media that in the meantime has been removed, showed how the anonymous activists filled the hollow steel cast with concrete and screwed the sign to the ground during the early hours of the morning. "We hope that this will initially create irritation and give people a task," one of the activists said on camera. At the beginning of October, they sent an open letter to the district, demanding that the memorial be preserved at the site. An online petition that was launched at the same time supported this idea and gained more than 3,300 signatures.

Ferat Koçak, an activist of color and member of the Left Party, also signed the petition and can imagine keeping the monument in its current location permanently. As Oranienplatz is one of the central squares in Kreuzberg, the many people who linger and walk in the park will see it, he told *taz*, the daily German newspaper (Hartmann 2020). In his opinion, the district will agree to the demands and preserve the monument. A spokeswoman for the district also announced that there is a general will to maintain it. Therefore, the memorial itself should not be replaced. Instead, the open cases of racist killings, especially against people in police custody, such as Oury Jalloh, should be solved and the perpetrators brought to justice.

Figure 1.1: A memorial on Oranienplatz was erected overnight by anonymous sculptors at the end of September 2020. Photograph: Natasha A. Kelly

Reclaiming the African Quarter

Berlin is itself a monument that tells (hi)stories and creates memories, many of which have been written in and into the city, be it in the names given to certain districts, areas, or streets, or in the political efforts made by Black communities from the colonial period to the present day. In the 20th century, Berlin was divided and stripped of its capital status, only to regain power after reunification and the expansion of the East. Today, Berlin is one of the most important capital cities in Europe and in the world. But, above all, it is "the mind of the beast," [9] a former colonial metropolis where in 1884–5 the idea to divide Africa among the German Empire and other European and non-European states was born (Aitkin and Rosenhaft 2015).

A relic from this time in history is the city's African Quarter in the Wedding district. One might assume that it was named because of the number of Africans who have lived there. But this is not the case. The Quarter was built around 1900 on the outskirts of Berlin, linking the surrounding green spaces and forests with the city. It was initially constructed to include Germany's largest "human zoo," in which African people and animals were to be exhibited (Honold 2004). Despite this history, a noticeable number of Africans have been drawn there in more recent times, most of them coming to Germany as students or refugees. On arrival in Berlin, they were sent directly to Wedding by friends or acquaintances, mainly because of the cheap rents in the working-class neighborhood. And if we believe the white German historian Ursula Trüper, Africans should in fact live there, not only because of the Quarter's name, but because she believes that this district should be associated with the city's present rather than with its past.[10]

This idea surely contradicts the original intention of the Quarter, if we take into consideration that Hamburg businessman and animal trader Carl Hagenbeck wanted to create a site that would surpass his earlier successes. In 1874, he organized the first major "human zoo", a so-called "Laplander Exhibition", where he had put the Sámi people from northern Europe on show in what spectators were to believe were their traditional homes (Dreesbach 2012). Hagenbeck planned to exceed this early sensationalism that would

---

9 Author's note.
10 "Afrika im Wedding", June 20, 2010 (https://issuu.com/afrikawedding/docs/afrika-im-wedding)

become the model for all those that followed, and with the new African Quarter he hoped to overshadow Berlin's first colonial exhibition, which had opened in Treptower Park on May 1, 1896 attracting around 7 million visitors.

Partly organized by Germany's Foreign Office and partly financed privately, the exhibition was intended to rekindle public interest in the German Empire after years of mismanagement and public scandals. It featured exhibits on colonial hygiene and medicine, a common theme at the time, replicas of administrative buildings, and examples of colonial goods such as ivory and cocoa. The spectacle lasted for almost six months and was originally designed to compete with earlier world exhibitions in Paris and London, to promote the German economy, and to demonstrate the growing global importance of the country and its capital. The most popular attraction, however, was the replica African and Melanesian villages, populated with over 100 individuals from overseas (ibd.).

Hagenbeck's ambitions to turn the African Quarter into a "human zoo" were thwarted by the outbreak of World War One, however, as his business contacts pulled out. Yet, the city of Berlin already had a design in place, with its "African Street" (Afrikanische Straße) at the center, an urban monument constructed in 1899 to symbolize the power of the German Empire. Linked to it were other streets: Lüderitzstraße in 1902, Guineastraße in 1903, and Transvaalstraße in 1907. Nachtigalplatz, Windhuker Straße and Swakopmunder Straße followed in 1910. These explicit references were supplemented by names of places and countries that were not directly under German rule but played a key role in the colonial division of the continent, such as "Congo Street" (named after the main arena of Belgian colonialism, as described in Chapter 2) and "Zanzibar Street," both dating from 1912. (The island of Zanzibar was annexed by the German Empire in 1885 but given to Great Britain just five years later in exchange for the island of Heligoland in the North Sea.) Over 50 years, from 1899 to 1958, street names with African and colonial references were added, the most recent being "Ghana Street," named in 1958 shortly after Ghana's independence from Great Britain. Many people are unaware that parts of Ghana that formerly belonged to Togoland were once colonized by Germany before its Empire was forced to give up its colonies to the Allies as a result of the Treaty of Versailles after World War One (Honold 2004).

Untouched by the war, the African Quarter was developed and estates built, such as Friedrich-Ebert-Siedlung, where residents established small gardens and built sheds, in contrast to other areas in the Wedding of the 1920s and 1930s. Most of these gardens were small and disorganized, but the "Dauerkolonie Togo" (Permanent Colony Togo), founded in 1939, stood out. Incorporating the colonial and imperial ideology ascribed in the Quarter's name, the title of the allotment re-enacted the colonial past and became a symbolic contribution to the "cultivation" of an allegedly "uncultivated" territory. This actively supported the National Socialist Party's propaganda on recolonizing the African continent, which, for the Black community in Berlin, corresponded with the sign displaying the garden's name in big bold letters above its entrance. The title of the garden association was changed to "Kleingartenverein Togo" (Small Garden Association Togo) in the 1980s, but, after numerous disputes and following public and financial support from the mayor's office as well as from other Social Democratic politicians, it eventually changed to "Dauer-Kleingartenverein TOGO" (Permanent Small Garden Association Togo) in 2014. With this renaming, the African Quarter actually moved a step toward becoming more "African" (Faust 2014).

In 2011, the district council decided to make the African Quarter an official site of learning about and remembrance of German colonialism, its perception, and the struggle for independence of African states. With funding from Aktionsräume Plus, a program that aimed to improve socio-spatial and urban development, the project involved residents, schools, young people, and various civil society actors. The objective was to create better opportunities for the residents of this low-income area, with education given priority in order to open up new perspectives, especially for young people. The initiative was also linked to the basic goal of identifying urban problem areas more quickly and more precisely through improved networking, communication, and coordination at the level of the senate and the districts and finding solutions among all those involved on an interdisciplinary basis. By embedding German colonialism and its implications in a modern understanding of democracy, human rights, and peaceful coexistence, this approach extended beyond a shocking reminder of past injustices and instead offered a compelling contribution to the decolonization of Berlin's society and culture.

A board of directors was set up to advise on the selection of projects and to involve activists and experts from Black communities as equal partners. In this context, tours of the African Quarter were organized on various occasions and for different audiences. A digital map of the 22 streets was also developed to provide a descriptive, methodical, and didactic overview of the area with audio files, graphics, pictures, historical documents, poems, songs, and interviews.[11] One year later, a memorial plaque was placed on the corner of Otawistraße/Müllerstraße, referring to the history of the African Quarter. Instigated by the Street Initiative, a group of African and Afro-German organizations and their allies, the information board includes two texts that reflect the multiple perspectives of the area's history – one written by the Social Democratic Party, the second by the Street Initiative (Diallo and Zeller 2013).

In 2007, the editorial offices of the African magazine *LoNam* had already moved to Wedding, realizing that it was the best place to sell the 10,000 copies of each issue. While not sugar-coating the facts, the magazine wanted to distance itself from negative media coverage. As the editorial team states on *LoNam*'s homepage:

> In doing so, we want to differentiate ourselves from the Afropessimistic media, which mainly show war, famine and misery, as well as from those that only emphasize the positive things about Africa.[12]

The bimonthly magazine was launched in March 2005 and is written in German for both Germans and Africans living in Germany. Since the publication depends on its readers, it was a good choice to move to the African Quarter, editor Hervé Tcheumeleu explained to *taz* (Vollmuth 2008). Being located in the heart of Wedding, the news it reports on occurs right on its doorstep and a lot of readers often drop by the office to offer first-hand information.

Furthermore, the Vera-Heyer-Archiv, a library for Black literature and media run by the non-profit organization Each One Teach One (EOTO), opened its doors in the African Quarter on March 21, 2014, the International Day for the Elimination of Racial Discrimination. Vera Heyer was an Afro-German born in 1946 and raised in a children's home near Frankfurt am Main. She began collecting and cataloging the works of Black authors in the 1970s. Her vision to one day open a library to the public was finally realized in 2014, almost 20 years after her untimely death. EOTO has pursued Heyer's dream and has grown over the years to become a reference library with

---

11 African Quarter, a place of learning and remembrance, Berlin. Digital map with texts and sound recordings: http://www.3plusx.de/leo-site/
12 LoNam das Afrika-Magazin: https://www.lonam.de/about/

more than 7,000 books. Today, it is part of a democracy program funded by the Federal Ministry for Family Affairs, Senior Citizens, Women and Youth.[13] The name Each One Teach One was coined by critical resistance movements in times of enslavement and colonialism to highlight the importance of access to formal education and the need to share knowledge within Black families and communities.

As part of the area's resurgence, the Wedding Renaissance swept through the district, with the goal of changing its negative perception – at least during the weekend of September 11–13, 2020, when the festival took place. Based on the Harlem Renaissance in the USA, Black German artists, poets, authors, and musicians took over the neighborhood, reclaiming the space and creating a temporary site for freedom of Black expression. In the same way as the Harlem Renaissance had laid the foundation for the Civil Rights Movement in the USA 100 years earlier, the event was decentralized throughout the district and aimed to comment on and critique the existing racial structures of German society. One of the organizers, Hassanatou Bah, spoke to *RosaMag*, a Black online lifestyle magazine that has been documenting the multifaceted worlds of Black women in Germany, Austria, and Switzerland since 2019:

> The Wedding Renaissance stands for Black Unity, Black Power, and Black Excellence. It's mostly about Black cohesion. Black Unity means becoming a unit, promoting solidarity among Blacks and expanding the community. Black Power is about our collaboration in Berlin, Germany, and around the world. This is where our Black Excellence draws. Work that reaches beyond the German borders, to Africa, to the Black diasporas in the USA and Americas (Parbey 2020).[14]

Although Wedding has been developing positively for the Black community over the years, there is still a long way to go before the African Quarter is no longer associated with its colonial past. However, with the renaming of important streets in the area, as shown below, the African Quarter is rewriting urban history from a Black perspective and moving a step closer to altering the perception of Black people in Germany and beyond.

---

13 Website of the non-profit organization EOTO: https://www.eoto-archiv.de/
14 Translated by the author.

Remembering Black German Liberation

Technically, the history of resistance is as old as the history of colonialism itself. After the success of the first Pan-African conference in London in 1900 (see Chapter 3), the first Pan-African Congress took place in Paris in 1919. Germany had just been defeated in World War One, and with the signing of the Treaty of Versailles the country's colonial empire had ended. The world was changing inexorably, becoming increasingly unstable. Aiming to decolonize the African countries and to unify the peoples who had been torn apart by arbitrary colonial borders, Pan-Africanism continued to emerge as a link between many African liberation movements and the African diaspora. Influential in this growing resistance of the late 1910s and early 1920s were Black intellectuals and workers who shared the vision of a unified African state and the end of racial hierarchies and exploitation. W. E. B. Du Bois, Marcus Garvey, and George Padmore are considered among the most important pioneers of this era. However, there were numerous Black feminists, who were also influential in the rise of the Pan-African movement: Maria Mandessi Bell from Cameroon, the sisters Paulette and Jeanne Nardal from Martinique, Mabel Dove Danquah from Ghana and Claudia Jones from Trinidad among others.

Between 1892 and 1894, during the heyday of German colonialism, Du Bois spent formative years of his young adult life in Berlin, where he studied at Humboldt University, formerly known as Friedrich-Wilhelm University. Throughout this period, he experienced Germany as a "culture in search of a nation" (Du Bois 1940: 136). With this quote, Du Bois described not only his lived experience as a marginalized Black man in the USA, but also Germany's social structure at the end of the 19th century. Attracted by Otto von Bismarck's idea of a social system, Max Weber's implementation of social legislations, and August Bebel's foundation of the Social Democratic Party, Du Bois returned to the USA after his grant for further studies was rejected. Back home, he did not simply translate German ideas into US thinking; he also merged aspects of German Romanticism with his own concerns for disenfranchised and underprivileged African Americans (Kelly 2016).

In 1958, Humboldt University awarded him an honorary doctorate, and for over 20 years the American Studies Program at the university has been honoring his legacy with two lecture series: the W. E. B. Du Bois Lectures and the Distinguished W. E. B. Du Bois Lectures. Organized by the Senate

Department for Culture and Europe and the Historical Commission of Berlin, a porcelain memorial plaque for the civil rights activist was unveiled at his former Berlin address at Oranienstraße 130 in August 2019 (Conrad 2019). And in January 2022, a plaque was installed on the ground floor of Humboldt University's main building next to the entrance to the Orbis Humboldtianus, a club for international students. The memorial was designed by Haitian-born, Berlin-based artist Jean-Ulrick Désert and consists of three glass panels showing a group photograph of Du Bois and other students, presumably from 1894, and two later portraits of the sociologist. Its color scheme is based on the Pan-African flag and thus refers to the Pan-African movement.[15]

Du Bois is the first African American to be dignified in this way by Humboldt University; he is also the first person to be honored as a former student. Yet, it is important to stress that many young Africans like Maria Mandessi Bell came to Germany during the colonial period to be educated, but the majority were trained as office or domestic workers. Others frequently served as interpreters for African languages at colonial research centers and with the colonial administration offices, and many worked in the entertainment industry. However, no matter where they came from,

Figure 1.2: Memorial plaque in honor of the scientist, writer, and civil rights activist W. E. B. Du Bois, installed in the main building of Humboldt University. Photograph: Natasha A. Kelly

---

15 "Gedenktafel für den Schwarzen Bürgerrechtler und Soziologen W.E.B. Du Bois", January 28, 2022 (https://www.hu-berlin.de/de/pr/nachrichten/januar-2022/nr-22126-1)

Black people were never fully integrated into German society. The political debate about the so-called *Mischehengesetze* (mixed marriage laws) that ignited in the German colonies led to the categories of race and nation intersecting and forming the foundation of German citizenship law. As a result, German nationality could subsequently be gained only through German blood, a fact that leads a large part of the German public to continue to perceive Black and German as an oxymoron to the present day (El-Tayeb 2001).

One African who came to Germany from Cameroon at the age of 20 was Martin Dibobe. Together with other Africans he was "exhibited" for six months at the colonial show in Treptower Park, mentioned above. Following this, he stayed in the Weimar Republic, as Germany was called during the interwar years, got married – despite administrative difficulties – and started working for the Berlin railway in 1902

Figure 1.3: At the entrance to the metro station Hallesches Tor in the Berlin district of Kreuzberg, there is a large photograph of Germany's first Black train operator, Martin Dibobe. Photograph: Natasha A. Kelly

(Oguntoye 1997). A photograph of him in his uniform is hanging on the staircase of the Berlin subway station Hallesches Tor in the district of Kreuzberg. However, it is unclear how or why this memorial is actually there.

Presumably, the photograph was not primarily set up to commemorate Black presence in Germany, but to exotisize Dibobe as Berlin's first African train driver who also became a local celebrity. In 1906/07, he was sent to Cameroon on behalf of the Reich government, where he was to consult in the construction of the local railway. But during his stay, he became aware of the social and economic injustices of the colonial system and returned to Germany to fight for equal rights of Africans, joining the League for Human Rights, founded in 1914, and becoming active in the Social Democratic Party (SPD). [16]

Against the backdrop of the forthcoming end to German colonial rule in Africa and the budding colonial revisionist propaganda of the National Socialists after World War One, Dibobe sent a letter to the Weimar National Assembly and a corresponding petition to the Reich Colonial Office, signed by himself and 17 other Black German men in June 1919. However, although demanding equal rights for Africans and PAD, Martin Dibobe and his followers committed to the former protection treaties of 1884 that had constituted the power of the German Reich over Cameroon and therefore argued for Germany retaining its colonies; an ambiguous decision. Accordingly, the signatories took a vow of loyalty and expressed the hope that the treatment of Black people living in the country would be better than under the imperial government (Gerbing 2010).

Neither the Weimar National Assembly nor the Reich Colonial Ministry responded. Then, on January 10, 1920, the Versailles Treaty came into force, through which Germany lost its colonies to the other colonial powers. Shortly after, Dibobe was laid off at the Berliner railway and planned to return to his home country, however, the now French colony of Cameroon would not let him enter and Dibobe was forced to move to Liberia. There his trail and name fall into oblivion. After Black organizations recapitulated his biography, a commemorative plaque equivalent to the one for Du Bois was put up at his former home at Kuglerstraße 44 in Berlin-Prenzlauer Berg on his 140th anniversary, on October 31, 2016 (Djahangrad 2016).

But despite rewriting colonial history from a Black perspective, the city continues to hold numerous remnants of German colonialism that are not too gratifying. From 1883 to 1921 the chocolate factory "Felix & Sarotti" relocated its production facilities to the "Sarotti-Höfe" in Berlin Kreuzberg, Mehringdamm 53-57, which is still named after it today. Criticism of the racist stereotype of the advertising character of the "chocolate-brown Sarotti-M*" (advertising quote) had been growing since the 1960s, so that in 2004 it was redesigned as the "Sarotti magician of the senses". Instead of carrying a serving tray in his hand, he now throws stars into the air while standing on a crescent moon, his skin color golden instead of brown (Koal 2021).

---

16 "Berlin postkolonial: Erinnerung an Martin Dibobe", November 16, 2021 (https://migrations-geschichten.de/berlin-postkolonial-erinnerung-an-martin-dibobe/)

The discriminatory meaning of the M-word can be traced back to the hostility toward non-Christians in the early 13th century. This connotation was eventually replaced by racist biological arguments in the course of the European Enlightenment. The German philosopher Immanuel Kant, for example, spread the view that Black people could be educated only as servants, an idea that supported the degradation of Black people and underlined the word's derogatory meaning. According to analysis by numerous linguists, the word has always had a negative connotation, which is why it is abbreviated to the letter "M" today (Arndt 2011). Arndt suggests:

> [T]he term should be deleted without replacement because it would be paradoxical to look for a substitute for a racist term. In order to function, any substitute needs knowledge of an "avoided" racist concept and inevitably has to reproduce it. As a result, a term that whites use to designate Black people and to portray their supposed superiority is absolutely dispensable (Arndt 2011).[17]

Another remnant of German colonialism is the so-called "Herero stone" in the New Garrison Cemetery in Berlin-Neukölln, a large granite boulder that was moved there in 1973 from a barracks in Kreuzberg, commemorates the German soldiers of the *Schutztruppe* (protection force) who participated in the genocide against the Hereo and Nama in today's Namibia between 1904 and 1908. In 2009, after long protests from citizens' associations, the Neukölln District Office finally set a stone plaque in the ground next to the boulder, which also commemorates the war's victims. To this day it is the only official memorial in Berlin for the crimes of German colonialism. Yet, the Herero living in the city like Israel Kaunatjike would have preferred a different neighborhood for it (Habermalz 2018).

Renaming Streets and Rewriting Urban History

In central Berlin, the above-mentioned Congo Conference was held in the Reich Chancellery on Wilhlemstraße 77 in the late 19th century. The chancellor at the time, Otto von Bismarck, had invited to Berlin delegates from

---

17 Translated by the author.

the USA and the Ottoman Empire as well as representatives of the European powers – Austria-Hungary, Belgium, Denmark, France, Great Britain, Italy, the Netherlands, Portugal, Russia, Spain, and Sweden-Norway – to negotiate previous and future territories and to establish free trade and trading routes throughout the African continent. The final document, the Congo Act[18], formed the basis for the colonization of Africa, without taking any account of existing social, economic, or political structures.

Today, an information board stands where the former chancellery was located and reminds tourists and locals alike of this episode of colonial history. It is one of 31 boards set up along the Wilhelmstraße History Mile by the Senate Department for Urban Development between 1996 and 2007 that tell stories of Germany's past. Researched by German historian Laurenz Demps for the Topography of Terror Foundation, the recent boards were part of a street exhibition that took place in 2007. However, a lot of imagination is required when searching for traces of the past, as Berlin's modern buildings provide no information about the edifices in which German politics was made for decades. Andreas Nachama, managing director of the Topography of Terror Foundation, said: "Wilhelmstraße has lost its meaning, but not its memory."[19]

Figure 1.4: Collage of the old and new Wilhelmstraße used as a backdrop for Natasha A. Kelly's performance "M(a)y Sister #4: between avenui and kreuzberg," staged at HAU Hebbel am Ufer Theater in Berlin in 2018. Photograph: Doro Tuch

Despite this important milestone in German history, the country's involvement in colonialism did not begin in the 19th century but dates further

---

18 General Act of the Berlin Conference on West Africa, 26 February 1885: https://loveman.sdsu.edu/docs/1885GeneralActBerlinConference.pdf
19 "Neues aus der Geschichte der Wilhelmstraße", April 17, 2007 (https://www.tagesspiegel.de/berlin/neues-aus-der-geschichte-der-wilhelmstrasse/835380.html)

back to the unjust actions of officer and explorer Otto Friedrich von der Gröben in the 17th century. In the spring of 1682, Electoral Prince Friedrich Wilhelm of Brandenburg assigned him an expedition to the coast of West Africa, where Otto von der Gröben was sent to establish a permanent armed military base. Later known as Großfriedrichsburg, the fort became the first German colony on the West Coast of Africa in today's Ghana. Selling over 20,000 Africans to the Americas and the Caribbean, and losing many more in the process, the fort became a deadly point of no return characterized by Germany's trafficking of captured Africans. Furthermore, Großfriedrichsburg served to support and protect Friedrich Wilhelm's Brandenburg African Company for almost three decades until the elector sold it to the Dutch West Indies Company in 1717.[20]

On the occasion of the first German colonial exhibition mentioned above, the bank of the River Spree in Berlin's Kreuzberg district was named Gröbenufer after Otto von der Gröben to celebrate Germany's colonial dominance. Criticism of this honor began to arise centuries later after the UN recognized colonialism and enslavement as the main causes of modern racism at the world conference in Durban in 2001. Following the initiative of members of the community, postcolonial organizations, and civil society, including the Initiative of Black People in Germany (ISD) who had come together under the umbrella of the non-profit development policy advocacy Berliner Entwicklungspolitischer Ratschlag, the Green Party put forward the suggestion to rename the street[21] on the grounds that by founding Großfriedrichsburg and leading the Brandenburg African Company, Otto von der Gröben had actively participated in transatlantic enslavement and therefore had committed a crime against humanity. At the end of 2007, the district assembly in Friedrichshain-Kreuzberg accepted the proposal and the decision was made to rename the riverbank in 2009.

---

20 Website of the the Black Central European Studies Network (BCESN), a network of historians spread across four different time zones and located on two different continents: https://blackcentraleurope.com/sources/1500-1750/founding-a-slave-trading-colony-in-west-africa-1682-1683/

21 "Umbenennung des Gröbenufer in May-Ayim-Ufer Hier: May-Ayim-Ufer aus postkolonialer Aufklärungs- und Erinnerungsperspektive gestalten", May 27, 2009 (https://gruene-xhain.de/umbenennung-des-groebenufer-in-may-ayim-ufer-hier-may-ayim-ufer-aus-postkolonialer-aufklaerungs-und-erinnerungsperspektive-gestalten/)

According to the implementing regulations of the Berlin Roads Act[22], a street can be renamed only after a person with an outstanding personality and an interest in the city as a whole. Additionally, this person must have died more than five years previously and the rules state that the historical context must not be changed and that women should be given greater consideration. This provided a basis for Gröbenufer to be renamed after the Afro-German poet, pedagogue, and Kreuzberg resident May Ayim, who became internationally renowned through her German-language spoken word performances. She can be considered the most prominent representative of the Afro-German movement.

Inspired by African American scholar, poet and civil rights activist, Audre Lorde (after whom the district council (BVV) decided to rename the northern part of Manteuffelstraße in Berlin-Kreuzberg in February 2019), May Ayim was co-author and co-editor of one of the foundational works of the Black German community: *Showing Our Colors: Afro-German Women Speak Out.*[23] This was the first publication to criticize ongoing colonial injustices and was the first in which the self-determined and self-defined terms "Black German" and "Afro-German" appeared – and, with them, the possibility for a postcolonial discourse in German politics and society presented itself (Kelly 2016). A formal rededication and the installation of the new street signs took place on February 27, with the street officially being renamed May-Ayim-Ufer on March 4, 2010 (Kelly 2015).

Nearly a decade later, the district council finally decided on new street names in the African Quarter; this took effect on April 1, 2019. Debates on changing the street names had dominated the area since the early 20th century. In March 1939, for example, the National Socialists had renamed Londoner Straße as Petersallee to glorify Carl Peters (1856–1918), a colonial commissioner in former German East Africa, where he led a cruel regime over the native population that eventually resulted in his arrest and dismissal. In 1946, the renaming of Togo Street was discussed; a proposal was submitted to the municipal as-

---

22 "BVV-Beschluss 0384/II Verfahrensweise bei Straßen (Plätzen) und deren Neu- bzw. Umbenennungen vom 20.06.2002", June 29, 2002 (https://www.berlin.de/kunst-und-kulturmitte/geschichte/erinnerungskultur/strassenbenennungen/)
23 The first book to be published by Black German women was *Farbe bekennen: Afro-deutsche Frauen auf den Spuren ihrer Geschichte* edited by Katharina Oguntoye, May Ayim (fomerly Opitz) and Dagmar Schultz in 1986. The English-language translation was published in 1992 with a foreword by acclaimed African American feminist Audre Lorde.

sembly again in 1987, but did not gain majority support. In 1986, the focus had shifted back to Petersallee, which was not renamed but instead rededicated to Hans Peters (1886–1966), who was active against Nazi rule and cofounded the Berlin State Constitution after World War Two. Yet, the rededication from Carl to Hans Peters was never officially legalized – all that happened was that small signs were attached explaining the eponym. And while Carl Peters had been dismissed from colonial services in 1891–2 for torturing and murdering his African maid Mabruk and sexually assaulting a Chagga girl, Jogodja, Adolf Lüderitz (1834–86), the first German landowner in today's Namibia, swindled land from the Nama chief Joseph Frederiks, who believed he was selling five British miles, each 1.6 kilometers in length, but instead sold 7.5 German miles. Additionally, Gustav Nachtigal (1834–85), a scientist who mainly explored the Islamic culture of North Africa, can be held responsible for bloody military action in Cameroon and the occupation of Togo.[24]

Figure 1.5: May-Ayim-Ufer, located on the River Spree in Berlin's Kreuzberg district. Photograph: Doro Tuch

After decades of effort and with the support of residents, the decision was finally made to reclaim the African Quarter and create a pro-African district in the heart of Berlin, with Petersallee, between Müllerstraße and Nachtigalplatz, renamed Anna-Mungunda-Allee. Anna Mungunda was the first female Herero activist to fight in the Namibian independence movement against the occupation of the coun-

---

24 Information about the renaming of streets in the African Quarter in Wedding, Berlin-Mitte https://www.berlin.de/kunst-und-kultur-mitte/geschichte/afrikanisches-viertel-609903.php

try by South Africa. Between Nachtigalplatz and Windhuker Straße, Petersallee was renamed Maji-Maji-Allee, commemorating the 1905–7 Maji Maji Uprising in Tanganyika, the most significant African challenge to German colonial rule. Lüderitzstraße is now known as Cornelius-Fredericks-Straße, named after a Nama leader who, together with Hendrik Witbooi, the leader of the Khowesin, actively waged a guerrilla war against the Germans in Namibia. The Nachtigalplatz is now called Manga-Bell-Platz, after Rudolf Duala Manga Bell, the king of the Duala people in Cameroon and the leader of the resistance against the illegal expulsion of the Duala from their traditional settlement areas during the German colonial era (ibd.). And, after an extensive participation process involving civil society, the previous Wissmannstraße in Berlin-Neukölln, which formerly honored the colonial officer Hermann von Wissmann, who was responsible for the suppression of the East African coastal population, was also renamed in the spring of 2021. Instead of a colonial ruler, the street now carries the name of Lucy Lameck, a Tanzanian politician who campaigned for women's rights and the Pan-African ideal.[25] Renaming streets allows the perspective of African people or groups and PAD to be inscribed as subjects – and not objects or victims – into national urban history.

However, the community's project of the heart remains the renaming of M*-straße, which refers to the racist name for Black people mentioned above, something that has been demanded by the Black community for more than two decades. According to the city chronicler Friedrich Nicolai, it was named as early as 1706, at a time when King Friedrich I of Prussia claimed rule over the colonial fortress Großfriedrichsburg (Nicolai 1779). An underground railway station was first opened in 1908 with the name Kaiserhof and was later renamed Thälmannplatz. From 1986 onward it was called Otto-Grotewohl-Straße, and in 1991, after reunification, it was renamed M*-straße to match the street.

For more than 30 years, the community has been fighting to rename both the station and the street. And since 2014, there has been an annual festival at the underground station in Berlin-Mitte organized by associations from the Black community. As the street name is directly linked

---

25 The new Lucy-Lameck-Straße – renaming and supporting program https://www.berlin.de/ba-neukoelln/aktuelles/veranstaltungen/die-neue-lucy-lameck-strasse-umbenenung-und-rahmenprogramm-1075274.php

to the history of enslavement, the event takes place close to August 22/23, the former being the day of the outbreak of the Haitian Revolution in 1791 and the latter the International Day for the Remembrance of the Slave Trade and its Abolition. At the festival, speeches, poetry, and music are followed by the symbolic renaming of the street. Today the street is partly residential but there are also numerous companies (e.g. a Hilton hotel) and institutions located there, including the embassies of Peru, Chile, and Lichtenstein.

Figure 1.6: Collage of an imagined Anton-Wilhelm-Amo-Straße created as a backdrop for Natasha A. Kelly's performance "M(a)y Sister #4: between avenui and kreuzberg," staged at HAU Hebbel am Ufer Theater in Berlin in 2018. Photograph: Doro Tuch

Those arguing for the street to be renamed, including Bündnis Anton Wilehlm Amo Erbschaft (Anton Wilhelm Amo Inheritance Alliance) have suggested Anton Wilhelm Amo, the first Black professor at a German university (see the Introduction), who fought for the rights of Black people in Europe. Adopting his name would maintain the reference to the history of the enslavement of Black people and their life in the African diaspora. And despite the renaming being opposed by many residents who believe that the "M" word is not racist, the district assembly of Berlin-Mitte approved the suggestion in August 2020, as did the district office in March 2021.[26] At the time of writing, the rededication and renaming ceremony have not yet taken place, as lawsuits filed by residents are pending (Schmoll 2022).

Since 2020, the association Decolonize Berlin has been committed to critically examining the past and present of colonialism and racism in the city. Some 250 people from 30 associations, some of which are Black, individual

---

26 "Mohrenstrasse: Berlin farce over renaming of ‚racist' station", BBC, July 9, 2020 (https://www.bbc.com/news/world-europe-53348129)

activists, and representatives from five districts and six senate administrations have so far taken part in the participatory process in order to formulate concrete proposals. An interim report by the coordination office summarizes the first results.[27] However, let us not forget that we might have moved a meaningful step forward, but there is still a long way to go until Berlin's past ceases to cast a shadow on the future of Black people in Berlin, Germany, and beyond.

References

Aitken, Robbie and Eve Rosenhaft (2015): *Black Germany: The Making and Unmaking of a Diaspora Community, 1884-1960*. Cambridge University Press.

Arndt, Susan (2011) "Mohr_in" in Susan Arndt and Nadja Ofuatey-Alazard (eds.), *Wie Rassismus aus Wörtern spricht. (K)Erben des Kolonialismus im Wissensarchiv deutsche Sprache. Ein kritisches Nachschlagewerk*. Münster.

Conrad, Andreas (2019): "Vordenker der schwarzen Bürgerrechtsbewegung. Gedenktafel für den US-Soziologen W.E.B. Du Bois". *Der Tagesspiegel*, August 27, 2019 (https://www.tagesspiegel.de/berlin/vordenker-der-schwarzen-buergerrechtsbewegung-gedenktafel-fuer-den-us-soziologen-w-e-b-du-bois/24944188.html)

Diallo, Oumar and Joachim and Joachim Zeller (2013) *Black Berlin. Die deutsche Metropole und ihre afrikanische Diaspora in Geschichte und Gegenwart*. Berlin.

Djahangrad, Susan (2016):"Vom Forschungsobjekt zum Zugführer", Der Tagesspiegel, November 1, 2016 (https://www.tagesspiegel.de/berlin/deutsche-kolonialgeschichte-in-berlin-vom-forschungsobjekt-zum-zugfuehrer/14764698.html)

Dreesbach, Anne (2012): "Colonial Exhibitions, 'Völkerschauen' and the Display of the 'Other'", European History Online (EGO), published by the Leibniz Institute of European History (IEG) (http://www.ieg-ego.eu/dreesbacha-2012-en)

---

27 A city-wide concept of Berlin's colonial past. Coordination point at Decolonize Berlin e.V.: https://eineweltstadt.berlin/themen/dekolonisierung/ein-gesamtstaedtisches-konzept-zu-berlins-kolonialer-vergangenheit/

Du Bois, W. E. B. (1940) *Dusk of Dawn: An Essay toward an Autobiography of a Race Concept*. New York.

El-Tayeb, Fatima (2001) *Schwarze Deutsche: Der Diskurs um "Rasse" und nationale Identität 1890–1933*. Frankfurt am Main.

Faust, Joachim (2014): "Wie lange dauert es noch mit der "Dauerkolonie Togo"?", *Weddingweiser*, June 14, 2012 (https://weddingweiser.de/wie-lan ge-dauert-es-noch-mit-der-dauerkolonie-togo/)

Gerbing, Stefan (2010) *Afrodeutscher Aktivismus. Interventionen von Kolonisierten am Wendepunkt der Dekolonialisierung Deutschlands 1919*. Frankfurt am Main.

Habermalz, Christiane (2018): "Koloniales Nicht-Gedenken in Deutschland", Deutschlandfunk, February 16, 2018 (https://www.deutschlandfunk. de/erinnerungskultur-koloniales-nicht-gedenken-in-deutschland-100. html)

Hartmann, Jannis (2020): "Denkmal für Opfer von Rassismus. Am richtigen Platz," *taz*, October 15, 2020, https://taz.de/Denkmal-fuer-Opf er-von-Rassismus/!5717616/

Honold, Alexander (2004): "Afrika in Berlin - Ein Stadtviertel als postkolonialer Gedächtnisraum," iz3w Nr. 278/279 (2004), S. 56ff., https://www. freiburg-postkolonial.de/Seiten/Honold-Berlin.htm

Kelly, Natasha A. (ed.) (2015) *Sisters and Souls. Inspirationen durch May Ayim*. Berlin.

Kelly, Natasha A. (2016) *Afrokultur "der raum zwischen gestern und morgen."* Münster.

Kelly, Natasha A. (2021) *Rassismus. Strukturelle Probleme brauchen strukturelle Lösungen*. Zurich and Hamburg.

Koal, Kilian (2021): "Auf den Spuren des Kolonialismus in Berlin"January 1, 2021 (https://storymaps.arcgis.com/stories/3f3fb58c4a764882b9310ce8e8 1a89b6)

Nicolai, Friedrich (1779): *Beschreibung der Königlichen Residenzstädte Berlin und Potsdam und aller daselbst befindlicher Merkwürdigkeiten* (https://www.di gitale-sammlungen.de/de/view/bsb10722593?page=5)

Oguntoye, Katharina (1997) *Eine afro-deutsche Geschichte. Zur Lebenssituation von Afrikanern und Afro-deutschen in Deutschland von 1884 bis 1950*. Berlin.

Oguntoye, Katharina, May Opitz, and Dagmar Schultz (eds.) (1986) *Farbe bekennen. Afro-deutsche Frauen auf den Spuren ihrer Geschichte*. Berlin.

Parbey, Celia (2020): "Wedding Renaissance – Für ein neues Schwarzes Selbstverständnis. Im Gespräch mit Hassanatou Bah", *RosaMag*, September 8, 2020 (https://rosa-mag.de/wedding-renaissance-fur-ein-neues-schwarzes-selbstverstandnis/)

Schmoll, Thomas (2022): "Symbol „rassistisch-imperialistischer Ideologien"? Gegner sieht Verfassungsbruch", Welt, March 13, 2022 (https://www.welt.de/politik/deutschland/article237478001/Umbenennung-der-Mohrenstrasse-Gegner-sieht-Verfassungsbruch.html)

Vollmuth, Hannes (2008): "Das afrikanische Viertel", *taz*, September 24, 2008, https://taz.de/Wedding/!5175370/

Chapter 2
Black Brussels

Sibo Rugwiza Kanobana

The resurgence in the global focus on racism following the police killing of George Floyd in the USA in May 2020 was also reflected on the streets of the Belgian capital, Brussels. And while Floyd's death was the initiating event that brought together a diverse crowd of 15,000–20,000 people on June 7, 2020, under the banner of Black Lives Matter, the demonstration was also an opportunity to bring to the fore a decades-long antiracism struggle that had been ignored for too long by authorities and established media. A taboo appeared to have been lifted, although it is too early to say whether there will be a lasting effect. As a result, Black Belgians suddenly seemed to play a critical role in understanding how to shape a more inclusive and antiracist future. And while, until recently, immigration and cultural difference had been the only legitimate ways to speak about racism, the acknowledgment of the colonial past, which includes addressing the traces of that colonial past in public space, achieved a central position in the struggle against racism.

In different ways, the monuments, plaques, statues, etc. reminiscent of the colonial past have become tools for the struggle against systemic racism, the advocacy of the African diaspora's interests, and the legitimation of the African diaspora in the public sphere. Symbols of racial oppression, including statues of King Leopold II, who was responsible for the deaths of millions of Africans during his rule, have legitimately become instrumental. After more than a decade of acts that were considered vandalism, such as defacing and daubing King Leopold II statues and other colonial symbols throughout Belgium with red paint, in June 2020 the authorities decided to remove a bust of Leopold II in Brussels and one in Ghent, as well as a statue in the city of Antwerp. The latter was set on fire before it was taken down. Attitudes toward these problematic symbols seemed to be changing.

This could be viewed as a step forward for Africans, who have been present in the Low Countries (Belgium and the Netherlands) since the Renaissance (Earle and Lowe 2010; Hondius 2011; 2008), although their numbers have been substantial only since the 1990s. In the 1950s, facing a lack of labor following World War Two, Belgium employed immigrant workers for its industry and infrastructure (Van Mol and de Valk 2016). However, while many Western European governments chose to recruit workers from their colonies, Belgium did not; instead, it arranged with Mediterranean countries to bring in temporary workers (De Smet 2016; Lafleur, Martinello, and Rea 2015; Martinello and Rea 2003). This scheme was in line with its colonial policy. As Eva and Erik Swyngedouw explain:

> The colonial administration excelled in discouraging and controlling migration. During the colonial period, migration to Belgium was extremely limited. Officially, there was no migration. (Swyngedouw and Swyngedouw 2009: 71)

This was for two reasons: first, a shortage of workers for the industrial and agricultural exploitation of Congo itself in the 1950s, resulting in considerable internal forced migration within Congo; and second, a concern that Congolese immigration would undermine the imagined racial homogeneity of Belgium (Kagné 2001: 6). As a result, the Black presence in Belgium was limited mostly to students and diplomats from Congo, Rwanda, and Burundi until the 1980s (Arnaut and Ceuppens 2009; Demart et al. 2017; Demart 2013a; Grégoire 2010; Kagné 2001; Mayoyo Bitumba 1995). The instability in the region following the Rwandan genocide in 1994, the fall of Mobutu in 1997, and the ensuing devastating wars in Congo prompted a significant wave of Congolese, Rwandans, and Burundians to settle in Belgium in the 1990s. In addition, other African immigrants joined the growing population.

Today, the number of People of African Descent (PAD) in Belgium is estimated to be about 250,000 (Demart et al. 2017). However, they are not one community per se but rather several communities due to their different countries of origin, home languages, religious affiliations, immigration trajectories, family histories, educational backgrounds, etc. Yet, they appear to share a common experience of racialization, what Pap Ndiaye, called "a community of experience" (Ndiaye 2009). The French sociologist working on Blackness in France, who was appointed Minister of Education and Youth by French President Emmanuel Macron in 2022, said that they share a common interest in addressing racism and the colonial legacy. However, racism and its link with coloniality has been partially obscured because, in Belgium, discourses of diversity, multiculturalism, racism, etc. have been dominated by a focus on Belgians of Moroccan and Turkish origin, often lumped together as Muslims (Demart et al. 2017; Arnaut and Ceuppens 2009). Thus, issues of inequality and racial discrimination are essentially understood in cultural, religious, and migratory terms, erasing the coloniality of power that informs the logics of racism (cf. Quijano 2000). As a consequence, Belgium suffers from a textbook example of "white amnesia" (cf. Hesse 2002) in which Black resistance against colonialism is forgotten. Moreover, Belgians like to think of themselves as part of a small, insignificant, and powerless nation that has had little historical impact (Mincke 2016). Consequently, they are usually unaware of the atrocities Belgian governments, businesses, and industries were involved in to create the wealth the nation knows today. Still, although Belgium lost its colonial possessions 60 years ago, the spirit of colonization is still to be found in the streets of its cities, undoubtedly so in Brussels (Njall Soiresse 2017).

There are a lot of physical traces of the colonial past in Belgium's public space, with a high concentration in Brussels (cf. Stanard 2019). Depending on how one counts them, there are at least 74 explicit references in the city to people and places linked to Belgian colonization (Jacobs 2018), although Lucas Catherine, a Belgian historian, counts 101 places, just including street names that refer to men directly responsible for the colonial endeavor along with numerous buildings, squares, and avenues that do not refer directly to colonialism but were built as a direct consequence of colonialism (Catherine 2006). Meanwhile, since the early 2000s, several activist associations and community organizations in Brussels, whose members are majority, but not exclusively, of African descent, have been at the forefront of making the Black presence and the significance of the Black experience heard. Some recent publications explore the history and achievements of these organizations (Grégoire, Kanobana, and Demart 2023; Debeuckelaere and Abrassart 2020). But there is still a lot of work that needs to be done, and addressing in detail the social significance of these organizations and how they emerged would exceed the focus of this chapter. However, the celebration of the 50 years of independence of Congo in 2010 can be considered a key moment in bringing that legacy into the mainstream (cf. Demart and Abrassart 2016). In the process, the role of public space, and of a Brussels urban landscape that is scattered with traces of colonialism, has served as a medium for making coloniality and racism visible and a subject to be addressed in earnest.

Efforts to decolonize public space in Brussels became undeniably visible in 2008, although the first public action seems to have taken place in 2005 following the decision to renovate the *Monument aux Pionniers Belges au Congo* (Monument to the Belgian Pioneers in Congo) in the Parc du Cinquantenaire. However, 2008 was a landmark year. Writer, philosopher, and activist Théophile de Giraud performed a critical act of protest against the huge equestrian statue of Leopold II on Place de la Nation (formerly known as Place du Trône), by climbing it and painting it red from its head to its waist; the first commemoration of the Unknown Congolese Soldier, organized by Black associations, took place at the Memorial for the African Campaign (see Figure 2.2) (Catherine 2018; Ben Yacoub and Abrassart 2016); and the first decolonial Brussels city tour was organized, explicitly denouncing the murderous aspects of Belgian colonization (Imbach 2008).

Out of the latter emerged CMCLD (Collectif Mémoire Coloniale et Lutte contre les Discriminations)[1], an influential unincorporated association of Pan-African activists from all parts of Belgium. Its members were initially exclusively PAD, and, as its name makes clear, the collective makes explicit the all too often ignored link between colonial legacy and the struggle against racism. The collective challenges a mainstream reading of colonial history, which is imbued with images that too often present colonialism as benevolent. Today, CMCLD continues to organize guided city tours that highlight the violent, racist, and exploitative aspects of the colonial past and are aimed at challenging a frequently glorified official history of Belgian colonialism (Imbach 2008). For example, CMCLD has pushed for the display of plaques with information that would contextualize certain street names and monuments, for the renaming of existing infrastructure, and for the establishment of new infrastructure with names of people – and, most importantly, of women – who fought against colonization and for the freedom of people.

However, there seems to be considerable resistance among politicians as well as in the media. Advocacy to address the colonial patrimony and the traces of Belgium's colonial past, in order to understand current forms of inequality and discrimination, has been going on for more than a decade, but with very little effect in political decision making and wider public dis-

---

1 CMCLD homepage: https://www.memoirecoloniale.be/a-propos/nos-realisations

courses (Lismond-Mertes 2018). It appears simpler to honor the South African President Nelson Mandela by naming the new Brussels rugby stadium the Nelson Mandela Stadium, or to condemn US and French imperialism, than to have an honest conversation about Belgium's colonial aberrations. It also seems easier in Brussels today to glorify those who oppressed and exploited rather than to honor those who fought for freedom and equality (Njall Soiresse 2017). As Achille Mbembe writes:

> The long humiliation of Blacks and their invisibility are still written in golden letters on the entire surface of the territory. (Mbembe 2006: 5)[2]

As the advocacy for a recontextualization of several colonial monuments has progressed, so too has investment in the creation and consolidation of new traces of the Black presence in Brussels.

Matonge: Where Black Belgians Meet

One of the most important imprints has grown organically: the neighborhood of Matonge, which itself is now home to two important symbolic markers of the Black presence in Brussels – Lumumba Square and a prominent artwork, both discussed below. Matonge takes its name from a lively and fashionable neighborhood in Kinshasa, the place where Congolese Soukous and Ndombolo music took root and where artists such as Papa Wemba and Koffi Olomide emerged. Brussels' Matonge, which is situated in the Ixelles municipality at the Porte de Namur (Namur Gate), developed in the late 1960s in the area surrounding the African House (Demart 2013a). The African House was a residence for students from the Belgian Congo, established when the Belgian authorities started timidly to accept Congolese to study at Belgian institutions of higher learning.

Consequently, the building became the first meeting place of Congolese students who lived in Brussels. After the independence of Congo, the neighborhood became a place of reference, with boutiques, hairdressers, groceries specializing in African food products, restaurants, and bars; it became

---

2 Translated by the author. In the original: "La longue humiliation des Noirs et leur invisibilité sont encore écrites en lettres d'or sur toute la surface du territoire."

a space reminiscent of the Matonge neighborhood in Kinshasa. While the area emerged from the fact that African students were assigned to live there, it never became a space of predominantly Black residence (Demart 2013a). Indeed, residents of African descent are estimated to constitute only 8 percent of the people who live in Matonge (Swyngedouw and Swyngedouw 2009). From the 1960s onward, Matonge became first and foremost a meeting place for Africans living in or visiting Belgium, a social and economic center, not a place to necessarily settle. Matonge "functions, both symbolically and materially, as a key signifying place in the construction of Congolese diaspora identity, while shaping a new form of 'glocal' urbanity in Brussels" (ibid.: 72).

Therefore, it is not surprising that this neighborhood is a place of Black political mobilization (Demart 2013b) and also the location of the two most remarkable explicit imprints of Black presence in Brussels: not only Lumumba Square (see Figure 2.4) but also, about 120 meters from the square, the gigantic reproduction of a Chéri Samba fresco. The original is to be found in the infamous Africa Museum, in the Afropea exhibition room that focuses on the history of the African presence in Belgium. Entitled *Matonge–Ixelles. Porte de Namur! Porte de l'Amour?* (Matonge–Ixelles. Gate of Namur! Gate of Love?), it was installed on June 9, 2002 on the walls of a derelict building at an important crossing in the neighborhood. It was the result of a long struggle by different associations, among them several with strong links to the African diaspora, and it represents the very first example of African contemporary art in a Brussels public space (CEC 2002). Originally, the work was meant to be there temporarily. It disappeared from view in 2006 after the renovation of the building it concealed. However, efforts were made to establish the work of art permanently and it returned in 2010 on the façade of another building at the same crossing between Chaussée de Wavre and Chaussée d'Ixelles at the Porte de Namur (Bouhbou 2010).

The painting is based on the location itself. It represents a street scene of Matonge in Brussels, showing in the rear a mixed crowd of Black, Brown and white people filling its streets, and in the front people having a drink on a terrace while watching others. The fresco's production was part of an initiative to trigger an intercultural dialogue at the heart of the Matonge neighborhood, an urban space that is renowned for its African imprint and is a meeting place not only for Blacks but for many Asians and South Americans (CEC 2002; Demart 2013a). The project was also part of a neighborhood revitalization program, which was led by the Ixelles municipality in collaboration with associations, local shopkeepers, and residents. CEC (Coopération Éducation Culture), an NGO established in 1970 that focuses on cooperation, education, and culture, invited the internationally famous Congolese artist Chéri Samba to create a painting inspired by the neighborhood. Chéri Samba is best known for paintings showing and commenting on everyday life in Congo, almost always including text in French and Lingala. Samba's work highlights social problems such as poverty, corruption, racism, sexism, health, and crime. He explained that he seeks to appeal to people's conscience and that artists must make people think. Moreover, Samba has been invested in nourishing and refashioning a common identity across the African diaspora and he usually paints himself at the center of his visual social commentaries (Samba and Magnin 2004).

Figure 2.1: Chéri Samba's Porte de Namur. Port de l'Amour? fresco.
Photograph: Sibo Rugwiza Kanobana

This work of art is no different: it features a self-portrait of the artist with text in French and Lingala commenting on what Matonge is and represents. Underneath the self-portrait are the words:

> Matonge–Ixelles. Gate of Namur! Gate of Love? I have traveled around the world, never have I seen a city like Brussels and a neighborhood like Matonge in Ixelles where everybody interacts with everybody (over 100 nationalities in this neighborhood alone). Difficult to describe in one word what Matonge is – Brussels or Brussels itself. Brussels is a mythical city. Brussels is paradise.[3]

---

3 Translated by the author. In the original: "Matonge–Ixelles. Porte de Namur! Porte de l'Amour? J'ai sillonné le monde entier, jamais je n'ai vu une ville comme Bruxelles et un

These words seem to straightforwardly praise Brussels and Matonge for their multiculturalism, but stating that Brussels is mythical and a paradise reveals a certain irony, or even sarcasm. The gate of entry to Matonge is the old city gate whose name refers to the town of Namur to the south of Brussels. This is also the name of the metro station and bus stops where one should alight if visiting Matonge. The name Namur forms an imperfect rhyme with *amour* (love), but Samba doesn't claim that the Porte de Namur is a gate of love. Rather, he questions it and wonders whether it can be such a place. This ambiguity is all the more apparent because, at first glance, the bright colors, the smile on Samba's face, and the crowd give an impression of happiness and post-racial conviviality. However, this combines with a text in which an older white man says "What I see here surprises me, since when do Africans read?,"[4] as well as comments such as "I don't like to stay too long in this neighborhood"[5] and "This neighborhood is invaded"[6] – but also "You have to be in a society where everybody's mixing."[7]

As a result, this impressive work of art that dominates the urban landscape of Matonge expresses the tensions and contradictions that are connected to a multicultural context that is imbricated with a colonial legacy. There is no naïve celebration of a supposedly post-racial society here, but a honest engagement with the past, the present, and the future, in which Black and white Belgians are not only onlookers but participants who interact with each other, acknowledge racism, but also envision a common tomorrow. Meanwhile, the 12 by 15 meter reproduction that hangs on the front of a large building has become iconic, not only of the Matonge neighborhood and the African diaspora in Brussels but also of Brussels as a whole. It appears to be there to stay, unmoved for a decade now, and cherished by the majority of

---

quartier comme Matonge d'Ixelles où tout le monde se mêle (plus de 100 nationalités dans ce seul quartier). Difficile de décrire en un mot ce qu'est Matonge – Bruxelles ou Bruxelles elle-même. Bruxelles eza ville mythique. Bruxelles eza lola (paradis)" (Samba 2002: 1).

4 Translated by the author. In the original: "ce que je vois ici m'étonne, depuis quand les Africains lisent-ils?"

5 Translated by the author. In the original: "je n'aime pas rester longtemps dans ce quartier."

6 Translated by the author. In the original: "ce quartier est envahi.."

7 Translated by the author. In the original: "Il faut être dans une société où tout le monde se mêle."

Brussels' citizens for the honesty, ambiguities, contradictions, and tensions it expresses.

Black Voices of Resistance

The push to create a voice for Africans in Belgium can be traced back to activist Paul Panda Farnana (cf. Tshitungu 2012). Born in 1888 near Banana, in Bas-Congo, he traveled to Belgium in 1900, accompanying a Belgian colonist who died shortly after his arrival. Farnana was placed in the custody of the man's sister and was educated at the School of Horticulture and Agriculture in Vilvoorde, a Brussels suburb, subsequently continuing his education in Paris at an institute for tropical agriculture. When World War One broke out, he enlisted in the Congolese Volunteer Corps and became a German prisoner of war in August 1914, remaining in Germany until the war ended (Brosens 2014). On his return to Belgium, he became involved in politics and founded the Union Congolaise in Brussels and "became known in Belgium and abroad for speaking out for African rights" (Stanard 2016: 236).

Each year, during the commemoration of the capture of Tabora in 1916, a turning point in World War One after Germany's defeat in Africa in which Congolese troops played a key role (Catherine 2014), Panda headed a delegation of the Union Congolaise to the Grand Place in Brussels asking for recognition of the African war effort. Eventually, in 1927, at his insistence a monument paying tribute to the Congolese soldiers who died during the war was inaugurated in Léopoldville (present-day Kinshasa), the then capital of the Belgian Congo, named after King Leopold II. However, when he returned to Congo, he died in mysterious circumstances, most probably by poisoning. Nobody knows who was responsible for his death, but what is known is that Farnana was disliked by the authorities and was considered to be a Congolese who upset the colonial order.[8]

Historians argue that it is because of Farnana, dubbed the first Congolese intellectual, and his activism for African rights that Belgian authorities enacted a policy of isolation, prohibiting Congolese from immigrating to Belgium in order to avoid ideas such as freedom and equality finding their way

---

8 See the 2014 documentary by Françoise Levie, *Panda Farnana, un Congolais qui dérange*, at https://www.youtube.com/watch?v=bNpqcC8MerI.

back to the colony (Stanard 2016; Kagné 2001; Etambala 2019). However, the Black subject – note, not citizen – of the Belgian kingdom continued to play not only an important economic role but, during World War Two, a military one. An estimated 22,000 soldiers and carriers of the Force Publique, as they were called, fought in Ethiopia alongside British troops and participated in expeditions to West Africa, Egypt, Jordan, Syria, Iraq, and Burma. However, members were denied the right to march as victors alongside Allied troops in the cities of Europe. The Belgian government in exile explicitly objected, afraid that the honoring of Congolese troops might trigger political ideas that would jeopardize the colonial capitalist order (Braeckman 2020). After independence, the Belgian authorities abandoned the soldiers. None of the Congolese veterans ever received a pension to support their families. The only thing that they "received" was a monument in Brussels – the Memorial for the African Campaign, erected in 1970 in the municipality of Schaerbeek – which was ignored until it was reappropriated by the African diaspora in Belgium (ibid.).

The memorial presents two profiles of soldiers, stylized in stereotypical ways. They both sport the traditional headgear for colonial troops of the time: the white officer with a pith helmet and the Black soldier with a fez. However, the differences are not only to be found in their hats but also in their facial features. The Black soldier is presented with thick lips and a chubby nose, while the white one has thin lips and a pointy, straight nose. This memorial suggests that both are equal; they cross hands as a collaborative gesture. It is a remarkable monument for two reasons: first, because it was erected in tribute to all the operations carried out in Africa, from the so-called anti-slavery campaigns in the late 19th century

Figure 2.2: The Memorial for the African Campaign.
Photograph: Merijn Van de Pol (creative commons)

until World War Two; and second, because it is the only known monument on which the white and Black protagonists face each other, at the same height, without the white man dominating the Black "other."

The uniqueness of the monument and the important story it tells have led Brussels PAD associations to organize an alternative and activist ceremony every November 11 since 2008, to commemorate the Unknown Congolese Soldier. This is equivalent to the official Armistice ceremony at the monument for the Unknown Soldier at the Congress Column in central Brussels (Catherine 2018). Thus, for more than a decade, Belgium's African communities have laid claim to this monument, using it as a place of remembrance of the African contribution to European history and also of Black suffering and exclusion.

However, the memorial is still problematic for several reasons. First and foremost, the aesthetics perpetuate racial stereotypes and obscure the racist oppression and violence that were part of everyday life in the Force Publique. Second, while it presents an image of racial equality, it is in fact an excuse to exclude and ignore the African war effort from the regular war commemorations, most notably the annual World War One Armistice commemoration in the center of the city. Third, not only does the memorial erase the fact that the Force Publique was made complicit in the terror that the colonial authorities inflicted on the Congolese people, it also underwrites an obsession with military achievements and the glorification of war – or, as Achille Mbembe eloquently states:

> That so many of these monuments are dedicated to the glory of soldiers and servicemen indicates how deep the habit of massacre now lies in our collective unconscious. (Mbembe 2006: 3)[9]

Yet, even if we take this pertinent critique into consideration, the yearly commemoration of the African war effort is of great importance in understanding the humanity of African traces in Belgian history and the common history we, of all races, share. It is an example of how monuments can be reappropriated to bring people together even if they have been erected to divide. Consequently, as Clette-Gakuba and Vander Elst (2018) explain, the political action

---

9 Translated by the author. In the original: "Qu'autant de ces monuments soient consacrés à la gloire des soldats et des militaires indique à quel niveau de profondeur gît désormais, dans notre inconscient collectif, l'accoutumance au massacre."

in which the reappropriation of colonial monuments is situated is not just about a restitution of the past, but just as much a way to communicate the emancipatory struggles and active transformation of a still racist present.

This became a focus in 2018, during ceremonies for the centenary of the Armistice. Belgian, British, and Canadian flags flew next to those of former British colonies at the Tomb of the Unknown Soldier at the Congress Column, yet there was no Congolese flag, although hundreds of thousands of Congolese played a leading role in the outcome of the conflict. And this was not due to a lack of interest on the part of Black organizations to include this part of history in the official ceremony. Their efforts and requests were systematically rejected (Demart and Dibua Athapol 2018). This is an example of how Belgium has a difficult time dealing with its colonial past; that the Black presence is erased and ignored at the center – in this case, at the official ceremony, where only white Belgians were commemorated next to other nationalities, but not the formerly colonized Congolese subjects of Belgian Congo.

Since 2007, several Black activist associations have demanded that the authorities and the royal family include the African contribution to the war effort in official Armistice commemorations. As a result, in 2016, the Belgian government laid a wreath in front of the Memorial for the African Campaign. That year was also the centenary of the capture of Tabora, which marked the beginning of the end of the German Empire (Roulette 2018), but the ceremony was not a moment of inclusion; rather, it was one of racial segregation. And it did not happen every year. After 2016, the official ceremony went back to its white normalcy and no formal presence of state officials was to be found again at the African memorial during Armistice celebrations. Even if the history of the Battle of Tabora is widely acknowledged as divisive, it is only seen as a white individual achievement. Indeed, a memorial in the city's Forest municipality honors one person for this battle, who is presented as a white man who "singlehandedly" won the Battle of Tabora: General Charles Tombeur, knighted as Baron of Tabora.

Patrice Lumumba Square: Claiming Black Spaces

An important symbol of Black presence in Brussels and recent addition to the city's public space is Patrice Lumumba Square. It was officially inaugurated on June 30, 2018, on the Democratic Republic of Congo's (DRC's) day of independence. Standing at the entrance to a central location for African peoples – the Matonge neighborhood (described above) – the square is the result of more than a decade of advocacy for public space that pays respect to the murdered first prime minister of the DRC. Community organizations with strong Afro-Belgian affiliations, such as Belgian Afrodescendants Committee (BAMKO), Change, CMCLD, and Groupement des Femmes Africaines Inspirantes et Actives (GFAIA), played a central role to achieve this (CMCLD 2018), along with other collectives and efforts by individual intellectuals and local citizens (Duval and Delobel 2018; Lismond-Mertes 2018). Most advocates had initially proposed another location, a square in the municipality of Ixelles behind Saint Boniface church, in the heart of Matonge. An informal street plaque with the name had already been put there by activists, and, thanks to a Belgian NGO's cyber intervention, if you search for it in Google Maps, you will find Futur Place Lumumba. Yet, the Ixelles municipality refused to use that location (Ben Yacoub and Abrassart 2016) and rejected the idea of a square named after Lumumba, arguing that he was not a unifying figure (Duval and Delobel 2018). Eventually, an interpellation by Zoubida Jellab, a councilor for the Ville de Bruxelles municipality, got the ball rolling for the establishment of a Lumumba Square at Ville de Bruxelles's border with Ixelles – i.e., at the Porte de Namur, the gate of entry to the Matonge neighborhood in Ixelles (Lismond-Mertes 2018).

Figure 2.3: The informal Square Lumumba behind Saint Boniface church. Photograph: Sibo Rugwiza Kanobana

The question remains whether the establishment of the square can be considered a change in the way in which public authorities in Belgium are addressing colonial history and its recollection. While it is a step in the right direction, one cannot deny that negationist forces in relation to colonial crimes are still at play within state structures (cf. Clette-Gakuba and Vander Elst 2018). Moreover, the square cannot be called a "proper" square, which is what the initial Place Lumumba activists strived for. The "real" square is officially a triangular crossing of three streets, with a low volume traffic, surrounded by houses and trees, and featuring the terrace of a local bar. The official Place Lumumba, however, is just a little piece of the sidewalk[10] (Braeckman 2018), limited to a narrow strip 15 meters by 50 meters, between the taxi stand at the metro station's exit and Avenue Marnix, a large avenue with heavy traffic that is part of the Brussels ring road, nicknamed *la petite ceinture*, that circumvents the city center. Consequently, no buildings will ever have Lumumba Square as an address (Lismond-Mertes 2018).

Figure 2.4: The official Lumumba Square sign at the Porte de Namur. Photograph: Sibo Rugwiza Kanobana

In essence, Lumumba Square is limited to a plaque, which is nearly invisible compared with the large advertisements surrounding the square. As historian Elikia M'Bokolo said during his speech at the inauguration, this plaque may be a revolution, but it is not enough. A square without a statue, monument, or other symbol may become a subtle way to perpetuate a failure to acknowledge the value of the person who embodies the Congolese will for independence and sovereignty. The mayor of Ville de Bruxelles municipality appeared to be aware of this in 2018, as he explained in an interview with *Le Soir*, a Francophone Belgian daily newspaper. He claimed that the municipality wanted something strong to be added to the square. Therefore, next to the plaque, a monument would be displayed in the months following the inauguration. The authorities reportedly freed up money to finance a call for artist pro-

---

10   Translated by the author. In the original: "un bout de trotoir."

posals for such a monument (Biermé 2018). But two years later nothing had happened and the mayor's spokesperson refuted the statement from 2018 by announcing that "There will be no statue" and claiming that "There was no agreement about that, it was only a lead [to explore]" (cited in Galindo 2020).

Maybe a statue of another individual is not what is needed (cf. Mbembe 2006), but, while there may now be a street sign referring to a Lumumba Square and a plaque with some contextualization, the municipality still honors Belgian colonists who committed crimes against humanity in its public space in a much more prestigious way. Elikia M'Bokolo addressed this at the inauguration, when he pointed out that the establishment of a Lumumba Square should logically lead to a questioning and revisiting of other public spaces that are directly linked to colonialism. He asked the crowd whether it could accept that the square was only named after Lumumba, without any further spatial planning, while not too far away a bust in a park glorifies Émile Storms, a colonist, assassin, and criminal (Bouffioux 2018), and just 300 meters away a huge monument glorifies King Leopold II, the man who symbolizes the horror that was inflicted on Congo when it was colonized by the Belgians.[11] These monuments, next to so many others, legitimize the colonial conquest by obscuring its destructive character (Clette-Gakuba and Vander Elst 2018). Furthermore, the problem is that the authorities viewed the inauguration of the square as an event for African communities, not as a Belgian event. However, it is essential that it is not seen as a memorial for associations of PAD, but as a tool of inclusive citizenship that aims to decolonize Belgian society as a whole (Njall Soiresse 2018). The question is indeed whether a country that self-identifies as democratic chooses disunity and dissension by holding on to its colonial symbols, or whether it wants to move forward and create an inclusive society in which the African diaspora does not need to legitimize itself, and in which the public space is respectful of all its citizens, Black and white, past and present (Vincent 2020).

Moreover, Ludo De Witte points to the danger that we could end up in what Herbert Marcuse called "repressive tolerance" (Wolff, Moore, and Marcuse 1970: 81–123), where one thing is tolerated in order to rebuke another. The danger is that the establishment of Lumumba Square may be taken as a tool not for decolonizing society as a whole, but rather to mute any further

---

11 Meanwhile the Emile Storms bust was removed by authorities on June 30 2022.

efforts at decolonization. Yet, a street sign or a plaque is not enough; it is not even a beginning. In a best case scenario, it is a letter of intent. Indeed, more and deeper work is needed, mentalities have to change, and the whole of the public space should be decolonized, including teaching history differently and stimulating the artistic, historical, and political work necessary to revisit colonial history (Duval and De Witte 2018).

All these critiques highlight that the decolonial nature of a Lumumba Square has not achieved much if it is not matched with other important tasks that are meant for all Belgians, whatever their racial or ethnic background. However, this is long-term work, and, in the meantime, the revisiting and reappropriation of colonial monuments and the wider public space by PAD is taking place, organically, step by step, without necessarily the official involvement of the authorities. Conclusively, and as also shown in the examples of Lumumba Square and the Armistice celebrations, public space seems to unceasingly play a critical role in the decolonial processes with which Brussels needs to engage, in order to create a common destiny that is not blind to humanity's past perversions, contemporary flaws, or future obstacles.

References

Arnaut, Karel and Bambi Ceuppens (2009) "De Ondiepe Gronden En Vage Grenzen van de Raciale Verbeelding in Vlaanderen" in Karel Arnaut, Sarah Bracke, Bambi Ceuppens, Nadia Fadil, and Meryem Kanmaz (eds.), *Een Leeuw in Een Kooi. De Grenzen van Het Multiculturele Vlaanderen*. Antwerp: Meulenhoff-Manteau.

Ben Yacoub, Joachim and Gia Abrassart (2016) "La Chasse aux Spectres Monumentaux dans la Belgique Congolaise" in Sarah Demart and Gia Abrassart (eds.), Sarah Demart and Gia Abrassart (eds.), *Créer en Postcolonie: 2010--2015 Voix et Dissidences Belgo-Congolaises*. Brusssels: Palais des Beaux-Arts.

Biermé, Maxime (2018) "Porte de Namur: Le Combat de Patrice Lumumba Récompensé," *Le Soir*, April 18, sec. Région: Bruxelles, https://plus.lesoir.be/151815/article/2018-04-18/porte-de-namur-le-combat-de-patrice-lumumba-recompense

Bouffioux, Michel (2018) "L'Histoire Que Nous Raconte le Crâne de Lusinga," *Paris Match Belgique*, March 22, https://parismatch.be/actualites/so ciete/129682/le-crane-de-lusinga-interroge-le-passe-colonial-belge

Bouhbou (2010) "Chéri Samba: Porte de Namur! Porte de l'Amour?," Sanza 08 [blog], June, https://bdmurales.wordpress.com/2010/06/17/cheri-samba-porte-de-namur-porte-de-lamour/

Braeckman, Colette (2018) "Bruxelles: Un Bout de Trottoir Pour Sceller le Retour Symbolique de Lumumba," *Le Soir [online]*, June 30.

Braeckman, Colette (2020) "Les Soldats Congolais (Inconnus) dans les Guerres Belges," *Le Soir* [online], June 26, https://plus.lesoir.be/309755/article/2020-06-26/les-soldats-congolais-inconnus-dans-les-guerres-belges

Brosens, Griet (2014) "Congo on Yser: The 32 Congolese Soldiers in the Belgian Army in the First World War," *Cahiers Bruxellois/Brusselse Cahiers* 1E (XLVI): 243–55.

Catherine, Lucas (2006) *Wandelen naar Kongo: langs koloniaal erfgoed in Brussel en België*. Berchem: EPO.

Catherine, Lucas (2014) *Des tranchées en Afrique: la guerre oubliée des Congolais contre les Allemands en 1914–1918*. Translated by Jacquie Dever. Brussels: Aden.

Catherine, Lucas (2018) "Chronologie Partielle de la Contestation des Statues Coloniales en Belgique,," *Bruxelles en Mouvements*, November.

CEC (2002) "Chéri Samba: Mantongé–Ixelles. La Porte de Namur! La Porte de L'Amour?," CEC Depuis 1977 [online], https://www.cec-ong.org/cec-depuis-1977/la-porte-de-namur-la-porte-de-l-amour/

Clette-Gakuba, Véronique and Martin Vander Elst (2018) "Une Tentative de Décolonisation de la Statue de Léopold II," *Bruxelles een Mouvement* 297 (November–December): 19–23.

De Smet, François (2016) "'L'appel d'air' ou la Victoire des Peurs," Myria: Centre Fédéral Migration [online], [online], https://www.myria.be/fr/evolu tions/opinion-migration-lappel-dair-ou-la-victoire-des-peurs

Debeuckelaere, Heleen and Gia Abrassart (eds.) (2020) *Being Imposed Upon*. Eindhoven: Onomatopee.

Demart, Sarah (2013a) "Histoire Orale à Matonge (Bruxelles): Un Miroir Postcolonial," *Revue Européenne des Migrations Internationales* 29 (1): 133–55, https://doi.org/10.4000/remi.6323.

Demart, Sarah (2013b) "Riots in Matonge and ... the Indifference of Public Authority?," *Brussels Studies*, July, https://doi.org/10.4000/brussels.1168

Demart, Sarah and Gia Abrassart (eds.) (2016) *Créer en Postcolonie: 2010–2015 Voix et Dissidences Belgo-Congolaises*. Brussels: Palais des Beaux-Arts.

Demart, Sarah and Georgina Dibua Athapol (2018) "L'Armée Coloniale Belge et les Commémorations du Centenaire de la Ière Guerre Mondiale: Georgine Dibua Athapol," *Edt. Kwandika de Bamko*, 5: 1–5.

Demart, Sarah, Bruno Schoumaker, Marie Godin, and Ilke Adam (2017) *Burgers Met Afrikaanse Roots: Een Portret van Congolese, Rwandese en Burundese Belgen*. Brussels: Koning Boudewijn Stichting and Fondation Roi Baudouin.

Duval, Jérôme and Ludo De Witte (2018) "Entretien Avec Ludo de Witte Lors de l'inauguration du Square Lumumba à Bruxelles." Liège: Comité pour l'Abolition des Dettes Illégitimes (CADTM).

Duval, Jérôme and Robin Delobel (2018) "Patrice Lumumba in Brussels: A Square against Forgetting." Liège: Comité pour l'Abolition des Dettes Illégitimes (CADTM).

Earle, T. F. and K. J. P. Lowe (eds.) (2010) *Black Africans in Renaissance Europe*. New York: Cambridge University Press.

Etambala, Zana Mathieu (2019) *Congo 1876–1914. Veroverd, bezet, gekoloniseerd*. Amsterdam: Amsterdam University Press.

Galindo, Gabriela (2020) "Brussels Drops Plans for Statue of Congo's Murdered Prime Minister," *Brussels Times*, June 23, https://www.brusselstimes.com/brussels/118082/brussels-drops-plans-for-statue-of-congos-patrice-lumumba-murdered-prime-minister-independence-leader-ixelles/

Grégoire, Nicole (2010) "Identity Politics, Social Movement and the State: 'Pan-African' Associations and the Making of an 'African Community' in Belgium," *African Diaspora* 3 (1): 159–81, https://doi.org/10.1163/187254610X505709

Grégoire, Nicole, Sibo Kanobana, and Sarah Demart (2023) "Troubles to Define: The Emergence of Black Studies in Belgium" in Nicole Grégoire, Sarah Fila-Bakabadio, and Jacinthe Mazzochetti (eds.), *Black Studies in Europe: A Transnational Dialogue*. Evanston IL: Northwestern University Press.

Hesse, Barnor (2002) "Forgotten Like a Bad Dream: Atlantic Slavery and the Ethics of Postcolonial Memory" in David Theo Goldberg and Ato Quayson (eds.), *Relocating Postcolonialism*. Oxford: Blackwell.

Hondius, Dienke (2008) "Black Africans in 17th Century Amsterdam," *Renaissance and Reformation/Renaissance et Reformation* 31 (2).

Hondius, Dienke (2011) "Access to the Netherlands of Enslaved and Free Black Africans: Exploring Legal and Social Historical Practices in the Sixteenth–Nineteenth Centuries," *Slavery & Abolition* 32 (3): 377–95, https://doi.org/10.1080/0144039X.2011.588476

Imbach, Pauline (2008) "Promenade Anti-Coloniale à Bruxelles, l'Ancienne Métropole du Congo." Liège: Comité pour l'Abolition des Dettes Illégitimes (CADTM).

Jacobs, Thibault (2018) "Empreintes du Congo Belge dans l'Espace Public Bruxellois," *Bruxelles en Mouvement* 297 (November–December): 13–16.

Kagné, Bonaventure (2001) "L'Immigration d'Origine Subsaharienne Avant 1960: La Belgique Découvre 'l'Africain'," *Courier Hebdomadaire* 1721.

Lafleur, Jean-Michel, Marco Martinello, and Andrea Rea (2015) "Une Brève Histoire Migratoire de La Belgique" in Gildas Simon (ed.), *Dictionnaire des Migrations Internationales: Approche Géohistorique*. Paris: Armand Colin.

Lismond-Mertes, Arnaud (2018) "Une Place Lumumba à Bruxelles," *Ensemble*, September.

Martinello, Marco and Andrea Rea (2003) "Belgium's Immigration Policy Brings Renewal and Challenges," Migration Information Source, October, https://www.migrationpolicy.org/article/belgiums-immigration-policy-brings-renewal-and-challenges/

Mayoyo Bitumba, Tipo-Tipo (1995) "Migration Sud/Nord: Levier Ou Obstacle? Les Zaïrois En Belgique," *Cahiers Africains* 13.

Mbembe, Achille (2006) "Que Faire des Statues et Monuments Coloniaux?," *Africultures. Les Mondes en Relation*, article 4354, March 16, africultures.com/que-faire-des-statues-et-monuments-coloniaux-4354/

Mincke, Christophe (2016) "La Légende Dorée de La Petite Belgique Cache un Racisme Rampant," *Le Monde*, March 23, sec. Tribune, https://www.lemonde.fr/idees/article/2016/03/23/la-legende-doree-de-la-petite-belgique-cache-un-racisme-rampant_4888744_3232.html

Ndiaye, Pap (2009) *La Condition Noire: Essai sur une Minorité Française*. Folio actuel 140. Paris: Gallimard.

Njall Soiresse, Kalvin (2017) "L'Espace Public Belge, Révélateur du Déni Colonial," *Politique: Revue Belge d'Analyse et de Débat*, 18 July, https://www.revuepolitique.be/lespace-public-belge-revelateur-du-deni-colonial/

Njall Soiresse, Kalvin (2018) "Square Lumumba: Décoloniser les Espaces et les Esprits," *Politique: Revue Belge d'Analyse et de Débat*, July, https://www.revuepolitique.be/square-lumumba-decoloniser-les-espaces-et-les-esprits/

Quijano, Anibal (2000) "Coloniality of Power, Eurocentrism, and Latin America," *Nepantla: Views from the South* 1 (3): 533–80.

Roulette, Damien (2018) "Les Congolais Grands Oubliés des Commémorations de l'Armistice de 14–18 ?," RTBF.Be, November 14, https://www.rtbf.be/info/belgique/detail_les-congolais-grands-oublies-des-commemorations-de-l-armistice-de-14-18?id=10072856

Samba, Chéri and André Magnin (2004) *J'aime Chéri Samba*. Arles and Paris: Actes Sud and Fondation Cartier pour l'Art Contemporain.

Stanard, Matthew G. (2016) "Interwar Crisis and Europe's Unfinished Empires" in Nicholas Doumanis (ed.), *The Oxford Handbook of European History, 1914–1945*. Oxford and New York: Oxford University Press.

Stanard, Matthew G. (2019) *The Leopard, the Lion, and the Cock: Colonial Memories and Monuments in Belgium*. Leuven: Leuven University Press.

Swyngedouw, Eva and Erik Swyngedouw (2009) "The Congolese Diaspora in Brussels and Hybrid Identity Formation: Multi-Scalarity and Diasporic Citizenship," *Urban Research & Practice* 2 (1): 68–90, https://doi.org/10.1080/17535060902727074

Tshitungu, Antoine (2012) "Comment Construire une Mémoire Historique Objective de la Colonisation loin des Clichés sur les Africains?" in *Actes de La Conférence "Lutte Contre les Discriminations au Regard de l'Histoire et de la Mémoire Coloniales: État des Lieux."* Brussels: Collectif Mémoire Coloniale et Lutte contre les Discriminations.

Van Mol, Christof and Helga de Valk (2016) "Migration and Immigrants in Europe: A Historical and Demographic Perspective" in Blanca Garcés-Mascareñas and Rinus Penninx (eds.), *Integration Processes and Policies in Europe*. Cham: Springer International Publishing, https://doi.org/10.1007/978-3-319-21674-4_3

Vincent, Sachka (2020) "60 Jaar Dipenda, Tijd Voor Een Beeldenstorm?," *Rekto:Verso*, June 30, https://www.rektoverso.be/artikel/60-jaar-dipenda-tijd-voor-iconoclasme

Wolff, Robert Paul, Barrington Moore, and Herbert Marcuse (1970) *A Critique of Pure Tolerance*. Beacon Paperback 328. Boston MA: Beacon Press.

Chapter 3
Black London

Olive Vassell

The United Kingdom's capital city, London, is famous for its history and monuments. In recent times, however, many of the city's markers have been criticized for being symbols of enslavement and racism. In 2020, such representations became the focus of protests following the police killing of George Floyd in the USA. Demonstrators gathered in Windrush Square, (a longtime site of activism for Black residents which will be discussed in more detail in the next section), while others went into the center of the city, targeting memorials to those who had brutalized and marginalized racial and ethnic groups in the name of the empire. This included a statue of noted slaveholder Robert Milligan outside the Museum of London Docklands, which was removed by the institution just days after another statue of a slaveholder, Edward Colston, had been torn down and thrown into the river in southwest England by antiracism protesters. Museum officials acknowledged that the monument was part of the ongoing problematic regime of whitewashing history and disregarded the effects of Milligan's crimes.[1]

These demonstrations were just some of the many outcries against police killings abroad and at home; police brutality in the UK is not new and has often led to uprisings of the Black population. In 1995, for example, protests erupted after the death in police custody of Wayne Douglas, a young Black man.[2] Officers said that Douglas, aged 26, had been arrested for suspected burglary and had died of a heart attack while in custody. But witnesses told a

---

1 "Robert Milligan: Slave trader statue removed from outside London museum", June 9, 2020 (https://www.bbc.com/news/uk-england-london-52977088).
2 "1995: Riots break out in Brixton", December 13, 1995 (http://news.bbc.co.uk/onthisday/hi/dates/stories/december/13/newsid_2559000/2559341.stm).

Black newspaper, the *Caribbean Times*, that he had been severely beaten. One eye witness later told a 1996 inquest into Douglas's death that a police officer had knelt on his head while he was handcuffed and that he was held face down on the ground by at least four others (mudlark121 2016).

Windrush Square was the site of some of the first Black Lives Matter (BLM) antiracism protests in the UK. On July 9, 2016, demonstrators rallied there after the police killing of Philando Castile and Alton Sterling in the USA, as happened in Berlin.[3] The previous day protestors had marched to the country's ruling body, the Houses of Parliament. In August the city was one of four - others were Birmingham, Manchester and Nottingham - that took part in a "national shutdown" to protest deaths in police custody, racist border policing, and everyday racism. Activists simultaneously blocked roads in these cities, including one to Heathrow airport, chosen partly because it was where Angolan deportee Jimmy Mubenga died after being restrained by private security guards in 2010. The latter were acquitted of manslaughter in 2014. The protests coincided with the fifth anniversary of the police shooting of Mark Duggan, a 29-year-old Black British father of six who was killed in North London in August 2011. His murder ignited riots across the capital and in other English cities.

However, these early BLM protests did not spark as much interest as those in 2020. As a result of the reactions to Floyd's killing, London mayor Sadiq Khan, for example, advised that monuments honoring historical figures with legacies of enslavement would be reviewed, explaining that they reflected the wealth gained from enslavement and that they ignored the contributions of many communities (Onibada 2020). Khan, who is of Pakistani origin, had previously supported the call for a British slavery museum and a memorial for Stephen Lawrence, a Black teenager who was murdered in 1993 by a gang of white youths in a racially motivated attack.

Additionally, Khan announced the establishment of the Commission for Diversity in the Public Realm to review and improve diversity in London's public space. He said:

---

3 "Freedom! Freedom!': Black Lives Matter activists take over Brixton's Windrush Square", July 10, 2016 (https://www.swlondoner.co.uk/news/10072016-freedom-freedom-black-lives-matter-activists-take-brixtons-windrush-square)

Our capital's diversity is our greatest strength, yet our statues, road names and public spaces reflect a bygone era. It is an uncomfortable truth that our nation and city owes a large part of its wealth to its role in the slave trade and while this is reflected in our public realm, the contribution of many of our communities to life in our capital has been wilfully ignored. This cannot continue. We must ensure that we celebrate the achievements and diversity of all in our city, and that we commemorate those who have made London what it is – that includes questioning which legacies are being celebrated. The Black Lives Matter protests have rightly brought this to the public's attention, but it's important that we take the right steps to work together to bring change and ensure that we can all be proud of our public landscape.[4]

However, not everyone agrees with his plan to review monuments to controversial figures. When graffiti was found on a statue of the country's wartime prime minister, Winston Churchill, labeling him racist for his support of eugenics and his role in the 1943 Bengal famine, far right groups such as Britain First clashed with police while "defending" it. The UK prime minister, Boris Johnson, also swore to do the same, arguing that antiracism protesters should attack the substance of the problem, not the symbols. However, he did pledge to establish a commission to tackle inequality and to build more monuments celebrating Black Britons (Johnson 2020). The commission's report, which was issued in 2021, was widely criticized for its denial of institutional racism. Simukai Chigudu, a Zimbabwean-born associate professor of African politics at Oxford University, said the focus on statues during the 2020 protests has been revealing because monuments record a particular version of the past – one that is open to change. He argues that a statue's meaning is not fixed and should instead be collectively and consistently reviewed over time. Thus, figures who no longer enjoy pride of place in public view should be put in museums and learned about there (Onibada 2020).

Meanwhile, two new memorials to Black Britons were signed off on in East London after the 2020 protests. The Hackney Council announced that it had commissioned them to honour the borough's Windrush Generation,

---

4 "Mayor unveils commission to review diversity of London's public realm", June 9, 2020 (https://www.london.gov.uk/press-releases/mayoral/mayor-unveils-commission-to-re view-diversity).

Figure 3.1: Veronica Ryan's Custard Apple (Annonaceae), Breadfruit (Moraceae), and Soursop (Annonaceae), 2021. Source: Courtesy of the artist, Paula Cooper Gallery, New York, and Alison Jacques, London. Photograph: Andy Keate, 2021

people who came to the UK from the Caribbean between 1948 and 1971. One is a series of marble and bronze sculptures depicting Caribbean fruit and vegetables, inspired by Montserrat-born sculptor Veronica Ryan's childhood visits to Ridley Road Market, a popular shopping location for African and Caribbean people in the area. The memorial was unveiled on the first day of Black History Month (October 1) in 2021 (Tandoh, Mohdin, 2021).

The second sculpture, *"Warm Shores,"* by Thomas J. Price is outside Hackney town hall. It is a bronze of a man and a woman created from composites of 30 residents connected to the Windrush Generation (Abrams 2022). The council also announced that it will review statues and the naming of landmarks, streets, parks, and other public spaces to make sure that they reflect local diversity. Explaining the plan, Mayor of Hackney Phillip Glanville said that it was part of the borough's mission to also specifically recognize Black history (Aron 2020a).

The following year, in February 2021, Khan announced the 15 members of the commission who represent a range of leaders from the arts, architecture, community engagement and business sectors and include People of African Descent (PAD) such as social rights activist Toyin Agbetu, art historian and curator, Aindrea Emelife and business owner, Binki Taylor. They will work with a board and local authorities. However, even before the 2020 BLM protests, London's Black communities had been pushing for public recognition of their identities and contributions.

Figure 3.2: Thomas J. Price's, Warm Shores, was unveiled on Windrush Day in June 2022. Photograph: Mr. Gee, 2022

Brixton's Windrush Square: A Performative Space for Black British Identity

Windrush Square in South London epitomizes how Black residents are using spaces to create a sense of belonging and identity. The name pays public tribute to the *Empire Windrush* and its passengers, which brought one of the first large groups of postwar Caribbean immigrants to Britain in 1948. The square is located in Brixton, a district in Lambeth, one of London's 32 boroughs. It was the first area to welcome the Caribbean-born immigrants whose arrival would change the nation's social landscape forever.

Arthur Torrington, the chair of the Windrush Foundation, which he cofounded in 1996 with former passenger Sam King (since deceased), said that the borough provided shelter for men, women, and children while many found their first jobs in this neighborhood.[5] Brixton was also where these new residents purchased food from their birthplaces and where publications such as *The Weekly Gleaner* and *West Indian Gazette* were available to satisfy their need for news from "home." It was also a place to meet fellow countrymen and find brief respite from the daily onslaught of pervasive racism. This chapter of Black British history reflects the area's shifting cultural dynamism.

Before the *Empire Windrush*, the square was originally part of Rush Common; it became known as Tate Gardens after the widow of English sugar merchant Sir Henry Tate purchased the land in 1905 to open a public garden. Tate had earlier funded a public library in nearby Brixton Oval, and a bust of him still stands outside the library today. In 1998, the local government reclaimed more public space from the Common, naming it Windrush Square to mark the 50th anniversary of the arrival of the *Empire Windrush*. Over the years, the square has been a place of social significance and resistance. Its location, flanking the seat of local government, Lambeth town hall, has only added to its importance. In 1955, for example, the town hall hosted a "No Colour Bar Dance." The mayor of Lambeth invited 180 "English" people and 180 "West Indians" to a dance to help address racial tensions, made visible through the hostility whites directed at their Black neighbors. Some 30 years later, in the 1980s, the square became a focal point for protests against apartheid in South Africa.

Its importance to Black Britain has only increased through the years. When, in 2010, Boris Johnson, then mayor of London, reopened the square after it had been closed for rehabilitation and expansion – two spaces once separated by a road were combined – residents were given the opportunity to change the name, but they decided to keep it the same. In recognizing the space's importance to Black residents before its redevelopment, Lambeth council wrote in the minutes of a committee meeting in 2006 that the square was an expression of Brixton's diversity and culture. This underscores the assertion that "place names are more than innocent spatial references or passive artifacts; they are embedded in social power relations and struggles over the identities of places and people" (Kearns and Berg 2002).

In 2014, the square was central to a milestone in Black life, becoming the home of the first repository of Black British history, the Black Cultural Archives. As a cultural and documentation center for people in the UK with

---

5 Torrington, Arthur, interview with Arthur Torrington, by author. London, July 13, 2020.

a direct or distant African family background, the archives trace the history of Black people from the Roman occupation onward. It emerged as a result of several factors, including the death of 13 young Black people in a South London house fire in 1981, which many Blacks believed was intentionally set by white racists.[6]

After receiving community donations – documents and photographs – educator and Black historian Len Garrison, supported by community and public funding, spearheaded an effort to catalog the collection which officially opened at 1 Windrush Square in July 2014. The organization believes that its location is appropriate not only because of its role in recent Black British history but also because it is on the site of two houses built during the Georgian period (1714–1830s), which coincides with a time of significant Black representation in Britain: an estimated 10,000–20,000 PAD lived in 18th-century London.[7] For poet Benjamin Zephaniah, who attended the opening, cultural geography was also key. He described the location as the heart of the Black community for his mother's generation (Dickens 2014).

Furthermore, three years later, on June 22, 2017, Windrush Square bore witness to another first in the UK: a memorial honoring African and Caribbean troops who fought for Britain in World Wars One and Two. The monument was conceived by the Nubian Jak Community Trust, a commemorative plaque and sculpture scheme that has highlighted the contributions of Black people in Britain. Founded in 2006 by Dr. Jak Beula, an entrepreneur and cultural activist, the trust had issued 36 blue plaques (permanent historical markers) around the country by 2020. Its London awardees include singer Bob Marley (2006) and pioneering Black newspaper publisher and activist Claudia Jones (2008). Beula said that the decision to create the memorial for the more than 2 million African and Caribbean military servicemen and servicewomen who participated in the two World Wars was an effort to correct a historical omission and to ensure that young people of African and Caribbean descent are aware of their ancestors' contribution to those wars.[8]

---

6 "The New Cross Massacre", n.d. (https://blackhistorystudies.com/resources/resources/the-new-cross-fire/)

7 Black Cultural Archives – Our Story", n.d. (https://blackculturalarchives.org/our-story)

8 "First ever memorial to African and Caribbean Service Personnel unveiled in Brixton", June 22, 2017 (https://www.gov.uk/government/news/first-ever-memorial-to-african-and-caribbean-service-personnel-unveiled-in-brixton)

Figure 3.3: The African and Caribbean War Memorial, 2017. Photograph: Vincenzo Albano / Art UK

Like other commemorations to Black figures, the process of creating the memorial was difficult. Beula said that it had first been scheduled to be placed at Tilbury Docks, London's principal port, which is northeast of the capital, but logistical issues delayed the project for three years before it found a home in Windrush Square.[9]

The next year saw the Windrush scandal engulf London and the nation. It stemmed from the UK Home Office's hostile environment policy, a set of administrative and legal measures intended to make staying in the UK so difficult that those designated as non-permanent residents would leave voluntarily. Thousands of people of Caribbean heritage were wrongly detained, denied legal rights, threatened with deportation, and even removed from the country or refused re-entry (Local Government Association n.d.).[10] Following the scandal which included the resignation of the then Home Secretary, the government officially backed a five-year effort to recognize Windrush Day, the anniversary of the arrival of Caribbean people on the *Empire Windrush* mentioned earlier.

---

9 Interview with Jak Beula, June 18, 2020.

10 "Commonwealth citizens without status," n.d. (https://www.local.gov.uk/topics/communities/commonwealth-citizens-without-status)

In 2019, the square's future as a site of Black memorialization was called into question when Prime Minister Theresa May announced that a new memorial to the Windrush Generation would be erected in Waterloo, a railway station where many immigrants arrived. Trinidad-born actor and TV personality Baroness Floella Benjamin chairs the Windrush Commemoration Committee, which made the recommendation to house the memorial in Waterloo Station. She said that the location was symbolic because thousands of Windrush pioneers, including herself, had arrived at the station when they first came to London.[11] Not all members of the community agreed. Local activists condemned the site and the process through which it had been selected. Torrington said that the government had been arrogant and was treating the Caribbean community like children, imposing a monument on its behalf (Busby 2019).

Opponents of the Waterloo site argued that the memorial should be located in Windrush Square, which had become identified with Caribbean people.[12] Those against the plan included Lambeth councilor Sonia Winifred, a cabinet member for Equalities and Culture, who started a petition to support the fight. She also wrote to Sadiq Khan, requesting his support for the campaign.[13] However, the £1 million monument by Jamaican sculptor and painter Basil Watson, which features three figures – a man, woman, and child – dressed in their "Sunday best" and carrying suitcases (Khomami 2022), was unveiled on Windrush Day 2022, along with the memorial in Hackney discussed earlier.

---

11 "Windrush memorial to be built at Waterloo station", June 22, 2019 (https://www.bbc.co.uk/news/uk-england-london-48724128)

12 Torrington, Arthur, interview with Arthur Torrington, by author. London, July 13, 2020.

13 "Lambeth urges Home Secretary to restore faith in the government – by bringing Windrush memorial 'home' to Brixton", (http://www.brixtonbuzz.com/2020/06/lambeth-urges-home-secretary-to-restore-faith-in-the-government-by-bringing-windrush-memorial-home-to-brixton/)

Figure 3.4: Cherry Groce Memorial Pavilion. Photograph: © Michelle Äärlaht 2

Meanwhile, in April 2021 the square saw the unveiling of a new memorial to a Black resident, this one for Cherry Groce, a local mother who was paralyzed after being shot by police in her home during a botched raid in 1985. She eventually died of her injuries in 2011. Groce's shooting again sparked an uprising over racism and police brutality. The memorial was the work of a foundation in her name, headed by her son, Lee Lawrence, and backed by prominent supporters including Lord Paul Boateng, the UK's first Black cabinet minister. Lawrence said that, although the project had faced enormous challenges, the community had never faltered in its pursuit of justice (Block 2020). At its unveiling, he called the memorial a fitting tribute to his late mother.[14] Designed by Black British architect Sir David Adjaye, the memorial is made up of a single column, symbolizing Groce's personal strength, while plantings on an attached pavilion represent hope. Its shape also echoes the lines of the nearby African and Caribbean war memorial. Lambeth council funded most of its £150,000 cost (Cobb 2020).

---

14 "Cherry Groce: Memorial unveiled for Brixton police shooting victim", April 25, 2021 (https://www.bbc.com/news/uk-england-london-56873938)

Pan-Africanism: Symbols and Plaques in Remembrance of a Political Movement

At the dawn of the 20th century, London's position as the center of Britain's colonial empire drew to it a host of advocates for independence from its rule. Beginning in the 16th century, the empire comprised nearly a quarter of the world's land surface and it counted more than a quarter of its total population by the 19th century.[15] Among those in the city were the creators of a new movement: Pan-Africanism. Two of London's most influential early Pan-Africanists, Henry Sylvester Williams and John Archer are remembered with plaques and, in Archer's case, with a building, school and street in his name.

Called the "father" of the movement, Williams advocated unity among all African peoples and coined the term Pan-African. He was born in Trinidad in 1869 and came to England in 1895 after a career as an educator in his homeland. Williams had also spent some time in the USA and Canada, cofounding the pioneering and innovative Coloured Hockey League in the latter. Once he arrived in London, he and three other Trinidadian lawyers became apprentices at Gray's Inn, the historic hub for law and legal professions in the city. Supporting himself by lecturing for the Church of England Temperance Society, Williams traveled throughout the British Isles. In 1898, he married a white English woman who worked as a secretary with the society and the couple would go on to have five children.

The year before, in 1897, Williams formed the African Association to publicize injustices against African people worldwide and to promote their interests. Williams was committed to the fight against colonialism, consistently denouncing British rule as the "heartless" cause of their plight. He even led a deputation of Trinidadians to meet MPs, becoming the first person of African descent to speak in the House of Commons in 1900 (Kegan cited in Fryer 1984: 280).

Williams believed in the power of the collective and that all Africans, as well as their descendants, belonged to one "race," were unified in culture, and shared historical experiences directly related to the European enslavement of Africans. With this in mind, he organized the first Pan-African conference on July 23, 1900, drawing 37 delegates and ten other participants and

---

15 "British Empire, historical state United Kingdom", Updated August 14, 2022 (https://www.britannica.com/place/British-Empire)

observers (Fryer 1984), including future Battersea mayor John Archer, composer Samuel Coleridge-Taylor, and the USA's most prominent Black activist and educator, W. E. B. Du Bois, who would later initiate the first Pan-African Congress in Paris in 1919.

The event was held at Westminster Town Hall (now Caxton Hall), a prominent venue in central London. In his opening address, its chair, Bishop Alexander Walters, acknowledged that the event was the first time that Black people from across the world had met to discuss their race, assert their rights, and organize themselves (Fryer 1984: 283). Attendees focused on issues including preserving the identity of the Black race and the need for the colonial powers to recognize the rights of all indigenous peoples. It ended with the African Association being renamed the Pan-African Association and an "Address to the Nations of the World," drafted by a committee headed by Du Bois, which was sent to heads of state where PAD were living and suffering oppression.

Two months later, delegates also petitioned Queen Victoria to review the treatment of Africans in South Africa and then Rhodesia, today's Republic of Zimbabwe. The conference was reported in the leading London newspapers of the time, although somewhat pejoratively. The *Westminster Gazette*, for example, observed that it "marks the initiation of a remarkable movement on history; the [African] is at last awake to the potentialities of his future" (Sivagurunathan 2007: 259–60). Williams also understood the power of the pen and founded the first publication for and by Blacks in the UK, *The Pan-African*, whose editors wrote in its first edition in 1901: "No other but a Negro can represent the Negro" (Kegan cited in Fryer 1984).

Returning from a stint in South Africa, where he had practiced law in Cape Town and helped to promote African interests in a white-dominated country, Williams hoped to run for the UK parliament, believing that Africa needed a voice in legislative authority and that his experience on the continent had prepared him to be that voice. He made the Colonial Office aware of his views (Mathurin 1976: 131). He was, however, unsuccessful in his quest and in 1906 decided to run for local office instead, as a Labour candidate for the St. Marylebone borough council. Williams' victory made him the first Black councilor in the country and one of only a few Black people to hold public office in the UK at that time.

Williams was well connected in his party and constituency. Even as he worked on behalf of residents, he used those connections to assist Africa and

PAD. He welcomed a wide variety of guests, including representatives of the Basuto nation, whom he helped to secure a meeting with the chairman of the Labour Party, Keir Hardie, regarding a land dispute with the British government (Westminster Council 2006). Williams was also actively advocating on behalf of Liberia. He met the nation's president, Arthur Barclay, on his 1907 official visit to London to discuss frontier issues and financial resources. Williams knew the nation's secretary of state, Frederick E. R. Johnson, who had played a prominent role in the 1900 conference. The following year he visited Liberia at Barclay's invitation but was chastised by the British government after the British consul sent home three confidential dispatches denouncing him. After his return to London, Williams decided to go back to Trinidad, where he died three years later at age 42.

In 2007, more than a century after his election and in recognition of his contribution to Marylebone, Westminster city council awarded Williams one of its green plaques for his work on the council (the body awards green plaques to honor the area's diverse cultural heritage and to highlight buildings associated with renowned people). The plaque is located on the front of his former home at 38 Church Street (Westminster City Council 2007).

A contemporary of Williams', fellow Pan-Africanist John Archer, was the first Black mayor in London, elected in 1913. He served various terms on Battersea borough council between 1906 and 1932. Archer was born in Liverpool to a Barbadian father and an Irish mother. He traveled the world as a seaman, living in the USA and Canada before he settled in Battersea with his wife, Bertha, a Black Canadian, in the 1890s. He studied medicine and ran a small photographic studio, getting involved in local politics as a supporter of the Liberal Party politician and trade unionist John Burns. His views were in part shaped by a play based on the novel *Uncle Tom's Cabin*, which his parents had taken him to see as a child (Creighton 2013). Active in Black politics, arguing for social justice and more rights within the African and Caribbean colonies, Archer was a close friend of the musician Samuel Coleridge-Taylor. In fact, they were both members of the African Association. Both were also representatives at Williams' first Pan-African conference.

In 1906, Archer was elected as a Progressive (Liberal) to Battersea borough council; at the same time, Williams won a seat as a councilor in Marylebone. Seven years later, in 1913, Archer was nominated for mayor. He triumphed despite a negative and racist campaign, including allegations that he did not have British nationality. He won by one vote, 40 to 39, against his fellow councilors. It is clear that Archer understood the global significance of this election, something that had never been achieved before. In his winning speech he said:

> I am a man of colour ... I am proud to be. I would not change my colour if I could ... my election tonight marks a new era. You have made history tonight. For the first time in the history of the English nation a man of colour has been elected as mayor of an English borough. That will go forth to the coloured nations of the world. (Phillips 2005)

His success was reported in the National Association for the Advancement of Colored People's (NAACP's) journal *The Crisis* in the USA in January 1914. Although thought to be the first Black man to be elected as a mayor in Britain, in reporting Archer's election the American *Negro Year Book* in 1914 also recorded that Dr. Allan Glaisyer Minns from the Caribbean had been elected mayor of the borough of Thetford, Norfolk in 1904 (Work 1914: 49).

Nonetheless, Archer faced prejudice in his new role and did not shy away from discussing it. He described receiving racist mail and questioned whether the opposition he faced was because of his color (Phillips 2005). He also continued his commitment to Black empowerment. In 1918, he cofounded the African Progress Union, becoming its first president and holding the post for three years. In a powerful speech at the union's inaugural meeting, Archer criticized Britain's view of Black people and people of color and pledged that they would claim their rightful place in the empire. He said that the association was demanding, not asking for, that right (Fryer 1984: 294). Furthermore, the organization's objectives were:

> to promote the general welfare of Africans and Afro-peoples; set up a social and resident club in London as a "home from home"; to "spread knowledge of history and achievements of Africans and Afro-peoples past and present"; and to create and maintain "a public sentiment in favour of brotherhood in its broadest sense." (Fryer 1984: 293)

The following year, Archer became a British delegate to the Pan-African Congress in Paris and later chaired the Pan-African Congress in London in 1921.

He continued to work in politics for the remainder of his life. At his death in 1932, age 69, he was deputy leader of Battersea council.

Archer is remembered in a number of ways in the area he once oversaw. Archer House, part of the Battersea Village estate, was named after him when it was built in the 1930s. Two local schools (one now closed) were renamed in his honour in 1986 and in 2018 and there is also a John Archer Way. In addition, two blue plaques have been unveiled at his residence and place of work. The first is on the site of his

Figure 3.5: A blue plaque for John Archer. Source: https://commons.wikimedia.org/wiki/User:Spudgun67

former photography studio and home and was created in 2010 by the Nubian Jak Community Trust. It was part of a project called "The John Archer Role Model Project" and was funded by the Heritage Lottery Fund. Three years later, English Heritage unveiled another blue plaque at his former Battersea home. In June 2020, Wandsworth council launched a campaign to erect a statue celebrating Archer's mayoral achievements, following calls from the local community group Love Battersea. The council said that it would make a small initial contribution to the memorial but hoped to raise more funds with community help (Aron 2020b).

The Caribbean Presence: Remembering Mary Seacole

To date, London has several statues of Black figures. Among them is the Bronze Woman, which features a mother and child and is the first statue to be displayed in England honoring a Black woman. Its creation, which celebrates the contribution of African-Caribbean people to the capital, was a community effort, spearheaded by the late Guyanese-born teacher, poet, and playwright Cécile Nobrega. Along with Olmec, a South London social enterprise firm, she worked for more than a decade to raise its cost of £84,000.[16]

Erected in Stockwell Memorial Gardens in South London near Nobrega's former home, it was unveiled by a group of Caribbean women in 2008. The occasion marked the 200th anniversary of the end of transatlantic enslavement and the 60th anniversary of the arrival of the *Empire Windrush*. Another more recent memorial to a woman, *Reaching Out*, was unveiled in August 2020 in an East London public art walk called The Line. Representing the "Black Everywoman," according to sculptor Thomas J. Price, it took two years to raise the funds to build the nine-foot bronze statue, which depicts a woman standing looking down at the phone she holds (Thorpe 2020). Megan Piper, director of The Line, said that the sculpture was pertinent and long overdue because it portrayed a contemporary Black woman rather than a historically celebrated white male figure (Paskett 2020).

In addition, the city's most prominent monument to a Black person also honors a woman, famed nurse Mary Seacole. The statue of the Jamaican-born immigrant stands proudly opposite parliament. It was unveiled in 2016, nearly 12 years after an official campaign to create it had begun. But the first efforts had in fact been made more than 20 years earlier, driven by residents of Caribbean origin seeking to restore the pioneering nurse to her rightful place in history; the statue celebrates a woman who is greatly admired by Black Britons.

Mary Seacole, who defied the British government to take care of soldiers during the Crimean War (1853–6), topped a 2004 list of 100 Great Black Britons. The list had been created after a British Broadcasting Corporation (BBC) poll in 2002 to find "Great Britons" failed to produce any Black winners. Patrick Vernon, a Black British former Labour councilor, launched an alternative campaign in October 2003 during Black History Month to raise the profile of Black contributions to Britain. He explained that Black British history was not recognized by the dominant society, although Black people had been in the country a thousand years and had helped to shape it (Bloomfield 2004).

---

16 "A Deeper Look into Stockwell's Bronze Woman Statue", August 12, 2019 (https://www.southlondonclub.co.uk/blog/a-deeper-look-into-stockwells-bronze-woman-statue)

Born Mary Jane Grant in Jamaica, Seacole was the daughter of a free Black woman and a white Scottish soldier. Her mother kept a boarding house for sick soldiers and taught Mary traditional African and Caribbean medicine at an early age. Seacole was proud of her heritage. In her autobiography, *Wonderful Adventures of Mrs. Seacole in Many Lands*, the first autobiography written by a Black woman in Britain (Robinson 2005: 213), she called herself a Creole and aligned with African slaves in the Americas (Seacole 1857: 14). After marrying Edwin Horatio Hamilton Seacole in Kingston, Jamaica, in 1836, from whom she received her surname, and after being widowed eight years later, Seacole traveled to England in 1854, attempting to volunteer as an army nurse in the war. Turned down by the British government, Seacole questioned whether racism was at the core of the government's refusal to allow her to join the war effort (Seacole 1857: 73–81; Gerzina 2003: 74).

Repeatedly faced with barriers from official organizations, Seacole was also rebuffed by the nurses who worked with Florence Nightingale, a contemporary nurse who later gained national recognition for her role in the war. Consequently, Seacole decided to go it alone and used her own resources to travel to Crimea to open an establishment to be called the British Hotel (Seacole 1857: 74). A partnership with a Caribbean acquaintance, Thomas Day, who had arrived in London unexpectedly, helped finance the trip. Accounts record that Seacole labored wholeheartedly, overcoming frequent thefts, particularly of livestock, at the hotel. Dr. Reid, a surgeon in the British army serving in the war, wrote a letter to his family in 1855 lauding Seacole's kindness and generosity (Simkin 2020).

When Seacole returned to England after the war ended in 1856, she was ill and destitute, narrowly avoiding bankruptcy. After prominent contributors, including members of the royal family, donated to a fund for her, she returned to Jamaica around 1860; however, the country had suffered an economic downturn in Seacole's absence. She bought land and built a house and a rental property. But, by 1870, Seacole was back in London, likely seeking to help in the Franco-Prussian War, according to historian Jane Robinson. Robinson believes that Seacole was spurned when she approached the husband of Florence Nightingale's sister, who was closely involved in the British National Society for Aid to the Sick and Wounded. Reportedly around this time, Nightingale wrote a letter to her brother-in-law implying that Seacole had kept a "bad house" in Crimea and was responsible for "much drunkenness and improper conduct" (Robinson 2005: 191).

Seacole eventually connected with members of the royal circle and became a personal masseuse to the Princess of Wales. She died in 1881 at her London home and was largely forgotten. The drive to recognize Seacole came nearly a century after her passing and was community-led. In 1973, the Lignum Vitae Club, a Jamaican women's organization in London, together with the British Commonwealth Nurses War Memorial Fund restored her grave in the Hammersmith cemetery where she had been buried. The Jamaican government enthusiastically supported the effort. According to a press release from the Jamaican High Commission in London dated November 20, 1973, the High Commissioner for Jamaica, Sir Laurence Lindo, and his wife Lady Lindo, who was president of the Lignum Vitae Club at the time, attended the unveiling of the "reconsecrated" grave. In addition, the High Commission reported that "[t]he Nurses Association of Jamaica will maintain it in repair forever."[17]

In 1979, a group of Caribbean women approached the MP for Hammersmith, Clive Soley, (now Lord Soley), asking him to join them at Seacole's gravesite. It had been almost a century since Seacole's death and her contributions had long been forgotten. However, Soley, who had lived through World War Two, said he appreciated Seacole's war efforts and those of the women who had come from the Caribbean in 1939–40 to help during the war (Soley 2018). Soley, who did not commit to helping then, would later help raise funds to build a statue in her honor. The plan to honor Seacole continued, however. In 1980, community activist Constance (Connie) Mark took up the mantle, cofounding the Mary Seacole Memorial Association. Her activism had begun in her Jamaican birthplace where she had experienced racism first-hand after being denied a pay increase while working as a medical secretary in the Auxiliary Territorial Service (ATS) during World War Two (Haigh 2018). Beula, who had met Mark when he was 17, said the activist made Seacole a household name. The Nubian Jak Community Trust would posthumously honor Mark in June 2008, with a blue plaque at the retirement complex named after Mary Seacole in Hammersmith, where Mark lived during the final years of her life.

---

17 "Mary Seacole's Grave Restored in London", November 26, 1973 (https://www.nlj.gov.jm/BN/Seacole_Mary/bn_seacole_mj_063.pdf)

Despite the efforts of stalwarts such as Mark, the Seacole statue met with considerable resistance. In a 2012 article in the conservative *Daily Mail* newspaper, opponents argued that Seacole's importance had been exaggerated by proponents of multiculturalism (Walters 2012). Meanwhile, supporters of Florence Nightingale also alleged that Seacole was overshadowing the former's achievements and that Seacole was not technically a nurse. Others tried to argue that naming her as a Black heroine was just political correctness because she was mixed race and not really Black (Gander 2016). This viewpoint focuses on a biological categorization rather than a social and cultural one, as this book prescribes. Meanwhile, in 2013, then Education Minister Michael Gove bowed to Seacole's detractors and removed her from the national curriculum, saying that students should learn about traditional figures such as Oliver Cromwell and Winston Churchill. The suggestion was met with outrage, leading him to make a U-turn shortly afterwards. Operation Black Vote, a non-profit organization created to broaden Black participation in electoral politics, played a central role in the fight to keep Seacole on the national curriculum, starting a petition that attracted more than 35,000 signatures.

Figure 3.6: The Mary Seacole statue. Source: https://commons.wikimedia.org/wiki/User:Sumitsurai

The job of realizing a Mary Seacole statue would eventually fall to the Mary Seacole Memorial Statue Appeal. Lord Soley chaired the charity which was set up in 2004. The group was renamed the Mary Seacole Trust after the statue was unveiled. Funded through donations from thousands of individual supporters, as well as from a small number of larger donors, the organizers raised more than £500,000. The chancellor of the exchequer (the UK government office that oversees public spending) also provided a £240,000 grant to help pay for the installation and a small memorial garden. Floella Benjamin unveiled the statue, which stands in the gardens of St. Thomas's Hospital. Tottenham MP David Lammy called the occasion a "seminal moment for Londoners, and for the Black community particularly."[18] Today, the statue symbolizes Mary Seacole's contribution as a nurse in particular and the contributions of Black people to British society in general.

Windrush Square, the symbols and plaques honoring London's Pan-African pioneers, and the Seacole statue demonstrate the importance of places – spaces grounded in reality in which humans have embodied personal meaning (Pedraza 2019) – that emphasize equality, justice, and democracy (Gieseking et al. 2014: 393). Such spaces contribute to one's racial identity (Winkler 2012) and belonging. In a city that was built on the backs of the enslaved, enriched by colonial oppression, and nurtured by populations of marginalized residents, PAD are insisting that these histories be made visible in the public domain – often claiming their own spaces – and that London clearly, unequivocally, and publicly acknowledges all who have contributed to its economic, social, and cultural development in the past and make a commitment to doing so in the future.

References

Abrams, Amah-Rose (2022) "'It's not a monument, it's a celebration': Windrush sculpture unveiled in Hackney," *Guardian*, June 22, https://www.theguardian.com/artanddesign/2022/jun/22/its-not-a-monument-its-a-celebration-windrush-sculpture-unveiled-in-hackney

Aron, Isabelle (2020a) "Hackney Is Getting Two New Sculptures to Honour the Windrush Generation," *Time Out*, June 22, https://www.timeout.com/london/news/hackney-is-getting-two-new-sculptures-to-honour-the-windrush-generation-062220

Aron, Isabelle (2020b) "There's a Campaign to Erect a Statue in Honour of London's First Black Mayor," *Time Out*, June 23, https://www.timeout.

---

18 https://www.bbc.com/news/uk-england-london-36663206

com/london/news/theres-a-campaign-to-erect-a-statue-in-honour-of-londons-first-black-mayor-062320

Block, India (2020) "David Adjaye Reveals Memorial for Black Woman Shot by Police in Brixton," *Dezeen*, July 8, https://www.dezeen.com/2020/07/08/david-adjaye-cherry-groce-memorial-brixton-london/

Bloomfield. Steve (2004) "The Top 10 Black Britons (But One May Not Be)," *Independent*, February 8, https://www.independent.co.uk/news/uk/this-britain/the-top-10-black-britons-but-one-may-not-be-68171.html

Brown, Mark (2019) "Bob Marley's London Home Gets One of Few Blue Plaques for Black Artists," *Guardian*, October 1, https://www.theguardian.com/music/2019/oct/01/bob-marleys-london-home-gets-one-of-few-blue-plaques-for-black-artists

Busby, Mattha (2019) "May's Plan for Windrush Memorial at Waterloo Met with 'Disgust,'" *Guardian*, June 22, https://www.theguardian.com/uk-news/2019/jun/22/windrush-generation-to-be-honoured-by-waterloo-monument

Cobb, Jason (2020) "Lambeth Council to Fund Extra 81,000 for Cherry Groce Memorial in Windrush Square," *Brixton Buzz*, August 7, https://www.brixtonbuzz.com/2020/08/lambeth-council-to-fund-extra-81000-for-cherry-groce-memorial-in-windrush-square-after-foundation-struggles-to-meet-target/

Creighton, Sean (2013) "Why John Archer Is Important," April 17, http://historyandsocialaction.blogspot.com/2013/04/why-john-archer-is-important.html

Dickens, Tim (2014) "Moving Celebration Marks Long Journey to the Black Cultural Archives Launch in Brixton," July 24, https://brixtonblog.com/2014/07/moving-celebration-marks-long-journey-to-the-black-cultural-archives-launch-in-brixton/23813/

Fryer, Peter (1984) *Staying Power: The History of Black People in Britain*. London: Pluto Press.

Gander, Kashmira (2016) "Mary Seacole Statue: Why Florence Nightingale Fans Are Angry the Crimean War Nurse Is Being Commemorated," *Independent*, June 24, https://www.independent.co.uk/arts-entertainment/florence-vs-mary-the-big-nurse-off-a7100676.html

Gerzina, Gretchen (2003) *Black Victorians*. New Brunswick: Rutgers University Press.

Gieseking, J. J., W. Mangold, C. Katz, S. Low, and S. Saegert (eds.) (2014) *The People, Place, and Space Reader.* New York: Routledge.

Haigh, Phil (2018) "Meet Connie Mark, the Tireless Activist Honoured by Today's Google Doodle," *Metro*, December 21, https://metro.co.uk/2018/12/21/meet-connie-mark-tireless-activist-honoured-todays-google-doodle-8272265

Johnson, Boris (2020) "Rather Than Tear Some People Down We Should Build Others Up," *Telegraph*, June 14, https://www.telegraph.co.uk/politics/2020/06/14/rather-tear-people-should-build-others/

Kearns, Robin A. and Berg L. D. (2002) "Proclaiming Place: Towards a Geography of Place Name Pronunciation," *Social & Cultural Geography*, 3 (3): 283–302.

Khomami, Nadia (2022) "Commonwealth Immigration: Windrush Generation 'Moved to Tears' as Monument Unveiled in London," *Guardian*, June 22 https://www.theguardian.com/uk-news/2022/jun/22/windrush-basil-watson-monument-unveiled-waterloo-station-london

Mathurin, Charles (1976) *Henry Sylvester Williams and the Origins of the Pan-African Movement 1869–1911.* Westport CT and London: Greenwood Press.

mudlark121 (2016) "Today in London's Murderous Policing History: Wayne Douglas Dies in Brixton Police Station, 1995," December 5, https://pasttenseblog.wordpress.com/2016/12/05/today-in-londons-murderous-policing-history-wayne-douglas-dies-in-brixton-police-station-1995/

Onibada Ade (2020) "Statues in the US and around the World Are Being Beheaded and Torn Down Amid Black Lives Matter Protests," *BuzzFeed*, June 20, https://www.buzzfeednews.com/article/adeonibada/statues-torn-down-monuments-us-uk-columbus-churchill-colston

Paskett, Zoe (2020) "Newly Unveiled Artwork Becomes the Third Public Sculpture Depicting a Black Woman in the UK," *Standard*, August 5, https://www.standard.co.uk/go/london/arts/thomas-j-price-reaching-out-sculpture-the-line-a4517076.html

Pedraza, Ishmael Nuñez (2019) "The Black Spatial Imaginary in Urban Design Practice: Lessons for Creating Black-affirming Public Spaces." MS thesis, University of Washington.

Phillips, Mike (2005) "Black Europeans: John Archer (1863–1932)," British Library Online Gallery.

Robinson, Jane (2005) *Mary Seacole*. London: Constable.

Seacole, Mary (1857) *Wonderful Adventures of Mrs. Seacole in Many Lands.* London: James Blackwood.

Simkin, John. "Mary Seacole," September 1997; Updated January 2020 https://spartacus-educational.com/REseacole.htm

Sivagurunathan, Shivani (2007) "Pan-Africanism" in David Dabydeen, John Gilmore, and Cecily Jones (eds.), *The Oxford Companion to Black British History*. Oxford: Oxford University Press.

Soley, Clive. "Lord Soley – The Story of a Statue," November 10, 2018 http://imagazineuk.com/lord-soley-the-story-of-a-statue/

Tandoh, Ruby (2021) "The Artist Celebrating the Windrush Generation," September 17, https://www.royalacademy.org.uk/article/veronica-ryan-sculptor

Thorpe Vanessa (2020) "Sculptor Unveils 'Black Everywoman' as UK Row over Statues and Race Grows," *Guardian*, July 19, https://www.theguardian.com/artanddesign/2020/jul/19/sculptor-unveils-black-everywoman-as-uk-row-over-statues-and-race-grows?fbclid=IwAR02GY2M3NzXp1yC3gnqiW9Q5HOe5-zLDnGQTRCF64Nd1Jdw-9dPEpWY-Dc

Walters, Guy (2012) "The Black Florence Nightingale and the Making of a PC Myth: One Historian Explains how Mary Seacole's Story Never Stood Up," *Daily Mail*, December 30, https://www.dailymail.co.uk/news/article-2255095/The-black-Florence-Nightingale-making-PC-myth-One-historian-explains-Mary-Seacoles-story-stood-up.html

Westminster City Council (2007) "Black History in Westminster." Edition 2. London: Westminster City Council Planning and City Development Department.

Winkler, E. N. (2012) *Learning Race, learning Place: Shaping Racial Identities and Ideas in African American Childhoods.* New Brunswick: Rutgers University Press.

Wood, Michael (2012) "Britain's First Black Community in Elizabethan London," BBC, July 9, https://www.bbc.com/news/magazine-18903391

Work, Monroe N. (ed.) (1914) *Negro Year Book: An Annual Encyclopedia of the Negro – 1914–1915*. Tuskegee AL: Negro Year Book Publishing Company, Tuskegee Institute Press.

Chapter 4
Black Luxembourg

Bernardino Tavares and Aleida Vieira

In the Grand Duchy, Black Lives Matter's (BLM's) impact has manifested itself on various levels of society, from rallies gathering together large numbers of people to artistic contestation tactics and the appropriation of public spaces, the mapping of buildings with colonial links, the defacement of monuments, and the renaming of streets, to mention just a few. All this happened in the context of uncovering Luxembourg's colonial past, which is directly connected to Belgian colonization (see Chapter 2) (Moes 2012).

Although the early BLM movements had already pushed bottom-up and top-down discussions on racism, no political measures had been put in place until the impact of BLM in 2020. The events of that summer were a sort of "wake-up call" and a sudden turning point, with Black people raising their voices against unequal conditions in modern postcolonial societies in Europe, including in Luxembourg. Additionally, newly created associations of People of African Descent (PAD), such as the feminist and antiracist associations Finkapé and Lëtz Rise Up (discussed below), have taken the lead and intensified their antiracist activities, shifting the conversation on race and racism from folklore to activism. As a result, the silencing of the colonial past has been broken.

At the European level, an earlier study entitled "Being Black in Europe" (BBE), carried out by the Fundamental Rights Agency (FRA) and published in 2018, had placed Luxembourg at the top of the list of European countries where perceptions of racism are very high. This is a serious matter in a country where almost half of the population are immigrants (Statec 2020). Finland is the only country where these perceptions are higher (Pauly 2019: 5). The BLM movement and the BBE study have fostered a wave of rallies as well as debates at conferences, including one that focused on "Being Black in Luxembourg" (BBL) and prompted studies on racism, a subject that previously had not been on the country's public radar.

In addition to calls for projects by the Ministry for Family Affairs, Integration and the Greater Region, the government also ordered the Luxembourg Institute of Socio-Economic Research (LISER) to conduct an unprecedented national survey on the experience and perception of racism among populations of color. Ordered by the Chamber of Deputies and coordinated by the Ministry, with the participation of Centre d'Étude et de Formation Interculturelles et Sociales (CEFIS), the data was made available in the three official languages of the country – Luxembourgish, French and German, plus English and Portuguese – and collected through a national online survey in 2021.

The poll was sent to random residents and asked: How widespread is racial and ethnic discrimination in Luxembourg? Which groups of people are mainly targeted? In which contexts and situations do residents perceive discriminatory acts and treatment? Where and how can action be taken to combat these issues? The team included only one Black person, whose participation in designing and evaluating the questionnaire was not very representative of the diverse voices of the Black community. In an interview, he pointed out that the LISER survey/study "does not reveal that there is very marked ideological racism in Luxembourg," and that, if compared "with the indicators of other countries, the figures in Luxembourg are less alarming than in neighbouring countries" (Queirós 2022).

This statement raises at least two questions concerning the study: Would the results have been more accurate if other Black experts were involved? And was the inclusion of only one Black researcher another form of "tokenism" and an attempt to soften and smooth over the results of the evaluation? Yet, it is important to underline that Luxembourg is taking its first steps toward opening up discussions on these hitherto avoided topics. However, there is still much to be done to bring new lines of reflection, as long as all parties are included in the search for the transformation strategies that are needed in order to eradicate racial oppression.

The study's findings were presented in March 2022 at a press conference attended by the Minister of Family Affairs and the researchers involved in the study. According to LISER, the data collected "will be used to identify the sectors in which specific actions are necessary" and will be "taken into account in the formulation of policy recommendations to combat racism and discrimination." However, to a certain extent, the study suffers from a lack of critical and disentangling voices that would better help society at large understand and unravel longstanding discrimination affecting Black people in Luxembourg. In an interview with the newspaper *Paperjam*, Sandrine Gashonga, the president of Lëtz Rise Up, underlined the wish that "discrimination based on race be treated as a transversal problem that concerns different ministries, mainly those of education and justice."[1]

As for the context of Europe in general, the category of race in Luxembourg is "seldom openly expressed in language" (M'charek, Schramm, and Skinner 2014: 471) in political and societal discourses, either written or spoken. Before the BLM movement, discussions about race and racism were taboo, despite longstanding racial discrimination against Africans and their descendants. Thus, the question of race has been an "absent-presence" (Law 2004) in Luxembourg, which "may temporarily appear in plain sight in a particular practice only to then disappear again beneath the surface" (M'charek, Schramm, and Skinner 2014: 471).

Nevertheless, for Antónia Ganeto, the president of Finkapé, despite resistance from Luxembourg governors, "the lines were moved, the taboo was slightly broken, and the denial is less present."[2] One would like to believe that the BLM movement has served as an additional stimulus to awaken Luxembourg's white population to the selective (in)visibility of Black people in the country, as well as to their struggles for the recognition of their past and future. We believe that, for Luxembourgish society in general, and especially for the community of African origin, the BLM movement has created an awareness and a need to reflect on their experiences and their positioning in the country, something that has not happened before. The Black population felt encouraged by this global movement to demand space for listening, taking measures, and introducing changes to ensure equal respect and recognition as part of Luxembourgish society. As we shall see below, there have been some catalytic moments of robust racial contestation embodied in the creation and activities of associations with African imprints, the use of art to

---

1 Translated by the authors. In the original: "les discriminations contre les personnes racisées soient traitées comme un problème transversal qui concerne différents ministères, notamment ceux de l'Éducation et de la Justice" (Frati 2020).
2 Translated by the authors. In the original: "Elle a permis de faire bouger les lignes. Le tabou est un peu cassé, le déni moins présent" (Frati 2020).

tackle "hidden" colonial links, as well as the organization of conferences and studies whose main topic is race and racism.

Traces of Black Representation in Urban Landscapes

In Luxembourg City and beyond, there are several street names and monuments honoring white Luxembourgers who were deemed important for their participation in colonization and who made a name for themselves from their colonial involvement. Although no monuments celebrating colonialism were torn down in the capital, contesting tactics were employed by protesters, collectives, and associations to denounce colonialism, calling for the decolonization of minds and (urban) landscapes. In their attempt to disentangle the Grand Duchy's past colonial connections and everyday racism under the motto "Lëtzebuerg dekoloniséieren" (Decolonize Luxembourg), Lëtz Rise Up collaborated with the activist artistic collective Richtung22 to document colonial memories emplaced in the city's landscape. Both organizations are presented in more detail below.

Their campaign tracked 28 spaces, including public buildings, private companies, and parks, that were linked to colonialism and grouped them into three main categories. The first group consisted of colonial routes of racism: for example, the location of Villa Louvigny and of the human zoos which took place in February 1900, and Charly's Gare, which was linked to the railway in the Congo. The second focused on colonial economy and wealth: for example, the neocolonial Boulevard Royal and the Cercle Cité, where colonial propaganda exhibitions were held in the presence of Prince Félix and the Grand Duchess Charlotte in 1933 and 1949 and where a conference was organized by the Fédération Internationale des Coloniaux et Anciens Coloniaux (FICAC or International Federation of Colonial and Former Colonial Civil Servants), of which Luxembourg was a member. The third group includes institutions located in the Athénée building, which is linked to the participation of Luxembourgers in the colonial war in Congo, and the German Dresdner Bank and its cooperation with the apartheid regime in South Africa. As these sites show, Luxembourg was active in European expansion although it did not have any colonies. Through a free guided tour – the first of which took place on June 26, 2021 – people would get to know these unknown links to colonialism.[3]

Furthermore, several monuments are located on the country's border with Belgium and illustrate Luxembourg's involvement in Belgian colonialism. In Arlon, for example, the statue of Leopold II was defaced by protesters.[4] Additionally, a group of activists from Richtung22 made an intervention on a bronze monument that depicts the profile of Nicolas Cito (1866–1949), a Luxembourgish colonial engineer who participated in Belgian colonization. The bronze is set above a fountain on the wall of a former primary school, now a high school in Bascharage, his childhood hometown. The monument was created to honor him as one of the so-called colonial pioneers (Clarinval 2021) who directed the construction of the railway line that connected the region of Matadi to Léopoldville (now Kinshasa, the capital of the Democratic Republic of Congo) in 1898 (Moes 2012).

The activists placed the monument behind a panel with a round upper opening, leaving Cito's head visible, but relegating him behind bars that allude to a prison window, thus indexing his colonial crimes and responsibility for "the 5,500 forced labourers who died during a railroad construction – of which Cito was the chief-engineer" (Spirinelli 2020; cf. Moes 2012). The lower part of the panel contained an updated text that commemorated the victims of these crimes. This plaque covered the official text, which celebrated Cito's colonial deeds. Below the updated text there was the Black fist, an iconic image of BLM. Additionally, the activists poured little red drops below the water tap, symbolizing blood.[5]

---

3 Lëtz Rise Up et Richtung22 unissent leurs forces dans une campagne comprenant des visites guidées à travers l'histoire occultée du pays: (https://www.letzriseup.com/d%C3%A9colonisons-le-luxembourg)

4 King Leopold's involvement in colonialism is explained in detail in Chapter 2.

5 Aktion gegen Denkmal in Niederkerschen, *Luxemburger Wort*, June 15, 2020 (https://www.wort.lu/de/lokales/aktion-gegen-denkmal-in-niederkerschen-5ee78528da2cc1784e35fb67)

Figures 4.1a and 4.1b: Original and updated images of the Nicolas Cito fountain in Bascharage. Sources: B. Tavares, August 19, 2021; Luxemburger Wort, June 15, 2020

The collective redesigned the monument as an act of "remembrance of European colonial culture" that has oppressed Black people in Africa, in European societies, and beyond (Clarinval 2021). Although the artistic redesign proved ephemeral – the contextual rectangular panel was removed shortly afterwards – the intervention has contributed to sensitizing society toward the oppression and brutality that monuments in public spaces often represent. The Luxembourgish historian cited above, Fabio Spirinelli, said in his insightful article that, as a student at the former primary school, he was not taught about the colonial meaning this monument carries and consequently simply did not know who Nicolas Cito was. Thus, Spirinelli underscores the importance of updating original monuments and street names, as exemplified by the artistic collective Richtung22. He calls for more public education about "colonial regimes, their racism, violence and plundering" (Spirinelli 2020). Perhaps, a recontextualization of colonial history would also be a sound educational tactic.

Indeed, there are still a number of buildings in the capital linked to Luxembourg's participation in colonization, with their histories unknown to the wider public. However, there was no public outcry until the BLM protests in summer 2020, when the organizations mentioned above started contesting these buildings' colonial links and connections. An inventory made by Richtung22 and Lëtz Rise Up, for example, identified a building called Cercle Municipal, in the center of Luxembourg City. It was used for meetings, colonial exhibitions, and propaganda by the Luxembourgish Colonial Circle (CCL), an association founded in 1925 by colonial officials that met regularly under Prince Félix and the government of the time. The association supported Luxembourg citizens in their colonial activities in Congo. Now, the property is used by officials for meetings with international partners. A second location is the former KBL (Kredietbank Luxembourg) building, now taken over by Quintet Private Bank. Its owners collaborated in financing the illegal sales of arms during the apartheid regime in South Africa.[6] However, research into colonial connections is still in its early stages.

Meanwhile, names such as Nelson Mandela appear as street names in other cities in the country, for example in Esch-sur-Alzette, Luxembourg's second largest city and one of the most multicultural. The municipal council decided to rename Rue des Boers[7] after the prominent South African leader in 2014 following a proposal from the leftist party Déi Lénk, a few days before the opening of an exhibition about Mandela at the National Resistance Museum in the city. The museum traces the history of Luxembourg under Nazi oppression from 1940 to 1945, from the perspective of the resistance movements. The exhibition "Nelson Mandela: From Prisoner to President" ran from April to September 2014 and was curated by the Apartheid Museum in Johannesburg.

---

6 For more examples, see Richtung22 and Lëtz Rise Up webpages.
7 Rue des Boers was named in the 1920s after the white settlers who supported white supremacy during the apartheid regime in South Africa (https://www.luxtimes.lu/en/luxembourg/esch-alzette-mandela-street-debate-continues-602d3d71de135b92363a4cd7)

Figures 4.2a and 4.2b: Original and covered images of the entrance to the former Mohrenapotheke or Pharmacie des N*. Sources: B. Tavares, May 10, 2021; Luxemburger Wort, August 21, 2020

Another building in the center of the capital became infamous for its problematic representation of Black people (Figure 4.2a). This building, which opened in the early 1800s, is called "M*apotheke" in German, or "Pharmacie des N*" in French, and is hard to ignore due to the ceramic representations of two African men standing at its doors. The "M*apotheke" was registered in 1803 by Alfred Lenoël (1774–1849), a Luxembourgish pharmacist. The German understanding of the word "M*" does not leave room for ambiguities and doubts as to its racist meaning (see Chapter 1). In 2007, the current owner, Claude Hostert-Pfeifer, renamed it Pharmacie Ginkgo as she considered the old name "inappropriate for the era in which we live" (Hostert-Pfeifer 2021). This echoes Spirinelli's assertion:

> [M]eanings of monuments need to be considered synchronically and diachronically. They can have different meanings to different people at a given time, and their meanings can change over time following a re-evaluation and sensitization. (Spirinelli 2020)

The two images were covered up in July 2020 (Figure 4.2b), presumably by officials. However, in contrast to the intervention against Cito's monument by Richtung22 mentioned above, it could be argued that this covering of the ceramic representations of the two African men constitutes a further act of official neutralization and invisibilization of Luxembourg's colonial links.

Over the years, some initiatives have taken place at the official level. For instance, in 1974, a street in Buschrodt (a village in the northern district of Diekirch) was named after Nicolas Grang (1854–83), who was born there and who was a colonial lieutenant, later promoted to a commander, in the Belgian colony of Congo. However, the street was renamed Um Schéckelt in July 2020. According to Marie-Paule Anzia, a physiotherapist on the former Rue Nicolas Grang, the name change is a consequence of the BLM movement in Luxembourg. The therapist explained in a telephone conversation that the municipality decided to rename the street because Grang had participated in the colonization of Congo and had "done things he shouldn't have." Anzia explained that the new name of the street, Um Schéckelt, refers to the idea of *"lieudit"* or *"lieu-dit,"* a French term for a small geographical area bearing a traditional name. An official from the municipality of Buschrodt, stated that, as far as she is aware, the name Schéckelt has no particular meaning but is linked to "a name from the village's historic past." These two interpretations lead us to believe that changing the street name was a result of the protests all over the world, including in Luxembourg, but also an attempt and a strategy to neutralize the Luxembourgish connection to the colonization of Congo – something that, before BLM, was completely ignored by the great mass of Luxembourgish society. The renaming process was overseen by the village's mayor and the historian Régis Moes, who is the curator for contemporary Luxembourgish history at the Musée National d'Histoire et d'Art (MNHA) (Heindrichs 2022).

As a result, the plaque honoring Nicolas Grang was transferred to the MNHA to be part of the 2022 exhibition on Luxembourg's colonial presence in Congo (Clarinval 2021). The temporary exhibition (April–November 2022) provided an overview of Luxembourg's little known colonial past. It allowed the public access to testimonies from private and institutional collections in the form of objects, artworks and photographs, advertising brochures, and press articles. By recalling historical facts and presenting numerous portraits of Luxembourg people involved in the colonial period, the MNHA displayed the complexity of colonial relations. Furthermore, nine people from today, whose lives are closely connected to Luxembourg and shaped by its colonial past, told their personal stories in interviews with the museum.

Even though the colonial era in a narrower sense has been over for more than 60 years, many citizens still experience its effects in their everyday lives. The MNHA's exhibition thus illustrated that Luxembourg does indeed have a colonial past.[8]

"Colonizing without Colonies": Luxembourg's Presence in Congo

In the public realm, only a few social actors recognize the Grand Duchy's active participation in colonization, as it did not have its own colonies. Some place the blame for the systematic suppression of Congo, which lasted until 1960, solely on the Belgians (Moes 2010; 2012; Spirinelli 2020). Others recognize that thousands of Luxembourgers enrolled in the Netherlands' military during the colonization of Indonesia, formerly known as the Dutch East Indies. According to the historians Bosma and Kolnberger, in the second half of the 19th century, young Luxembourgers

> saw enlisting in the army as part of their life cycle: serving in the Dutch East Indies for a relatively short period before returning home to start their own families, establish a business, or look for permanent work. (Bosma and Kolnberger 2017: 568)

In fact, the presence of Luxembourg in Congo manifested itself via the recruitment of young Luxembourgers as administrative colonial staff for Belgium. This occurred to such an extent that, in 1922, Luxembourgers gained the same status as Belgians in the colonies. It was declared by the Belgian colonial regime that those who aspired to work in the colony should have Belgian or Luxembourgish nationality (Mukuna 2020).

In addition, colonial propaganda and lobbying intensified in Luxembourg through local colonial associations, such as the CCL mentioned above. In collaboration with white Belgians, members of the CCL organized conferences and campaigns at Luxembourgish schools to incentivize new graduates to pursue colonial careers (Moes 2012; Mukuna 2020). One objective was to find posts for the surplus of highly educated Luxembourgers within the

---

8 "Luxembourg's colonial past", March 8, 2022 (https://www.mnha.lu/en/exhibitions/luxembourgs-colonial-past)

Belgian administrative colonial staff in Congo. Thus, recruitment of Luxembourgers was often financed by the government. The case of the engineer Nicolas Cito remains emblematic of the way in which the country has dealt with its colonial past.

A noteworthy illustration of Congo's presence in Luxembourg is embodied in the person of Jacques Leurs; he was the son of a white Luxembourgish father, a colonel in the Belgian Congo who worked in the rubber industry (cf. Hausemer 2018), and a Congolese mother named Tchaussi. In 1912, he became the first Luxembourger of African descent when he was brought to the country at the age of two to be educated and live with his grandparents. The filmmaker and writer Fränz Hausemer highlights that the move "constitutes a return of colonies never before experienced by the inhabitants of this country without colonies [i.e., Luxembourg]" (2018: 50). In his 2017 documentary film entitled *Schwaarze Mann: Un noir parmi nous* (A Black among Us), Hausemer recounts Jacques' experiences as an Afro-Luxembourger. It is based on interviews with Jacques' widow, Léoni Leurs, a white Luxembourgish woman, who describes the various racist challenges they faced as a interracial couple. According to Hausemer (ibid.), Léoni Leurs highlighted that the reason why she did not have a child with her husband was because "he would not have tolerated someone screaming at his son in the street: Here comes the N-word."[9]

After his graduation, Jacques Leurs became a well-known figure in the railway industry despite his exoticization. When World War Two ended, he became first secretary of the board of directors of the Luxembourg Railways and was active in the national association and in the International Confederation of Free Trade Unions. He also participated in politics and social activism in the Grand Duchy at that time. His biography and social status remind us of his German contemporary Martin Dibobe (see Chapter 1). Despite all of his contributions, however, there has been no official effort to honor Leurs' life with a plaque or a street name in Luxembourg's public space. Beyond a tendency to romanticize his life, the documentary portrays Jacques Leurs' challenging existence as "the first Black person in Luxembourg," which was complicated even further with the Nazi occupation in 1940. He was fired from his job at the railway company and had to resist the additional societal and political pressure to break up with Léoni Leurs that was enforced by the

---

9 Translated by the authors. In the original: "Do kënnt den N*."

racial laws introduced by the National Socialists in Luxembourg that same year (Hausemer 2018). The struggles Leurs faced due to his Blackness still exist today, albeit under a different guise.

It is important to note that countries such as Luxembourg, much like Norway (Chapter 5), and Poland (Chapter 8), are not deemed colonial powers; indeed, they did not officially possess colonies. Thus, they define and brand themselves as "colonial outsiders" (Purtschert, Falk, and Lüthi 2016). However, it is too narrow to understand colonialism as mainly a chronological or geographical marker. As Rizvi, Lingard, and Lavia (2006) put it, such an understanding is deeply problematic, as colonialism works transversally in time and space. Stoler (2016: ix) reminds us that there is a need to tackle "the temporal and affective space in which colonial inequities endure and the forms in which they do so." This view points to ruptures and continuities in the "colonial presence," which manifests in persistent racial inequities, immigration, and language regimes, to mention just a few.

There is a need to move beyond reductive national perspectives and to focus on colonial endeavors and practices across nation states and societies, whether or not they were deemed former colonizers. Several postcolonial and decolonial scholars and theorists have posited the continuity of colonial hegemony, "long after the departure and end of official colonialism" (de Souza 2017: 189). Thus, one should also acknowledge that colonization created knowledge and representation systems that became the basis of Eurocentricity with which the world was defined. In this sense, colonialism constantly involved the attempt to impose culture and customs onto *Others*, whether as a result of a belief in the racial and/or cultural superiority of the colonizing power; due to an evangelical desire to spread particular religions or cultural practices; or as a mechanism for establishing and consolidating political control as a core feature of our current global landscape (Butt 2013: 892).

The lived experiences of Black populations across several life domains (work, education, politics, etc.) have proven that colonial legacies are present and longstanding, not only in presumed "classic" colonial metropoles and colonies such as France, Portugal, and the UK and their former colonies in Africa, Asia, and the Americas, but also in those countries that self-proclaim and position themselves at the "colonial margins" (Purtschert and Fischer-Tiné 2015). Studying this will cast a light on "how colonial bodies of knowledge and practices have been borrowed, remoulded and disseminated within the scientific communities, everyday cultures and political arenas of these states" (ibid.: 7). All the colonial outsiders and their cities that were not considered colonial metropoles benefited (and still benefit) economically and politically from their entanglements with the more obvious colonial European powers. This was manifested through military and missionary involvements, trade, and the lobbying for colonial associations and careers, as in the case of Luxembourg.

Luxembourg has long been "marked by the scarcity of critical knowledge of colonialism as well as of acts of resistance against the persistence of colonial practices in postcolonial times" (Purtschert and Fischer-Tiné 2015: 4). As elsewhere, the BLM movement and the assassination of George Floyd have contributed to opening up more nuanced debates concerning racial inequalities. Together, Lëtz Rise Up, Finkapé, and Richtung22 have been at the forefront of uncovering Luxembourg's colonial past and spurring dialogue about it. To a large extent, these debates consist of a re-evaluation of monuments in public spaces designed to awaken today's society to the longstanding negative effects of colonialism and how it is manifested and embodied in these monuments. This is paramount in the construction of a better and fairer society. Thus, these associations can be considered catalysts that reveal Luxembourg's past and its contemporary forms of discrimination and inequality.

Cultural Associations with African Imprints

During the early 20th century, the presence of Luxembourgers in Congo did not trigger the mass immigration to Luxembourg of Congolese people, nor of any other Africans, as was usually the case with other colonial countries. The immigration of Italians swelled in the 19th century to support Luxembourg's iron and steel industries. After it had begun to decline due to Italy's economic growth, guest worker agreements between Portugal and Luxembourg were revised, intending to stop Cape Verdeans coming to Luxembourg through Portugal (Laplanche and Vanderkam 1991; Jacobs, Manço, and Mertz 2017; Tavares 2018). However, it is worth noting that, when Cape Verdeans started to come to Luxembourg in the 1960s, they held Portuguese citizenship before Cape Verde became independent from Portugal in 1975. Back then, the race category was officially and explicitly used to stop them entering the Grand Duchy (Laplanche and Vanderkam 1991; Jacobs, Manço, and Mertz 2017).

These agreements stipulated that only *"portugais de souche"* (white/European Portuguese) would be allowed to enter the country (Laplanche and Vanderkam 1991: 38; Jacobs, Manço, and Mertz 2017: 13). At that point it was made explicit that a person's race and ethnicity were the leading criteria for entering or being denied access to the state. After that, if Cape Verdeans did enter Luxembourg, it was only via family reunification processes or by crossing the borders secretly. Today, Cape Verdeans form the largest African group in the country (Statec 2020). However, they are constantly received with displeasure, as the government and society have exhibited racist ideologies that, to a certain extent, have influenced Luxembourg's perception toward Cape Verdeans, reflecting an iconic resonance of colonial imprints.

In line with the BBE study, the social worker Mirlene Monteiro, a Luxembourger of Cape Verdean origin and a member of the antiracism association Finkapé, presented the results of her study of second-generation Cape Verdeans in Luxembourg. According to her research, Cape Verdean descendants consider themselves Luxembourgers, despite having to deal with their sense of belonging being questioned by those who consider themselves "real" Luxembourgers. While trying to downplay the results of the BBE study, the Luxembourgish Minister of Family and Integration, Corinne Cahen, pointed out in a debate that she was shocked by Monteiro's results, which prove the existence of racism in the Grand Duchy, and invoked her personal experiences of discrimination based on her Jewish background. Another young Luxembourger of African descent, who has experienced racism both at school and at work, said that she was also shocked by the minister's feigned ignorance of the longstanding issue of racism in the Grand Duchy.[10]

With the exception of Cape Verdean immigration, little is known about Africans in the country. There is no study devoted to understanding immigration from mainland Africa to the Grand Duchy, despite the significant presence of Black people in its urban landscapes. Black Luxembourgers are quite noticeable thanks to their entrepreneurial spaces, such as small grocery stores, restaurants, and hair salons (Tavares 2018: 183), and associations, as well as in public spaces. In 2019, official statistics counted 11,411 African residents in the Grand Duchy (Statec 2020); this number is mis-

---

10 For more information on this debate, see https://www.youtube.com/watch?v=Zh282gIa8ww

leading, however, because dual citizenship, which many PAD hold, was not taken into account. In fact, if we included those with dual citizenship, the number of Cape Verdeans alone would be approximately the same as the number of all Africans recorded in the official statistics (cf. Jacobs, Manço, and Mertz 2017; Tavares 2018). Given these figures, it is no surprise that Cape Verde is the only African nation represented by an embassy in the Grand Duchy.

Nonetheless, there has been a proliferation of cultural associations with African imprints in Luxembourg. Currently, there are more than 50 that deal with the most pressing concerns of their community members, such as accommodation, unemployment, and official paperwork (Gerstnerova 2016: 7; cf. Tavares 2018). Often, these associations are used as a gateway to get by and embrace the discursive tropes of "integration." However, until recently, the ways in which the associations can operate to solve their members' existential socioeconomic problems to a large extent have been at the intersection of exoticization and commodification of their cultures – for example, during the annual Festival des Migrations.

This event, which began in 1983, is organized by the Comité de Liaison des Associations d'Étrangers (CLAE).[11] Associations connected to Africa, South America, Asia, and Eastern Europe, as well as to Portugal, are prominent during the festival. Most of the organizations involved are of African descent, while associations representing the USA, France, Italy, Germany, and Belgium are hardly seen. This is an interesting contrast, since the latter four countries represent the largest groups of immigrants in Luxembourg after the Portuguese. This paradoxical insight helps us better understand who is perceived as a "migrant" and who is not. The festival brands the host country as multicultural, multilingual, and inclusive, although there are persistent unequal policies preventing social mobility for residents born or with heritage from outside the country: for example, several government jobs (which are more prestigious and better paid) are limited to European citizens (Gerstnerova 2016).

---

11 CLAE was funded by the Ministry of Family and Integration in 1985. It is an association that campaigns for citizenship rights of residence, for the recognition and enhancement of cultures resulting from immigration, and for an open and united immigration policy in Luxembourg and in Europe. https://www.clae.lu/

Beyond Statec's numbers, however, information concerning Black Luxembourgers is limited. The little there is stems from newspaper articles covering issues relating to the "cooperation for development" that has existed between Cape Verde and Luxembourg since the 1990s (cf. Tavares 2018). Negative stereotypes of PAD, drug dealing, refugee crises, and deportation, for instance – are common in these reports, suggesting that there is still a pejorative image of Black people in the country. Academically, the experience of Africans in Luxembourg has remained uncharted terrain, despite longstanding experiences of racism and inequalities affecting mostly Black people in the Grand Duchy. Indeed, the BBL conference debate has further catalyzed nuanced public discussions about the country's links to colonialism. In its wake, several other debates and conferences in diverse sectors of society followed, organized by Lëtz Rise Up and Finkapé.

Finkapé started as an informal platform in 2019 and became a nonprofit association before BLM spurred calls to action in 2020. Literally, the name Finkapé means "stick foot tight" in Cape Verdean Creole; it can be loosely translated in English as "grit one's teeth" – the act of summoning up one's strength to face unpleasantness or overcome a difficulty. As written on its website, the name suggests the determination to struggle for a better life. The organization was created to tackle racism and other forms of discrimination and inequality PAD suffer. Since its inception, it has been active in denouncing the racism that members have experienced in their interactions, from school to work.[12] In an interview, Finkapé's president Antónia Ganeto stressed its engagement in tackling four intersecting axes of structural racism that affect Black people: "education, work, housing and gender".[13] In terms of its ideological background, she defined Finkapé as an antiracist, Afro-feminist, and decolonial association, committed to opening spaces of visibility, raising awareness, and bringing a critical point of view to challenges and pejorative ideas related to the Black population. Although very new, Finkapé has organized several activities – conference debates, training, and strikes – in collaboration with other institutional actors from the government and civil society, including Mirlene Monteiro.

---

12 "Finkapé. Le réseau Afrodescendant Luxembourg vous souhaite la bienvenue! (https://www.finkape.lu/)

13 Antónia Ganeto (the President of *Finkape*) in discussion with author Bernardino Tavares Facebook and telephone, Luxembourg city, Luxembourg, August 2021.

Lëtz Rise Up, founded in September 2019, aims to promote social transformation. This includes the restructuring of public institutions and the deconstruction of stereotypes and prejudices linked to racial and religious identity. For its members, however, social change starts with individual change and the self-awareness that they are being racialized in their own country, although their communities have been contributing to Luxembourg's development for centuries. To that end, in collaboration with Richtung22, Lëtz Rise Up has organized guided visits around the capital to highlight places linked to colonialism, as mentioned above. Beyond colonial memory, it focuses on education and legislation, which the organization believes are core areas in the fight against discrimination. Furthermore, this association collaborates with other public institutions, such as the University of Luxembourg and the UNESCO Chair in Human Rights, to bring together international experts on questions of institutional racism.[14]

What these two associations have in common is an activist, feminist, and political approach to unraveling racism and other forms of discrimination that are ingrained in the structures of society and polity. They are mostly composed of people of African origin and their descendants, who, in collaboration with stakeholders, are trying to disentangle racism and create a fairer society. The two associations have very similar objectives and philosophies. Both walk the same road to combat racism, gender bias, and other areas of discrimination, such as religion, sexual orientation, employment, and disability. Additionally, both of them stress the intersectionality of these forms of discrimination and inequality.

Unlike the two feminist and antiracist organizations, Richtung22 is a majority-white non-profit association founded by artists, filmmakers, and theater enthusiasts in 2010. Its aim is to regularize artistic professions and ensure fair working conditions. The collective is composed of students and young people from different professional backgrounds who use art, especially theater and cinema, as a social tool that they believe should be "inte-

---

14 "Understanding Institutional Racism in Comparative Perspective: From Lesson-drawing to an Agenda for Change," April 20, 2021 (https://eb6303ed-cff9-44f6-b5f4-16f0790b4040. filesusr.com/ugd/c7f16c_c762766a1e1a4ef18e52f13ffb85f0ba.pdf?fbclid=IwAR3XBMtJ3g sOkF1FlVrbrN5z1rDcw1mug1RIhhHiUc_9mOIde2Q9OHdA9Mk)

grated in the discussion [of social issues]".¹⁵ In 2020, the BLM movement did not escape its attention. Richtung22 collectively reunited a group of local artists to symbolically arrest one of the most prominent Luxembourgish figures of Congo's colonization, the engineer Nicolas Cito as mentioned above.

The establishment of these organizations means more future participation for Black Luxembourgers, who have already had two high-level political representatives. Both of Cape Verdean origin, the first is Natalie Silva, who was born in 1980 in the Grand Duchy and is the only Black mayor in Luxembourg, heading the town of Larochette. Silva stresses her belonging to the country, wondering about the "exceptionalism of her position," even after more than 60 years of Black presence in Luxembourg. Meanwhile, Monica Semedo, a former member of the Luxembourg Democratic Party, was elected in 2019 to represent Luxembourg in the European Parliament. Born in 1984, she said in a March 2022 debate:

> Mr. President, in my high school there were three black students out of more than 1,500. I was the first black TV host in Luxembourg, but not many were following, unfortunately. Once a boyfriend's mother told me "many black people are criminals, but you are different." No, I am not different. I am not an exception. There are many like me, and they deserve to have a fair chance to succeed. We have to get rid of the racist stereotypes, deconstruct prejudices and represent the full diversity of our society at all levels. We need equal access and opportunities for all in culture, education, media and sports, because they play an important role in the fight against racism. They have the power to change minds and to drive social inclusion.¹⁶

This does not necessarily mean that the Black population and their contributions are well perceived or well recognized. Moreover, these two Black women are not representative of the Black community in its entirety. According to

---

15 "Richtung 22: un film, une discussion, un coup de pied dans la fourmilière", May 3, 2013 (https://www.wort.lu/fr/culture/richtung-22-un-film-une-discussion-un-coup-de-pied-dans-la-fourmiliere-518400e1e4b08d4e6deobdbb)

16 https://www.europarl.europa.eu/doceo/document/CRE-9-2022-03-07-INT-1-131-0000_EN.html

Nancy Fraser (1995), redistribution "is tied to a vision of justice which means to achieve social equality through a redistribution of the material necessities for an existence as free subjects, while the conditions for a just society come to be defined as the recognition of the personal dignity of all individuals" (Honneth 2001: 43). To a certain extent, political (and societal) discourses have instrumentalized these women's positions to celebrate diversity associated with immigration in general.

The work was funded by the Luxembourg National Research Fund (FNR) C20/SC/14556610/DisPOSEG/TAVARES.

References

Bosma, U. and T. Kolnberger (2017) "Military Migrants: Luxembourgers in the Colonial Army of the Dutch East Indies", *Itinerario*, 41 (3): 568.

Butt, D. (2013) "Colonialism and Postcolonialism" in *International Encyclopedia of Ethics* [online]. Hoboken NJ: John Wiley & Sons.

Clarinval, France (2021) "Contextualiser," *d'Lëtzbuerger Land*, June 25, https://www.land.lu/page/article/193/338193/DEU/index.html

de Souza, L. M. T. M. (2017). Epistemic Diversity, Lazy Reason, and Ethical Translation in Postcolonial Contexts. In C. Kerfoot and K. Hyltenstam (eds.) Entangled Discourses: South-North Orders of Visibility. R 189 -208.

Fraser, N. (1995) "From Redistribution to Recognition? Dilemmas of Justice in a Post-Socialist Age," *New Left Review* 212: 68–93.

Frati, C. (2020) "Le racisme au Luxembourg, du tabou à la prise de conscience," *Paperjam*, June 5, https://paperjam.lu/article/racisme-au-luxembourg-tabou-a--2

Gerstnerova, A. (2016) "Migrant Associations' Dynamics in Luxembourg," *Ethnicities*, 16 (3): 418–31.

Hausemer, F. (2018) "Des lettres et un bébé noir," *Forum*, 381: 50.

Heindrichs, Tracy (2022): "Confronting Luxembourg's colonial past", *Delano*, March 2, 2022.

Honneth, A. (2001) "Recognition or redistribution?," *Theory, Culture & Society*, 18 (2–3): 43–55.

Jacobs, A., A. Manço, and F. Mertz (2017) *Diaspora capverdienne au Luxembourg: Panorama socio-économique, rôles dans les mouvements migratoires et solidarité avec le pays d'origine*. RED 21. Luxembourg: Centre d'Étude et de Formation Interculturelles et Sociales (CEFIS).

Laplanche, C. and M. Vanderkam (1991) *Di nos ...: nous, des Capverdiens au Luxembourg ...* Luxembourg: Centre National de l'Audiovisuel.

Law, J. (2004) *After Method: Mess in Social Science Research*. London: Routledge.

M'charek, A., K. Schramm, and D. Skinner (2014) "Topologies of Race: Doing Territory, Population and Identity in Europe," *Science, Technology, & Human Values*, 39 (4): 468–87.

Moes, R. (2010) "La collaboration coloniale belgo-luxembourgeoise au Congo," *Forum*, 299: 29–32.

Moes, R. (2012) *Cette colonie qui nous appartient un peu. La communauté luxembourgeoise au Congo Belge, 1883–1960*. Luxembourg: Fondation Robert Krieps and Éditions l'Lëtzeburger Land.

Mukuna, O. (2020) "Le Luxembourg et son passé colonial. Oser la décolonisation des esprits," *d'Lëtzbuerger Land*, July 24, https://www.land.lu/page/article/994/336994/DEU/index.html

Pauly, M. (2019) "Lëtzebuerg, rassistesch?," *Forum*, 401: 5.

Purtschert, P. and H. Fischer-Tiné (2015) "The End of Innocence: Debating Colonialism in Switzerland" in Patricia Purtschert (ed.), *Colonial Switzerland: Rethinking Switzerland from the Margins*. Basingstoke: Palgrave Macmillan.

Purtschert, P., F. Falk, and B. Lüthi (2016) "Switzerland and 'Colonialism without Colonies': Reflections on the Status of Colonial Outsiders," *Interventions*, 18 (2): 286–302.

Queirós, Madalena (2022): "Um terço dos portugueses sente-se vítima de racismo no Luxemburgo", Contacto, March 23, 2022 (https://www.wort.lu/pt/sociedade/um-terco-dos-portugueses-sente-se-v-tima-de-racismo-no-luxemburgo-623b46adde135b92360c4d33)

Rizvi, F., Bob Lingard, and Jennifer Lavia (2006) "Postcolonialism and Education: Negotiating a Contested Terrain," *Pedagogy, Culture & Society*, 14 (3): 249–62.

Spirinelli, F. (2020) "Toppling Symbols: Statues, the Colonial Past and the Public Space," June 21, https://www.c2dh.uni.lu/thinkering/toppling-symbols-statues-colonial-past-and-public-space

Statec (2020) "Population par nationalités détaillées 2011–2021," www.statistiques.public.lu

Stoler, A.-L. (2016) *Duress: Imperial Durabilities in Our Times*. London: Duke University Press.
Tavares, B. (2018) "Cape Verdean Migration Trajectories into Luxembourg: A Multisited Sociolinguistic Investigation." PhD dissertation, University of Luxembourg.

Chapter 5
Black Oslo

Michelle A. Tisdel

In Norway, numerous demonstrations were organized in response to the murder of George Floyd in the USA in May 2020. The "We Can't Breathe – Justice for George Floyd"[1] demonstration, arranged by the African Student Association (ASA) of the University of Oslo and the organization Afrikans Rising in Solidarity and Empowerment (ARISE), mobilized more than 15,000 people on June 5. It was Oslo's second and largest protest in response to the killing. The organizations sought to highlight the ongoing problem of structural racism and inequality in Norway, not just in the USA. In media interviews and statements, they referred to Norwegian examples of police violence and the police's use of excessive force, as well as to discriminatory attitudes and practices that have led to structural inequality and experiences of racism. The most egregious example of police violence in Norway is the case of Nigerian-born Eugene Obiora, who, aged 48, died in Trondheim in 2006 after police restrained him using a chokehold. Reportedly, the same policeman who killed Obiora had also been involved in another controversial case seven years earlier involving 21-year-old Ghanaian-born Sophia Baidoo, who was also restrained in a chokehold, but survived. Public opinion and debate surrounding these incidents pointed to discrimination, minority rights, and police brutality as issues of concern for antiracism organizations and activists.

The same protest transformed the historic Eidsvolls Plass (Eidsvoll's Square) in front of the Norwegian parliament into a new site of meaning in the symbolic landscape of Black Oslo. The concept "symbolic landscape"

---

[1] The original title of the demonstration was "We Can't Breathe – Rettferdighet for George Floyd."

describes a constellation of emotionally important components and highly visible venues that have different emotional significance for social actors in the public field (Ross 2007; 2009). The demonstration and the perceived messages of the organizers and protesters became central to a renewed racism debate that is still ongoing. As the site of a collective mobilization for anti-racism and social justice, the demonstration became a platform for voicing claims about historic inequality and articulating demands for new framings of equality and social justice.

In the following weeks, the public discourse quickly turned to definitions of racism, including everyday racism and structural racism in the Norwegian context. Many individuals with a so-called minority background shared personal narratives of discrimination and highlighted important examples of how individual incidents of discrimination contribute to systemic and structural inequality. In the public discourse that played out in traditional and social media, the stories were met with an array of responses, such as empathy and support, but also criticism and provocation. Debates focused on the claim that racism in Norway is still a hindrance to quality of life and social mobility. How could a country with such strong social democratic and egalitarian principles and anti-discrimination legislation be fertile ground for racism and structural inequality? Some critics commented that the demonstration illustrated, among other things, the importation of political issues, racism discourses, and 'identity politics' from the USA.

There were many different contributions to the racism debates, which ranged from serious and constructive to sensational and superficial. Nevertheless, the demonstrations had mobilized a new social engagement and political interest that highlighted issues of self-representation and historical visibility. Later that year, in October 2020, the organization Black History Month Norway kicked off its second celebration in Oslo. With a host of new prestigious institutional partners, such as the National Library of Norway, the National Gallery of Art, Architecture, and Design, and the Deichman Public Library, producing more than 15 events. Black representation and definitional power were central to the program theme, "From Fragments to History" (*Fra fragmenter til historie*).[2]

---

2 "Black History Month Norway 2020," May 18, 2021 (https://www.omod.no/post/black-history-month-norway-2020)

In addition, the Fritt Ord Foundation, a private non-profit organization that promotes freedom of expression, public debate, art, and culture, commissioned an analysis and report titled *Covering the Debate on Racism in Norwegian Media, 1 May 2020–31 August 2020*.[3] The report was prepared by Retriever, Scandinavia's largest media monitor and analyst. Described as a "media analysis of racism in the wake of the murder of George Floyd and the emergence of the Black Lives Matter movement," the report underscored a deep sense of "before" and "after" the demonstration.[4] It illustrated the national relevance of George Floyd's death as a catalyst for widespread demonstrations and public debate. The analysis also highlighted the media's active role in the Norwegian racism debate that ensued following antiracism solidarity protests around the country.[5] These debates also explored the issue of historical representation involving monuments and statues commemorating controversial persons such as Swedish scientist Carl von Linné (1707–78) and British statesman Sir Winston Churchill (1874–1965), as mentioned in Chapter 3.

Figure 5.1: The "We Can't Breathe – Rettferdighet for George Floyd" demonstration at Eidsvolls Plass in Oslo. Photograph: Lila Zotou, 2020

---

3 Homepage of The Fritt Ord Foundation (https://frittord.no/en/home)
4 Report Launch Event: "Covering the Debate on Racism in Norwegian Media," November 11 2020 (https://frittord.no/en/calendar/report-launch-event-covering-the-debate-on-racism-in-norwegian-media)
5 Demonstrations were also held in several cities, including Arendal, Aurland, Bergen, Hamar, Harstad, Skien, Sortland, Stavanger, Tromsø, Trondheim, and Volda.

The demonstrations that occurred in Oslo and around the country in June 2020 were not the first antiracism demonstrations held in the city. In October 1976, the Foreign Workers' Association,[6] along with antiracism allies and other immigrant and labor organizations, had staged an anti-discrimination and antiracism demonstration at University Square, a few blocks from Eidsvolls Plass. It was a response to anti-immigration policies, such as the 1975 immigration ban, and to increasing racism and structural inequality that impacted immigrant populations at the time (Røsjø 2007).[7] On May 8, 2007, OMOD Center for Social Justice and the Norwegian Centre Against Racism staged a protest outside the Ministry of Justice and Police, demanding an independent investigation into the death of Obiora.[8] In June 2021, ARISE and ASA commemorated the anniversary of the 2020 demonstration, acknowledging the continued relevance of antiracism and the need for collective action and responsibility.

The significance of Black spaces of representation in Oslo as contact zones – places or frontiers for "meetings" where "people geographically and historically separated encounter each other and establish ongoing relationships" (Pratt 1992: 6) – emerges through the interactions between people who meet and engage there. As a contact zone, the Oslo demonstration on June 5 engaged not only the 15,000 demonstrators but also those who observed and discussed their experiences. The demonstration had historical relevance and gave legitimacy to self-historicizing narrative practices about the value of Black lives and histories (see Espeland and Rogstad 2013: 128; Das 1995).

---

6 The Foreign Workers' Association (FAF), founded in 1972, focused on issues of human rights and the interests of foreign workers. Important mobilization issues for FAF were residence permits, family reunification, and discrimination in work life and the housing market. The association published the newspaper *Fremmedarbeideren* in 1974. The immigration ban that parliament introduced in 1975 affected many foreign workers (see Røsjø 2007).

7 On May 8, 2007, OMOD Center for Social Justice and the Norwegian Centre Against Racism staged a protest outside the ministry of justice and police, demanding an independent investigation into the death of Obiora.

8 Subsequent demonstrations were held in Oslo on May 19 and August 25, 2007 and January 4, 2008.

European Attraction Unlimited: A Temporary Site of Collective Memory

Examples of the social construction of space include the definitional power mobilized by the "Congolese Village," a temporary art installation constructed by Swedish-born Lars Cuzner and Sudanese-born Mohamed Ali Fadlabi in 2014. According to a text attributed to Will Bradley, artistic director of Kunsthall Oslo:

> The challenge in thinking through Lars Cuzner and Mohamed Ali Fadlabi's proposal to recreate the Congolese Village exhibit from Oslo's 1914 centenary exhibition is to escape the straightforward statement that it seems to offer.[9]

Fadlabi and Cuzner named the project after the London-based company European Attraction Unlimited, run by entertainment entrepreneur Benno Singer, who was the director of the Amusement Department at the 1914 exhibition that marked the centennial anniversary of the 1814 constitution. Adding to the numerous human zoos and colonial exhibitions that were celebrated in Germany (see Chapter 1) and other European countries, Oslo also participated in this colonial cultural tradition, staging *Kongolandsbyen* (Congolese Village) during the fair in 1914. Solidifying the dissolution of its more than 500-year union with the ruling kingdom of Denmark, the 1914 exhibition celebrated not just the centennial of the 1814 Norwegian constitution but also the nation's recent economic and cultural achievements. The exposition focused on industry, agriculture, and shipping, but organizers also aimed to entertain the public. There was an amusement park, which consisted of the Congolese Village, a Ferris wheel, a 700-meter roller coaster, and other attractions.

The staged Congolese Village presented 80 African inhabitants from Senegal in a theatrical setting. As many as 1.4 million spectators are reported to have visited the exhibition, where they encountered African adults and children, dressed in allegedly "traditional" clothes, using supposedly "authentic" tools and objects, and performing what were assumed to be "ordinary" African activities. According to newspaper reports, the village consisted of approximately 20 huts built by the "villagers," who cooked meals, sang, danced, and performed religious rituals (Graff 2004). At that time in Europe,

---

9 Website of Lars Cuzner: https://larscuzner.com/european-attraction-limited/

these productions were billed as entertainment but also as contributions to public information bordering on education, offering eager and curious Norwegians a unique opportunity to see Africans firsthand (many for the first time) and to observe them as "exotic" beings in their "natural" habitat engaging in everyday activities.

The archival evidence tells us, however, that the individuals in the 1914 "Congolese Village" were recruited from different Senegalese populations. The man whom newspapers referred to as "the village chief" (Ytreberg 2014a; 2014b) was Jean Thiam, a resident of Dakar, a jeweler and property owner who also participated in local politics. Thiam had taken part in the 1900 World Exhibition in Paris. Professor and media scholar Espen Ytreberg suggests that Thiam functioned as an employer or manager for the unidentified Senegalese. These elements further reveal the complex nature of Black representation in Norway – in 1914 as well as in 2014.

The extent to which the Congolese Village exhibition in 1914 provided Norwegians new insights into how Africans lived or merely reinforced racial stereotypes and ideas about a racial hierarchy is highly debatable. The public's reactions ranged from curiosity and excitement to discomfort and disgust. For example, some spectators seemed surprised or fascinated by the similarities between the demeanor of African and European children, while for others the exhibition confirmed the notion of African people and culture as primitive and inferior to civilized Europeans.

The 1914 jubilee exhibition took place in the then capital Kristiania, which later was renamed Oslo. A committee founded in 1908 had applied for funds from parliament and the Kristiania municipality. A total budget of 2,850,000 NOK[10] was approved to fund the exhibition, which covered 40,0000 square meters and included six thematic departments and 19 sections (Hammer 1928: 413–14). The government and Kristiania municipality contributed 500,000 NOK and 300,000 NOK respectively, while organizers hoped to raise an additional 800,000 NOK through a lottery and ticket sales (ibid.).[11]

As part of the celebrations of the 200th anniversary of Norway's constitution in 2014, the government funded the reenactment of the "human zoo," which

---

10 The equivalent of approximately 202,600,000 NOK or €21,325,500 in 2021.

11 The amounts are equivalent to the following 2021 values: 300,000 NOK (1908) is 21,325,500 NOK or €2,245,000 (2021); 500,000 NOK (1908) is 35,500,000 NOK or €3,750,000 (2021); and 800,000 NOK (1908) is 57,000,000 NOK or €6,000,000 (2021).

sparked debates with antiracism organizations. In recreating this critical event, Fadlabi and Cuzner's project sought to raise important questions about Black and African representation in Norway, the country's relationship to colonial history, and discourses about racism in 1914 and 2014. They also organized the conference "European Attraction Unlimited," which assembled experts and researchers in art and African history to probe the historical context of race, inequality, and representation surrounding the Congolese Village projects. Themes included Afrocentric historical perspectives, material conditions that enabled imperialism, ideologies of racial hierarchy, and the problematic industry surrounding human zoos or exhibitions that showcased indigenous peoples and traditions as "exotic" and "primitive" for white spectators.

The artists conceived the project as a public dialogue and experiment that would address historical patterns of injustice and asymmetrical power relations between Africa and Europe and their populations. This created an opportunity to question the material conditions and power relations that shaped perceptions of racism and representation in 1914 and 2014. Had understandings and practices of racism, "othering," and exotification really changed at all? To say that Fadlabi and Cuzner's project engaged the public is an understatement. Reactions ranged from amusement and curiosity, to concern, irritation, and provocation. Critics questioned whether a reenactment of a racist spectacle could effectively articulate a critique of racism in the past and the present. Others argued that any reenactment or replica of the 1914 Congolese Village could inadvertently reinforce racist attitudes and stereotypes (cf. Khan-Østrem 2014).

Another perspective was that the project might have benefited from the use of more archival evidence and information about the "villagers" in the 1914 exhibition. Ytreberg, for example, noted that the 1914 Congolese Village was part of a broader tradition of public display and information dissemination (Ytreberg 2014b). The 1914 jubilee exhibition program also featured a small farm operated by the Kalby family, Norwegian farmers from Midtskogen near Jessheim (Ytreberg 2014a). In this sense, both the Congolese "villagers" and the Norwegian farmers were human exhibits. The Norwegian family, however, was part of the agriculture and industry presentation, located inside the main exhibition area, and intended to illustrate Norwegian farming methods. In contrast, the Congolese Village was part of the entertainment department, separated from the "serious" exhibitions and located outside the entrance. Promoting European superiority, it was designed as a contrasting showcase of "exotic" people and culture from Africa.

European Attraction Unlimited and its 2014 Congolese Village project were a critical event, not only because they engaged the public in an important debate about racism and representation in Norway. Some of the most outspoken critics of the project were individuals from the Black community who feared that the mere replication of such a dehumanizing spectacle might retraumatize their members, not to mention delight anti-Black racists. As the editorial written by Nazneen Khan-Østrem suggested, amid the persistent denial of racism in Norway, the complicated debate among Norwegians of African descent – and the, at times, uncomfortable majority–minority interaction – the Congolese Village was a "mental state" (Khan-Østrem 2014). The art project was designed to mobilize taboos, stereotypes, and discomfort that obscure racism and inequality. Inadvertently, perhaps, the project also revealed the complexity of Black Oslo – its scars, vulnerabilities, and competing self-images.

Figure 5.2: Mohamed Ali Fadlabi and Lars Cuzner's "Congolese Village" recreated in Frogner Park in 2014. Source: https://commons.wikimedia.org/wiki/File:Kongolandsbyen_2014.JPG. Photograph: Bjørn Christian Tørrissen, 2014

In May 2014, after much controversy and debate, the artists reconstructed their model of the Congolese Village at the site of the 1914 village campus in Frogner. Instead of populating the recreated Congolese Village with African bodies, before the opening, the artists had published an open call for volunteers to participate in the village by displaying themselves. When the artists opened the attraction, the public became both collective spectators and spectacle, as individuals were left to ponder each other's curious and "othering gazes." In this way, Cuzner and Fadlabi further engaged the public in antiracist and postcolonial debates by creating a new spectacle that questioned existing understandings of what it means to perpetuate and challenge racism in the past and the present.

Colonial Innocence and Cultural Contestation

Power structures, material conditions, and sociopolitical factors have also influenced broader social processes, such as public debate and knowledge production. The construction and production of historical narratives, monuments, and memorial sites are manifestations of these processes (Trouillot 1995; Low 2000). In public discourses, many community leaders and activists have addressed different kinds of power and historical processes from the perspectives of minorities and People of African, Asian, and Caribbean Descent. Take, for example, human rights activist and cultural critic Khalid Salimi's book *Rasismens Røtter: Da Rasisme Kom Til Norge* (*The Roots of Racism: When Racism Came to Norway*) (1987). He discusses how racism, definitional power, and representation can be understood in relation to broader histories of European colonialism, extremist ideologies such as fascism and Nazism, as well as global inequality. In *Mangfold og Likeverd* (*Diversity and Equality*) (Salimi 1996), Salimi, a former leader of the Norwegian Centre Against Racism (1983–98), engages younger readers in a discussion about race relations in Norway, citing the need for knowledge grounded in respect for human dignity.

Consider, for example, that while scientist Carl von Linné developed his perspectives on the racial categories of *Homo sapiens sapiens*, the world was engaged in lucrative triangular economic activities – enslavement that trafficked Africans and traded goods between Africa, the Americas, the Caribbean, and Europe. From the Reformation in 1536 until 1814, Norway was part of the Danish Empire, which built the Christiansborg fort, now called Osu Castle in the current city of Accra, Ghana, between 1659 and 1661. At first, this stronghold became the seat of the Danish governor, who oversaw the colonized peoples and land on the so-called Gold Coast, but later the fort became an important support point for enslavement. The twin kingdom of Denmark and Norway was active with its route between Christiansborg on the Gold Coast of Africa and the Caribbean colonies, now known as Saint Croix and the US Virgin Islands, but formerly called the Danish West Indies.

As part of Denmark–Norway, many Norwegian residents and regions engaged in and benefited from the enslavement and trafficking of Africans during this period. In the 17th century, the Bergen businessman Jørgen Thormøhlen (1640–1708) invested in the city's shipping economy and became the largest ship owner and industrialist in the country. His good relations with Denmark's King Christian V led to Thormøhlen's appointment as commerce director (minister of trade) in 1682. Thormøhlen managed all trade with the Danish–Norwegian colonies in the Caribbean between approximately 1690 and 1700 (Mardal and Fossen 2020). It is said that because of this economic system, the period 1770–89 was a heyday for Denmark–Norway. However, the abolition of the trade in enslaved Africans in 1792 was not the end of enslavement; it took until 1848 for it to be abolished in their colonies.

There is ample scholarship and archival evidence to nuance and even refute notions of Norwegian colonial innocence, which underpin many denials of racism and the historical conditions of inequality that the Benjamin Hermansen bust and Ruth Reeses Plass address (to be discussed later). Two important examples are Bergen-based journalist Claus Fasting's (1746–91) anti-slavery writings and the works of activists of the Sámi movement, such as Elsa Laula Renberg (1877–1931) and Karin Stenberg (1884–1969) from the southern Sámi-speaking region of Sweden. As historian Aina Nøding explained, in the Danish–Norwegian and European context, Fasting was an early and unreserved opponent of enslavement, even though – or perhaps because – he had relatives and friends who profited greatly from sugar plantations in the Caribbean (see Nøding 2018: 201–5). In 1778, Fasting used his magazine *Provinzialblade* (Bergen, 1778–81) to argue against enslavement and to directly oppose the excuses of Danish and religious authorities, both in articles and through translations of stories of enslavement and the trading of Africans.

Furthermore, newspaper announcements from the 18th century confirm the presence of enslaved Africans and Caribbeans living in Norway with their Danish and Norwegian enslavers who had returned from the Danish–Norwegian colonies and the United Kingdom. On September 8, 1777, the year before Fasting published his antiracist writings, a baptismal announcement for a Black woman called "Christine" or "Juliana Maria" appeared in the newspaper *Bergens Adressecontoirs Efterretninger*: "This Negro belongs to Mad. Dischingthun who brought her from the West Indies to this place."[12] About ten years before Fasting's publication, the merchant frigate *Fredensborg* had already sailed from Accra to Saint Croix with a cargo that consisted of 265 Africans. Sugar, tobacco, mahogany, and ivory were in the hold when the ship sank on December 1, 1768 at Gitmertangen at the eastern end of the island of Tromøy in Norway. The wreck was found in August 1974. The examples above demonstrate Norway's role in enslavement and colonization, which can also be framed as a broader issue of social justice and part of the symbolic landscape of Black representation and history.

Many Norwegians do not regard Norway as a former colonist state because it was part of the Danish Empire. Moreover, there are no identified direct descendants of the Danish–Norwegian colonial populations in Norway. On the contrary, there is a strong belief that "Norway is so highly valued in the world because we have no colonial past," as former prime minister and current secretary general of NATO Jens Stoltenberg stated in 2013 (Tveit 2021). As social anthropologist Laurie McIntosh notes: "[T]he national self-image disregards the history of Norwegian maritime involvement in the transatlantic slave trade during Denmark–Norway's participation in colonial expansion" (2015: 312). Yet, many contemporary ideas about fundamental Norwegian self-image, values, and national cultural identity relate to ideas and traditions from the 19th century (Gullestad 2004: 192). "Norwegian national identity used to be defined in contrast to Danes, Swedes, and other Europeans who were white," according to social anthropologist Gullestad (ibid.: 193). "Now being white has become a more pronounced dimension of being Norwegian" (ibid.). In this regard, race, descent, and national self-image represent mutually referential but shifting ideas. Furthermore, there

---

12 The notice refers to the woman as a *"negerinde"* named Christine, who is baptized as Juliana Maria. "Denne Negerinde tilhører Mad. Dischingthun, som førte henne med sig fra Vest-Indien her til Stedet," *Bergens Adressecontoirs Efterretninger*, September 8, 1777, p. 2.

is more scholarship and archival evidence to muddy and even refute this notion of colonial innocence that underpins many denials of racism and the historical conditions of inequality. These processes are also part of cultural contestations and the social constructions of space in the symbolic landscape (cf. Low 2000; Ross 2007; 2009).

The political representation of Black Oslo is not only about the power to challenge, define, and disagree with the terms of belonging in society and in history. It also involves the ability to articulate and realize demands for Black historical representation. Even before the death of George Floyd, Bergen resident Irene Kinunda Afriyie articulated this need in her editorial "Norway Needs a 'Black History Month,'" published in the newspaper *Bergens Tidende* on February 28, 2020 (Afriyie 2020). "Norwegian history lacks, among other things, recognition of Africans who have been in Norway from the start," she writes. That is, the African diaspora in Norway did not begin with modern immigration. Afriyie points out that enslavement and Norway's role in colonization are also part of Black history in Norway. This framing of Norwegian history and Black Oslo also inspired Yacoub Cissé and Ann Falahat's book *Afrikanere i Norge gjennom 400 år* (*Africans in Norway throughout 400 Years*) (2011).

In addition to the aforementioned memorials, street art depicting PAD is also an important contribution to the public arena and political representation. Substitutes for official monuments are strategically located in neighborhoods associated with significant populations with African backgrounds. In Oslo's Tøyen neighborhood, for example, the municipality commissioned a mural by acclaimed artist Fadlabi. Fadlabi's mural *The Sky's the Limit* (2016), located at Jens Bjelkes 63C, depicts a Somalian man with brown skin, wearing sporty sunglasses, dressed in an astronaut suit, and holding a helmet (figure 5.3). In interviews, the artist has stated that he chose a Black role model for the artwork to inspire the community. The mural is the artist's message to the local youth: "Kids, if you work hard, everything is possible."[13] Fadlabi's work foregrounds the Black protagonist as a force of progress and autonomous action. Thus, the mural performs a monumental role in the public space and as a homage to Black Oslo.

---

13 Interview by NK with artist Mohamed Ali Fadlabi on June 2, 2016 (https://www.nrk.no/osloogviken/gatekunst-pa-toyen-1.12980157)

Figure 5.3: Fadlabi's The Sky's the Limit (2016). Photograph: Michelle A. Tisdel, 2022

In her acclaimed book *Rasismens Poetikk* (2019), author, slam poet, and educator Guro Jabulisile Sibeko addresses the importance of social categories and labels, describing "Black" and "Brown" bodies in Norway. By discussing the term *melaninrik* (melanin-rich), Sibeko illustrates the power of self-identification and labeling as engaged social action. Among relevant populations there is no consensus about which descriptive term is the best collective label for African diaspora populations. While personal experience may influence self-perception, historical factors, beliefs, and attitudes operating in society also influence the use and effect of accepted and emerging social categories. These social constructions all involve the "phenomenological and symbolic experience of space as mediated by social processes such as exchange, conflict, and control" (Low 2000: 128).

Community Organizing: Permanent Contact Zones as Official Sites of Memory

Political representation of Black Oslo in the symbolic landscape is the ability to attain rights and realize new forms of historical visibility through self-articulation and representation. The demand for political representation is predicated on a public dialogue in which a multiplicity of Black experiences and histories are valued and validated. Two permanent contact zones in the symbolic landscape are the bust of the slain teen Benjamin Hermansen (1985–

2001), born to a Ghanaian father and Norwegian mother, and Ruth Reeses Plass, which commemorates the African American singer, author, and activist Ruth Ann Reese (1921–90). The former holds somber relevance for Black Oslo because it pays tribute to 15-year-old Hermansen, who died after neo-Nazis attacked him with a knife on January 26, 2001, in the Åsbråten neighborhood in the Holmlia district. A brutal reminder of the persistence of racism and nationalism in Norway and Europe, Hermansen's death was a tragedy that left deep wounds in the imagined community of Black Oslo and the nation.

Every year since the tragedy, Åsbråten residents and others have been gathering at Hermansen's bust and lighting candles in his memory. The idea for the monument came from his friends in Holmlia and initially was a source of considerable discontent and disagreement among nearby residents. A group of members of the housing association were concerned that the statue would negatively affect the property value of their apartments.[14] Nevertheless, in November 2001, a bust of Hermansen, created by Norwegian sculptor Ivar Sjaastad, was unveiled at the site of his death. The inscription reads "Do not forget [Glem ikke], 26.01.2001," reportedly at the request of the teenager's friends.

Figure 5.4: Bust of Benjamin Hermansen (1985–2001) in the Åsbråten neighborhood in Oslo. Photograph: Michelle A. Tisdel, 2021

---

14 The results from a private communication with a colleague who conducted research on the case.

A miniature copy of the bust is awarded to schools that receive the annual Benjamin Prize for their work on antiracism. The prize is managed by the Norwegian Center for Holocaust and Minority Studies, a research, education, and documentation center in Oslo focusing on the Holocaust and other genocides, as well as "extremism, anti-Semitism, hate speech, and the situation of minorities in contemporary societies."[15] Holmlia Sports Club, the organization Vær Stolt (Be Proud), Holmlia School, and the Benjamins Minnefond (Benjamin's Memorial Fund) helped to arrange a ten-year celebration in January 2011.

In January 2001, residents with a so-called minority background made up 9,000 of the 32,000 residents of the Holmlia district that includes Hermansen's neighborhood Åsbråten (Buggeland et al. 2001). The popular teenager, a student at Holmlia High School, was involved in his local community through activities such as football and the local youth club. According to one newspaper article, the "Norwegian-African"[16] youth was aware of his skin color (ibid.). In a news interview with the Norwegian Broadcasting Corporation just six months before his death, Hermansen had discussed encountering racism and neo-Nazis at recent football tournaments in Denmark and Sweden.

After his murder, friends, local residents, and other mourners from greater Oslo placed photographs, flowers, candles, written messages, and other objects at the site, forming the first spontaneous site of memory commemorating Hermansen. A few days later, approximately 40,000 people participated in the torchlight procession and demonstration held on February 1, 2001 at Youngstorget; this became another significant venue for Black people in central Oslo. One newspaper summarized the significance of the gathering, saying that the country had not seen a rally of that size since the liberation after World War Two (Strand 2001). In 2011, a similar vigil was held at Youngstorget to commemorate Hermansen, who had become an important source of inspiration and a symbol for antiracism in Norway, ten years after his death. His killing was a critical event that created another new reference point and dialogue about racism and belonging.

The three assailants who had targeted Benjamin Hermansen had direct ties to the neo-Nazi group Boot Boys. His death was widely understood as

---

15 Quoted from the homepage of The Norwegian Center for Holocaust and Minority Studies (https://www.hlsenteret.no/english/)

16 "*Norsk-afrikansk*" is the phrase used in the newspaper article.

a racially motivated hate crime. A survey of the collection of the National Library of Norway illustrates the vast body of literature and news generated about Hermansen. More than 270 digitized books and 50 journal articles reference him. The digital library also contains nearly 4,000 relevant newspaper items. Social history, discrimination against national minorities and "new" minorities with a "migration background," racism, hate crimes, and extremism represent important subjects in the academic and popular works that reference Hermansen. He, along with other victims of racism in Norway, were featured on several protest posters during the demonstration in Oslo.

In January 2021, the Benjamins Minnefond, along with the local community of Åsbråten, the African Student Association (UiO), the Norwegian Centre Against Racism, and many other actors, staged virtual memorials for Hermansen, marking 20 years since his passing. Friends, neighbors, Prime Minister Erna Solberg, and a host of other individuals submitted video tributes about antiracism and Hermansen's significance. This suggests that many people link Hermansen's death to broader public issues of racism, injustice, inequality, and the very real danger of racial violence in Norway. Moreover, the commemorations of Hermansen suggest that his death has influenced knowledge production and new frames for imagining values, such as social justice, antiracism, minority rights, and democracy.

Ruth Reeses Plass, another contact zone of historical relevance, is in the Grünerløkka district in Oslo, located in front of the main gate of the former Schou Brewery. It lies at the intersection of Nybrua, where Trondheim Street starts and Thorvald Meyers Street ends. The name was adopted by the Grünerløkka Bydelsutvalg (District Committee) in February 2012 as part of a plan to increase the number of roads named after women. In a letter dated June 18, 2020, the socialist political party Rødt introduced a motion to the Grünerløkka Bydelsutvalg to investigate the cost and criteria for erecting a bust of Reese in the square.[17] Rødt also suggested that the committee involve Reese's collaborator and friend Cliff Moustache, who wrote the poem "Letter to U"[18] about Ruth Reese.

---

17 "Ny Sak: Statue av Ruth," letter to the Grünerløkka District Committee, June 18, 2020.
18 Cliff Moustache is the artistic director of Nordic Black Theatre in Oslo. In 1985, Reese and Moustache were founding members of the Oslo-based activist organization Artists for Liberation.

The year 2021 marked a century since Reese's birth in Hayneville, Alabama. However, she grew up in Chicago and was trained as a classical singer. In the early 1950s, she moved to Europe to pursue a singing career, settling in Oslo in 1958, where she lived for more than three decades. In Europe, Reese became known as "The Black Rose." Combining her

Figure 5.5a: Ruth Ann Reese. Photograph: Klaus Forbregd, 1959, NTNU University Library.
Figure 5.5b: Ruth Reeses Plass, Grünerløkka. Photograph: Michelle A. Tisdel, 2021

knowledge of African American cultural history with social justice activism, she significantly contributed to antiracism and the rights of women of color in Norway.

A vast body of archival material provides an insight into Reese's life and community involvement. Reese is well represented in the collections of the

National Library of Norway and the Oslo City Archives.[19] She published two books, her autobiography *Min Vei* (*My Way*) (1985) and *Lang Svart Vei* (*Long Black Road*) (1972), a collection of short essays on African American history. The books and chronicles illustrate Reese's desire to educate Norwegians about African American history and the individual and societal consequences of racism.

Reese was first interviewed for an article entitled "Vanskelig å være neger – også i Norge" (Difficult To Be a Negro – Also in Norway) in the magazine *Alt for Damene* in 1958 (Lekang 1958). We learn about her background and ambitions, and that she struggled to find housing in Oslo in the late 1950s. In the text "Vår hud er sort" (Our Skin is Black) published in the daily newspaper *Dagbladet* and others in July 1959, she observed:

> Most people in Scandinavia disagree with what is happening in South Africa and the American southern states, but it does not concern them. It's so far away. (Reese 1959: 4)

Reese's call to mobilize for antiracism and social justice received much attention. Her newspaper article ignited a debate about white complicity, denial, and misunderstandings of racial prejudice. Newspapers also printed letters of support, criticism, and comments from readers. The essay and the discussion it created can be regarded as a reference point in an ongoing dialogue on solidarity and European accountability in the struggles for anticolonialism and antiracism. Six months later, Reese followed up the article with the lecture "Rasehat og demokrati" (Racial Hatred and Democracy), which was held in January 1960 at the prestigious University of Oslo Aula.[20]

Reese worked to raise awareness about antiracism in Norway more than 60 years ago, at a critical time just before the mass immigration from Pakistan, Turkey, Morocco, and several other countries began. According to archivist Ellen Røsjø, Reese became "an inspiration for several of the new immigrants who came to the country in the 1960s and 70s" (Røsjø 2017: 31). "She took on the role of public educator in Norway – about Black Americans'

---

19 In the National Library's digital collection alone, Reese is mentioned in 150 books, 9,000 newspaper items and 113 journals. The Oslo City Archives manages the MiRA-Centre's private archive about Reese.

20 (1960) "Rasehatogdemokrati," In: Morgenbladet, January 22, 1960, 4.

music, culture, history and tradition" (ibid.). On October 25, 1990, during a program at the local culture house Slurpen, the organization SOS Rasisme awarded Reese an honorary lifetime membership for her antiracism work. Reese accepted the award, and then collapsed and died on stage while delivering her thank you speech.

Although many African American performing artists had worked and lived in Norway before, Reese was distinctive because she engaged in the public dialogue about the plight of Black people around the world. She had experienced firsthand the brutality of racism and racial segregation in the USA. Although she chose to live in Europe to pursue an international career as an artist, Reese felt a profound responsibility to participate in the ongoing Civil Rights Movement in the USA. Not only did she speak and write about the social movement for equality there, in 1959 she also advocated for stronger political action against apartheid in South Africa. She was an early collaborator with the Norwegian Students' Society and supported their efforts to create the South Africa Committee in Oslo and sponsor Black South African students to study in Norway. Moreover, her public presence and engagement from 1958 to 1990 was unprecedented for a Black woman in Norway.

Among Black Oslo's younger generation, her significance and that of the landmark Ruth Reeses Plass are still emerging. Reese introduced Black self-representation and historical awareness into the Norwegian public dialogue about racism and inequality. Although she challenged Norwegian stereotypes about race and discourses about social justice, Reese and Norwegians felt a mutual respect. She commented that in Norway she felt "human," because there was no explicit state-sponsored racism targeting People of African Descent (PAD), unlike in the USA. She also spoke openly about examples of racism in Norway, such as the use of Blackface and other practices.[21] "Ignorance has always been the source of fear and injustice," Reese told a journalist in 1959 (Blom 1959). Thus, she combined her appeal as an artist with her dedication to educate and mobilize the public about the inhumanity of racism and colonialism. By combining her activism and artistry, she spread a message of antiracism, social justice, solidarity, and social responsibility to thousands of Norwegian children and adults around the country.

---

21 Reese's criticism of Blackface in 1958 was written about by Einar Deisen in the national newspaper *Aftenposten*, June 27, 1958, p. 6.

Critical events and narratives involve knowledge production, collective action framing, and critiques of power (Espeland and Rogstad 2013). The ascription of meaning to George Floyd, the Congolese Village, Benjamin Hermansen, and Ruth Reese are all involved in this process and offer different frames for interpreting Black Oslo and its complexity. When a personal challenge or event takes on meaning in a collective action or narrative framing, it becomes a "public issue" that can reveal conflict and implicit power relations from a different perspective. These monuments and memory sites relate to critical events and narratives that hold significance for Black Oslo as a real and imagined community. Moreover, narratives about meaningful events and persons can reveal cultural contestation about asymmetrical power relations, claims for rights and equality, and how these histories are represented in the public field. Knowledge production involves analyzing and making sense of the world through remembering and self-historicizing, as well as through marking and encoding objects, events, social interactions, and spaces with value and sentiment (see Espeland and Rogstad 2013: 128; Das 1995).

References

Afriyie, Irene Kinunda (2020) "Norge trenger en 'Black' History Month," *Bergens Tidende*, February 28, p. 3.

Blom, Anton (1959) "Hennes hud er sort," *Arbeiderbladet*, August 15, p. 7.

Buggeland, Sven Arne, Tore Johansen, Tom Bakkeli, and Ole Morten Melgård (2001) "Skulle møte venn," *VG*, January 28, pp. 6–7.

Cissé, Yacoub and Ann Falahat (2011) *Afrikanere i Norge gjennom 400 år*. Oslo: Afrikanere i Norge.

Das, Veena (1995) *Critical Events: An Anthropological Perspective on Contemporary India*. Delhi: Oxford University Press.

Espeland, C. E. and J. Rogstad (2013) "Antiracism and Social Movements in Norway: The Importance of Critical Events," *Journal of Ethnic and Migration Studies*, 39 (1): 125–42, http://dx.doi.org/10.1080/1369183X.2013.723251

Fagerlid, Cicilie and Michelle A. Tisdel (2020) "Introduction: Literary Anthropology, Migration, and Belonging" in: Cicilie Fagerlid and Michelle A. Tisdel (eds.), *A Literary Anthropology of Migration and Belonging: Roots, Routes, and Rhizomes*. Cham, Switzerland: Palgrave Macmillan.

Graff, Sverre Bjørstad (2004) "En afrikansk landsby i Oslo," *ABC Nyheter*, October 22, https://www.abcnyheter.no/nyheter/2004/10/22/38883/en-afrikansk-landsby-i-oslo?gclid=EAIaIQobChMIo-SElLq18gIVGO-qyCh26igdrEAAYAyAAEgLpwvD_BwE

Gullestad, Marianne (2004) "Blind Slaves of Our Prejudices: Debating 'Culture' and 'Race' in Norway," *Ethnos (Estocolmo)*, 69 (2): 177–203.

Hammer, S. C. (1928) *Kristianias Historie 1878–1924. Bind 5*. Kristiania: I Hovedkommission hos J. W. Cappelen.

Khan-Østrem, Nazneen (2014) "Kronikk: Kongolandsbyen – en mental tilstand," *VG*, March 22, https://www.vg.no/nyheter/meninger/i/3ywq9/kronikk-kongolandsbyen-en-mental-tilstand

Lekang, Per (1958) "Vanskelig å være neger – også i Norge," *Alt for Damene*, September 10.

Low, Setha M. (2000) *On the Plaza: The Politics of Public and Culture*. Austin: University of Texas Press.

Mardal, Magnus A. and Anders Bjarne Fossen (2020) "Jørgen Thor Møhlen," Store Norske Leksikon, https://snl.no/J%C3%B8rgen_Thor_M%C3%B8hlen

McIntosh, L. (2015) "Impossible Presence: Race, Nation and the Cultural Politics of Being Norwegian," *Ethnic and Racial Studies*, 38 (2): 309–25.

Nøding, Aina (2018) *Claus Fasting: Dikter, journalist og opplysningspioner*. Oslo: Scandinavian Academic Press.

Pratt, Mary Louise (1992) *Imperial Eyes: Travel Writing and Transculturation*. London: Routledge.

Reese, Ruth (1959) "Vår hud er sort," *Dagbladet*, July 24, p. 4.

Reese, Ruth (1985) *Min Vei*. Oslo: Gyldendal. English translation: *My Way: An Autobiography*. London: Akira Press, 1987.

Reese, Ruth and Paul Shetelig (1972) *Lang Svart Vei*. Oslo: Tiden.

Røsjø, Ellen (2007) *Spor etter oss: "Oslos multikulturelle arkiver."* Oslo: Oslo Byarkiv.

Røsjø, Ellen (2017) "The Black Rose: Ruth Reese" in Kirsti Gulowsen, Unn Hovdhaugen, and Øystein Eike (eds.), *Oslofortellinger: Oslo Byarkiv – Byens Hukommelse*. Oslo: Oslo Byarkiv.

Ross, Marc Howard (2007) *Cultural Contestation in Ethnic Conflict*. Cambridge: Cambridge University Press.

Ross, Marc Howard (2009) *Culture and Belonging in Divided Societies: Contestation and Symbolic Landscapes*. Philadelphia: University of Pennsylvania Press.

Salimi, Khalid (1996): Mangfold og likeverd. Oslo: Cappelen

Salimi, Khalid, Mari K. Linløkken, and Antirasistisk Senter (1987) *Rasismens Røtter: Da Rasismen Kom Til Norge*. Oslo: Cappelen.

Sibeko, Guro (2019) *Rasismens Poetikk*. Oslo: Ordatoriet.

Strand, Trond (2001) "40.000 viste varme," *Bergens Tidende*, February 2, https://www.bt.no/nyheter/innenriks/i/vrpRm/40000-viste-varme

Tisdel, Michelle A. (2020) "Narratives of Competence and Confidence: Self, Society, and Belonging in Norway" in: Cicilie Fagerlid and Michelle A. Tisdel (eds.), *A Literary Anthropology of Migration and Belonging: Roots, Routes, and Rhizomes*. Cham, Switzerland: Palgrave Macmillan.

Trouillot, Michel-Rolph (1995): Silencing the Past: Power and the Production of History. Boston: Beacon Press.

Tveit, Marta Mboka (2021): Decolonization: A view from the North, *ECDPM Great Insights magazine*, Volume 10, Issue 1, March 23, 2021 (https://ecdpm.org/great-insights/call-change-young-people-africa-europe/decolonisation-view-north/)

Ytreberg, Espen (2014a) *En Forsvunnet by: Jubileumsutstillingen På Frogner 1914*. Oslo: Forlaget Press.

Ytreberg, Espen (2014b) "Fornøyelse ved det fremmede," *Morgenbladet*, May 16–22, pp. 28–9.

Chapter 6
Black Paris

Epée Hervé Dingong and Olive Vassell

Like many cities around the world, Paris erupted in protests after the George Floyd police killing in the USA in the summer of 2020. The largest was organized by activist Assa Traoré, the older sister of 24-year-old Adama Traoré, a young Black Frenchman who died in police custody in July 2016. Under the banner "Truth for Adama Traoré," the march drew 20,000 people who defied a government ban on demonstrations and stood in front of a Paris court to demand justice for Traoré. Four years earlier, Assa Traoré had founded Le Comité Vérité et Justice pour Adama (Committee for Justice and Truth for Adama), declaring that her brother had died because of a racist system and vowing to keep his name alive. And during the 2020 demonstration, she drew parallels between Floyd and her brother, saying that they both died at the hands of the police (Martirosyan 2020).

It is this same racist system that invisibilizes Black people in France and makes them feel like second-class citizens. Although they have long called for increased equality and visibility, little has changed. Unlike anglophone countries such as the USA and the UK, France does not know the number of its Black population. Statistics based on race and ethnicities are outlawed. Moreover, in 2018, race was erased from the constitution in the belief that France is a color-blind society.[1] However, as long as France's ethnic makeup is denied, ensuring that Black residents are fully represented throughout society will be problematic. This includes representations of history that accurately reflect Black contributions to the country. And while it is true that some have been recognized, like well-known African American entertainer

---

1 The concept of color-blindness refers to not seeing race, as a way to ignore structural racism.

Josephine Baker, who became the first Black woman to be reinterred in the Panthéon in November 2021, some 46 years after her death, few Black French people receive this highest honor.[2] Three Black men have been inducted into the institution so far – Félix Éboué, the governor general of French Equatorial Africa (1949); author Alexandre Dumas (2002); and writer, politician, and cofounder of the Negritude movement Aimé Césaire (2011) (to be discussed later), whose remains are in his birthplace, Martinique. The Panthéon is the final resting place of some of France's most illustrious citizens, including writers Victor Hugo, Rousseau, and Voltaire and famed chemist Marie Curie. Traditionally, the French president names those worthy to be moved to the centuries-old monument.

During the 2020 protests, a group of French internet users called for the commemoration of Black historical figures in public places, promoting the #JeVeuxUneStatueDe (I want a statue of) hashtag. Among the suggestions were Suzanne Bélair, known as Sanité Bélair, a freedom fighter, revolutionary, and Black female lieutenant in Toussaint Louverture's army, who fought against the reinstatement of enslavement in Haiti. She was caught, tried by a colonial court, and executed in 1802.[3] Yet, her contribution has not yet been acknowledged by French society. Nonetheless, one cannot ignore the number of renamings that have taken place in Paris since the demonstrations. They include a tribute to Claude Mademba-Sy, a soldier during World War Two; an alley near the Museum of Liberation in Paris's 14th arrondissement was named after him in August 2020. Sy, an unsung hero of the war, was an officer in France's Leclerc regiment and later cofounded the Senegalese army. He was the only Black person to enter Paris when it was liberated by the Americans (Chichizola 2020).

One month later the first statue of a Black woman in the city was unveiled in a public garden in the 17th arrondissement. It is of Solitude, a freedom fighter, born around 1772 to an enslaved African who was raped by a white sailor on the ship bringing her to the Caribbean. Solitude won her freedom after the French Revolution, but when Napoleon reinstated the enslavement

---

2 "Joséphine Baker to Enter French Panthéon of National Heroes," France24, August 22, 2021, (https://www.france24.com/en/france/20210822-jos%C3%A9phine-baker-to-enter-pan th%C3%A9on-of-france-s-national-heroes)

3 "#JeVeuxUneStatueDe sort les figures noires françaises des oubliettes," *Brain*, July 15, 2020, (https://www.brain-magazine.fr/article/page-president/62671-Statues)

system in the French colonies, she joined Guadeloupe's resistance movement. Napoleon's military forces arrested the then pregnant Solitude and sentenced her to death. She was hanged the day after giving birth. The garden where Solitude's statue stands is close to a statue of General Alexandre Dumas – a man of African descent – which was destroyed by the Nazis when they occupied the city.[4]

Meanwhile, future plans to honor the victims of enslavement with a national memorial were suspended after a disagreement over its concept. The idea was first announced in 2016, when then president François Hollande called for the building of a memorial or museum recognizing France's role during enslavement. The only current marker to victims is an often overlooked large bronze sculpture of chains on the city's Left Bank (Machemer 2020). In June 2020, four years after the initial announcement, the French ministry of culture and the ministry for overseas territories issued an open call for artists to create the memorial, which would be housed in the Tuileries Gardens. The monument was to be conceived in partnership with the organizations Comité Marche du 23 mai 1998 (CM98) and the Slavery and Reconciliation Foundation, which had both campaigned for it. The winning artist was due to be announced in the first half of 2021, with the piece expected to be completed by the autumn of the same year. A dispute over the submitted designs, however, halted plans.

As the push to pay tribute to Black French contribution continues, Black people are calling for the removal of monuments and markers honoring colonialists and proponents of enslavement and racism. The main focus is the statue of Jean-Baptiste Colbert, which sits in front of the French National Assembly, the lower house of the French parliament. The 17th-century minister under King Louis XIV authored the "Code Noir" for the French West Indies that outlined the rules and regulations of race and enslavement, describing enslaved peoples as *"êtres meubles"* (chattel). During the 2020 demonstrations, a member of the Brigade Anti Négrophobie committed a "political act," spray painting the statue with the words "state negrophobia."[5]

---

4 "Paris Inaugurates City's First Park Honouring a Black Woman," France24, September 26, 2020, (https://www.france24.com/en/20200926-paris-inaugurates-city-s-first-park-honouring-a-black-woman)

5 "France Colbert Row: Statue Vandalised Over Slavery Code," BBC, June 24, 2020, (https://www.bbc.com/news/world-europe-53163714)

Years earlier, in 2017, Louis-Georges Tin, president of the Representative Council of France's Black Associations (CRAN), had called Colbert the enemy of "liberty, equality, and fraternity," the motto of the French Republic. More recently, former French prime minister Jean-Marc Ayrault called for places bearing his name to be changed (Dussart 2020).

Renaming other contested memorials is also an item on antiracism agendas. This includes one to Georges Cuvier, who has a street named after him in Paris's 5th arrondissement. Cuvier conducted racial studies that provided part of the foundation for scientific racism, and he published work on the supposed differences between racial groups' physical characteristics and mental abilities. Shortly after the death of Saartje Baartman, a young South African woman who was brought to Europe, given the stage name the "Hottentot Venus," and paraded in so-called freak shows in London and Paris in the 19th century, Cuvier examined her body. He disparagingly compared her physical features to those of monkeys. Meanwhile, a street and metro station named after General Jacques-François Dugommier, a supporter of enslavement, whose name is also inscribed in the Panthéon, are also being challenged (Chadwick 2020).

Karfa Sira Diallo, founder of the organization Sharing Memories,[6] which preserves the memory of colonization and enslavement, explained in June 2020:

> [T]he death of George Floyd has made it possible for many to make a link between the racism inscribed in the walls of cities, monuments, and squares and the issue of racist police violence. (Gueye 2020)[7]

Diallo called for some of the symbols honoring colonial traders and supporters to be removed and the remainder to be contextualized with explanations to preserve the memory of the crime against humanity and to teach current and future generations about it (Dussart 2020). For the historian Françoise Vergès, the removal of these statues is a matter of "memorial justice," which has "nothing to do with the erasure of history" (Vergès 2020).

---

6 In the original: "Mémoires et Partages."
7 In the original: "La mort de George Floyd a permis à beaucoup de faire un lien entre le racisme sur les murs des villes, monuments et places et la question des violences policières racistes."

Château Rouge, Château d'Eau, and the Banlieues

A more accurate reflection of French history can be seen in cities such as Paris which has long been a center of Black life. The city's Black population grew quickly after World War Two and especially in the 1960s and 1970s, because France needed a workforce. Called *"Les Trente Glorieuses"* (The Glorious Thirty Years), a synonym for economic dynamism between 1945 and 1973, the period saw increased numbers of Africans and French Caribbeans arrive on France's shores. It was a symbiotic relationship. France needed more people to rebuild the country after the war and the newcomers needed to escape the economic crises, war, or other conflicts in their birthplaces. Many of them chose France, and especially Paris, because of the colonial relationship between the host country and their homelands. France was a powerful colonizer on different continents – Africa, the Americas, and Asia. At the end of the 19th century, as the second largest colonizing empire behind the UK, it was especially dominant in Africa (North, West, and Central). The population spoke the language imposed by its colonial masters, which was one of the major arguments used for recruiting workers from these regions.

In response, the French government created new housing projects in the suburbs (banlieues) for these new immigrants. Some 70 years later, the banlieues are still home to the Black working class who live outside Paris but work within the city; their modest incomes put the capital's highly priced accommodation beyond their reach. Although they live predominantly in places such as Saint-Denis, Créteil, Sarcelles, or Aubervilliers, there are areas special to the Black population within the city's walls. For the African diaspora, Château Rouge and Château d'Eau provide a connection to their culture. As far back as the 1960s, grocery stores selling food from their faraway motherlands helped Black communities adjust to their new country. And in the following two decades, especially the 1980s, the concentration of stores catering to Blacks also increased in the north of Paris, where African immigrants used to live before gentrification pushed them out.

Nicknamed "Little Africa," Château Rouge is located between the famous Sacré-Cœur basilica and Montmartre in the 18th arrondissement. It has been a hub for African businesses selling food, cultural products, cosmetics, and clothing for Black people since 1990. Meanwhile, further south, the smaller Château d'Eau, in the 10th arrondissement provides hairdressing services and cosmetics. These products are important to Black people, who did not see themselves represented in advertising images and traditionally have not been served by major cosmetics firms, which did not consider the market as profitable. After the riots of October and November 2005, when mostly French Arab and Black residents were involved in four weeks of urban violence in the banlieues, the government finally became aware that it was time to give more opportunities to minorities. In June 2005, French president Jacques Chirac started talking about stopping discrimination in France. "Discrimination is a poison for our democracy and our national cohesion," he said. On July 17, 2006, journalist Harry Roselmack became the first Black man to host the news on the leading French television channel TF1.[8] It was a beginning – and, since then, efforts to diversify have been moving forward step by step, even though there is still a long way to go.

The area is popular with independent traders originally from North and West Africa who sell cigarettes, hot corn, or drinks at metro exits. There are also a few restaurants serving food from the African continent. While both Château Rouge and Château d'Eau remain centers of Black economic life, the banlieues such as Sarcelles are home to a large Black community made up largely of people of Caribbean and African origin. The residents come from a variety of countries, with most Caribbean people from Martinique and Guadeloupe and Africans mainly from Senegal, Côte d'Ivoire, and Cameroon. But all face poverty, unemployment, and sometimes violence at higher rates than their neighbors in the center of Paris. French radio France Inter said that, according to a survey from November 2018 to January 2019, residents have 20 percent less chance of receiving a response when applying for a job offer and 30 percent less chance of being contacted again after a spontaneous application.[9]

The history of Sarcelles perfectly symbolizes a city built through post-World War Two immigration, although French colonization had already brought many Black people to the country. During the 1950s and 1960s, projects were created in order to house the *"pieds-noirs"* and Jews from Algeria. The *"pied-noirs"* were French and other people of European origin who were born in

---

8 TF1 découvre la télé couleur (https://www.liberation.fr/medias/2006/07/17/tf1-decouvre-la-tele-couleur_46234/

9 Discrimination à l'embauche : les résultats de la campagne de testing passée sous silence par le gouvernement https://www.franceinter.fr/economie/discrimination-a-l-embauche-les-resultats-de-la-campagne-de-testing-passee-sous-silence-par-le-gouvernement

Algeria during the period of French rule from 1830 to 1962 and had to return to France at the end of the Algerian War. They left everything behind in North Africa. Like them, Jews from Algeria also had to move to France and reestablish their lives when the former *département* became an independent country in 1962. As Algeria was considered a French *département* for almost a century, its independence was judged as blasphemy by the French government.

Figure 6.1: Monument to the African tirailleurs – the well-known soldiers who fought alongside the French during World Wars One and Two. Photograph: Epée Hervé Dingong, 2022

Among the immigrants were the sons and daughters of African *tirailleurs* – the well-known soldiers who fought alongside the French during World Wars One and Two. Following the oil crisis of 1973–9, which slowed immigration, new arrivals came to Sarcelles as families from the continent reunified. The soldiers are now honored in their descendants' place of settlement with a monument outside the train station.[10] Unveiled in May 2018, former Sarcelles's mayor François Pupponi and deputy mayor Youri Mazou-Sacko, a former community leader of Central African origin, were responsible for its erection. This monument has three parts: To the right and left are African soldiers with their special uniforms from World Wars One and Two. In the center an inscription reads: "In honor of the brave African soldiers who participated in the liberation of France."[11]

---

10 Le long combat des abolitions," (https://memorial.nantes.fr/en/the-long-struggle-for-abolition/)

11 In the original: "Honneur aux valeureux soldats africains qui ont participaté a la liberation de la France."

Unfortunately, in the year following its unveiling, the monument was defaced.[12] Sarcelles mayor Patrick Haddad called the action shocking, especially since the monument had been so recently erected. According to him, it was "fractured and cut in two" and could not be repaired; instead, it was rebuilt to look like it had before.[13]

This is not the only monument to Black people in Sarcelles. The area's significant Caribbean community has also seen the accomplishments of its heroes honored. One of the most prominent monuments is for Aimé Césaire (1913–2008). The Martinquais was one of a triptych – also known as *"les trois pères,"* which also included Senegalese-born Léopold Sédar Senghor (1906–2001), and Léon-Gontran Damas (1912–78), who was from French Guiana. They co-founded the anti-colonialist French literary, artistic, philosophical, and political movement Negritude, which will be discussed in the next section. Inaugurated in November 2010, in the presence of Césaire's grandson Christophe, the bronze bust was sculpted by Guadeloupean artist Jean-Claude Nasso, who is committed to the recognition of Caribbean culture. From the top of its black pedestal, at human height, it oversees the Place Jean-Pierre Passé-Coutrin, where it is located, as well as the lively surrounding Flanades district. A brief introduction written under the bust says: "Emblem of Negritude, in his life he defended humanism and cultural identity."[14]

In May 2013, former mayor of Sarcelles François Pupponi unveiled a statue as part of a genealogy project spearheaded by CM98, in tribute to the victims of enslavement. The marble monument was also created by Nasso and features a rectangular structure with a globe. It is engraved with 213 names – first names, surnames, and numbers – arbitrarily attributed to former slaves freed

---

12 "Sarcelles: ouverture d'une enquête après la profanation d'un monument aux soldats africains," November 19, 2019, Le Monde/Agence France Presse (https://www.lemonde.fr/afrique/article/2019/11/19/sarcelles-ouverture-d-une-enquete-apres-la-profanation-d-un-monument-aux-soldats-africains_6019700_3212.html)

13 In the original (translated by the author): "C'est très attristant et très choquant de voir cette profanation sur une mémoire relativement fragile car encore récente ... La stèle, 'fracturée en deux', n'est pas réparable, selon le maire: 'On partirait a priori sur une reconfection.'" https://www.lepoint.fr/societe/sarcelles-enquete-apres-la-profanation-d-une-stele-aux-soldats-africains-18-11-2019-2348088_23.php

14 Un buste en hommage à Aimé Césaire (https://www.leparisien.fr/val-d-oise-95/sarcelles-95200/un-buste-en-hommage-a-aime-cesaire-22-11-2010-1160410.php)

in Guadeloupe and Martinique in 1848. Of the 213 names, about 70 belong to the ancestors of Sarcelles residents. On the day of the unveiling, Caribbean residents surrounded Pupponi during the ceremony, rediscovering their ancestral history. CM98 has already retraced the route of 80 percent of some 157,000 Martiniquais and Guadeloupean enslaved who were given names after the abolition of slavery (Koda 2013). A similar monument can be found in Saint-Denis, another banlieue in the north of Paris.

A second monument to Césaire is located on the front and the first floor of the Langfus library building: a fresco created in November 2016 by painter Jean-François Perroy, alias "Jef Aérosol," in association with the Galerie Mathgoth. It reads "Justice listens at the gates of beauty"[15] and is part of the "100 Walls for Youth" project, a national contemporary urban art project to teach young people about strong values: respect, solidarity, diversity, and tolerance (Chaffotte 2016).

Figure 6.2: Mural depicting Aimé Césaire in Sarcelles. Photograph: Epée Hervé Dingong, 2022

Marking the Negritude Movement

Strongly influenced by the Harlem Renaissance in the USA, the Negritude Movement began in the 1930s after Césaire, Senghor, and Damas met as students in Paris and created the monthly journal *L'Étudiant Noir*. The publication attracted francophone writers of African descent and all three published works in the periodical; Damas published his first poems and Senghor his first articles. However, Negritude also drew on a burgeoning cultural

---

15 In the original: "La justice écoute aux portes de la beauté."

wave in Haiti (Bouchard 2009: 381), and its proponents had a connection to Pan-Africanism, discussed in Chapter 3.

In 1935, Césaire coined the word Negritude in the publication (Ako, cited in Miller 2010). The word encapsulated the self-affirmation of Black people and was an expression of a revolt against French colonialism and racism. He also used the term in his poem "Cahier d'un retour au pays natal" (Journal of a Homecoming), a landmark of modern French poetry and a founding text of the movement.[16] In his book *Discours sur le colonialisme* (1950), Césaire would later critique the hypocrisy of justifying colonization and questioned the use of colonialism as well as its impact, calling Europe indefensible for its actions (Nye 2016). With their work, Césaire, Damas, and Senghor brought about increased consciousness and awareness of the Black situation in France. The movement allowed Black people to see themselves through their own eyes and understand their own qualities. Negritude was based on the idea that a common African diaspora identity was needed to overcome the social and political rhetoric of French colonialism and the resulting domination. It gave Black people the ability to communicate to whites that, from now on, Blacks would be asserting themselves (Sprague 2018).

In addition to literature, Negritude was also a philosophy of African art, as Senghor insisted. When he first arrived in Paris at the end of the 1920s, modern European art was already drawing on *art nègre* (Black art). Pablo Picasso, in particular, had already taken to making African sculptures and masks. However, Senghor wanted Negritude to be the ideology behind African art, particularly the forms so characteristic of African masks and sculptures across different regions and cultures. He explained that African art was not created to reproduce or embellish reality but to establish the connection with what he labeled the *sub-reality* that is the universe of vital forces.[17] In 1956, Senghor argued that Black culture must acknowledge its own traditions but combine this with an open approach to new ideas and developments in art. Artist Ben Enwonwu articulated this in "Problems of the African Artist Today," which was published in the journal *Présence Africaine* the same year (Enwonwu 1956). He called for an international African art that responded

---

16 The poem can be found on this website: (https://dukeupress.wordpress.com/2018/04/18/poem-of-the-week-14/)

17 Négritude, Stanford Encyclopedia of Philosophy, *First published Mon May 24, 2010; substantive revision Wed May 23, 2018* (https://plato.stanford.edu/entries/negritude/)

to contemporary life and times but was also aware of traditional, local, and global influences:

> I will not accept an inferior position in the art world ... European artists like Picasso, Braque and Vlaminck were influenced by African art. Everybody sees that and is not opposed to it. But when they see African artists who are influenced by their European training and technique, they expect that African to stick to their traditional forms ... I do not copy traditional art. I like what I see in the works of people like Giacometti but I do not copy them ... I knew he was influenced by African sculptures. But I would not be influenced by Giacometti, because he was influenced by my ancestors.[18]

A decade later, Senghor organized the World Festival of Negro Arts in Dakar in 1966, providing the first occasion for many Black artists, musicians, writers, poets, and actors to participate in a global examination of African culture.

Meanwhile, Martiniquais psychiatrist and intellectual Frantz Fanon, a former student of Aimé Césaire, added practical and theoretical analysis of the traumatic effects of colonialism and racism to the discourse in his seminal works *Black Skin, White Masks* (1952) and *The Wretched of the Earth* (1961). In an attempt to retrieve dignity for Black people from the horrific ordeal of enslavement, the pioneering postcolonial theorist and activist used his experiences during the French occupation of Algeria to explain the violent effects the system had on both the colonizer and the colonized. Fanon argued that, as long as the systems of enslavement and colonization existed, Black people would develop a sense of self only through the eyes of the white man, who, at the same time, developed a sense of self-superiority. In accordance with this idea, Senghor described the Negritude movement as "the sum total of the values of civilization of the Black world."[19]

In the history of the movement, the women who helped shape it are often forgotten – Paulette Nardal and her sister Jane in particular. A true pioneer, Paulette was the first Black female engineer in her birthplace, Martinique.

---

18 Quoted from the website of the Tate gallery in the UK (https://www.tate.org.uk/art/art terms/n/negritude)

19 Négritude, Stanford Encyclopedia of Philosophy, *First published Mon May 24, 2010; substantive revision Wed May 23, 2018* (https://plato.stanford.edu/entries/negritude/)

Figure 6.3: Plaque for Jane and Paulette Nardal. Photograph: Epée Hervé Dingong, 2022

In 1920, she became the first Black person to study at the Sorbonne University in Paris, along with her sister; Paulette studied English and her sister literature. In 1928, the women joined the Pan-African newspaper *La Dépêche Africaine*. Additionally, Jane wrote the manifesto "Black Internationalism," a pioneering text about a united Black movement with African, African American, and Caribbean participation. In 1931, the sisters created *La Revue du Monde Noir* based on meetings in their salon in Clamart, a Paris suburb, where guests spoke French and English. They received poets, writers, musicians, and intellectuals from the Black diaspora, who shared drinks, music, and poetry, and often discussed topics such as colonialism, race issues, and other current political debates. Guests included Césaire, Senghor, and Damas (Terriennes 2021). In addition to writers, scholars, and musicians, the meetings also attracted visual artists who created works that not only acknowledged ancient African traditions but defined contemporary Blackness.

The Nardals were concerned about female inclusion:

> I have often thought and said, about the beginnings of *négritude*, that we were just unhappy women, my sister and I, and that is why we were never mentioned. It was understated because it was women talking about it.[20]

---

20 In the original (translated by the author): "J'ai souvent pensé et dit, à propos des débuts de la négritude, que nous n'étions que de malheureuses femmes, ma sœur et moi, et que c'est pour cela qu'on a jamais parlé de nous. C'était minimize, du fait que c'étaient des femmes qui en parlaient" (Grollemund 2018).

The women have been remembered, if only in a smaller way than their male peers. Based on a proposal from the Paris city hall and its council in November 2018, Mayor Anne Hidalgo approved the naming of a pedestrian walkway after the sisters. The following year, in August 2019, a plaque with the name "Promenade Jane and Paulette Nardal" was unveiled in the 14th arrondissement. It reads:

> Sisters, Women of Letters from Martinique Inspirers of the literary and political movement of Negritude Feminist militants[21]

The sisters' niece, singer Christiane Eda-Pierre, attended the unveiling, honoring her aunts who, as writers, philosophers, and teachers, laid the theoretical and philosophical bases of Negritude upon which Césaire, Senghor, and Damas built. Activists are now pushing to have a plaque for Paulette Nardal placed in the Panthéon. The Association Paulette Nardal at the Panthéon, whose members include Martiniquais filmmaker Euzhan Palcy, co-chair of the committee, has been bringing attention to her contribution to the feminist and Negritude movements, among others.[22] Her better-known colleague Césaire already has a plaque in his name in the Panthéon. Césaire passed away in 2008 and his body was taken back to Martinique. Three years later, in April 2011, in a national event presided over by the French president Nicolas Sarközy, the plaque was unveiled in the Parisian monument.

Other markers commemorating Césaire include the Quai Césaire in the 1st arrondissement. It was inaugurated in June 2013 and is part of the Quai des Tuileries. The site was chosen by the Paris municipal council in March 2013. The mayor of Paris, Bertrand Delanoë, hailed the memory of the Martiniquais poet who would have been 100 years old that year. The location is not far from another marker honoring an important figure of the Negritude movement. Initially known as Passerelle Solférino, a footbridge was renamed Passerelle Léopold-Sédar-Senghor in October 2006[23] to commemorate the

---

21 In the original: "Soeurs, Femme de Lettres martiniquaises / Egeries du Courant litteraire et politique / de la Négritude / Militantes feministe."

22 Paulette Nardal au Panthéon. Figure de Matrimoine National, Écrivaine, Feministe, et Précurseure du movement de la Négritude, (https://www.paulettenardalaupantheon com/en/)

23 Passerelle Leopold Sedar Senghor footbridge in Paris (https://www.eutouring.com/pas serelle_leopold_sedar_senghor.html)

100th anniversary of the birth of the Senegalese politician and poet, who was also the first president of Senegal, governing for two decades. Senghor was also the first African to be an elected member of the Académie Française.[24]

Another marker of the movement continues to educate today. The journal *Presence Africaine*, founded by Alioune Diop in 1947, set the tone, depth, and breath of decolonization aspirations of the Negritude movement. Early on, *Presence Africaine* was defined as the voice of the Black world in Europe, mainly in France. This voice contributed to proclaiming the end of white monologue and was a platform for many Black intellectuals and for creating awareness in the Black diaspora of its own condition (Lock 2013). As a magazine, it aligned with Pan-Africanism and gave voice to some already great figures of Negritude theory, including Césaire, Alioune Sarr, Senghor, Richard Wright, and Fanon, to name just a few.

In 1949, *Presence Africaine* expanded from its origins as a quarterly journal and became a publishing house and bookstore. Over the next several decades, a plethora of writers, such as Mongo Beti and Cheikh Anta Diop, also released books through the publisher. More than 60 years later, *Presence Africaine* continues to be an important cultural marker for Pan-Africanism and Negritude. Located in the 5th arrondissement, it is in the Latin Quarter, not far from the Sorbonne University. Inside, the space is a temple of books, housing a large selection of work from Black diaspora authors. Founder Alioune Diop died in 1980 and his wife, Christiane Yandé, took over. Today, professor and writer Romuald Fonkoua runs *Presence Africaine*.

Hidden Histories/Unwritten Stories

Black lives have long been hidden in plain sight in Paris. There are some markers celebrating their contributions, but the stories behind them are seldom told. One example is the street named after Chevalier de Saint-Georges in central Paris. Rue du Chevalier de Saint-Georges is located in the 1st arrondissement. De Saint-Georges was an accomplished 18th-century classical composer and champion fencer. He was born in Guadeloupe in 1745 to Georges de Bologne Saint-Georges, a married white French planter, and Anne (also called Nanon), an enslaved African of Senegalese origin owned

---

24 The Académie Française oversees the French language in France.

by his wife. When he was a young soldier he became colonel of the Legion of Saint-Georges, an all-Black regiment in Europe fighting for the Republic during the French Revolution. Although he was a brave soldier and an example of the country's brightest and best, he faced racism from a young age and witnessed the horrors of enslavement. But his skills spoke for themselves, earning him a special place in French history. However, this was largely ignored until December 2001, when he finally received an official tribute.

At that time, Paris counselor George-Pau Langevin (originally from Guadeloupe) and Paris mayor Bertrand Delanoë changed the name of Rue Richepanse to Chevalier de Saint-Georges. The original street name had been controversial as it honored Antoine Richepanse, a former governor of Guadeloupe under Napoleon Bonaparte who was in charge of the restoration of the enslavement system in Martinique and other islands in 1802. The French Revolution and Black revolts had resulted in the first attempt to abolish enslavement in 1794. As Dominique Taffin, from the Foundation for the Remembrance of Slavery, explained:

> Napoleon wanted to extend the French colonial empire to control the Caribbean. To colonize the huge land of Louisiana in North America, he needed workers so he restarted the slave trade. It was a colonial strategy. (Phalnikar 2021)

France permanently abolished enslavement on the mainland and in the colonies in 1848. Opponents of Richepanse had wanted to change the street name for many years, sending petitions and several letters to the city hall before Langevin and city officials stepped in. The process of changing a street name requires the approval of the mayor, who studies the case with advisers. Delanoë supported the renaming, calling the Rue de Richepanse "a permanent insult to the Afro-Caribbean population of Paris" (Henley 2002). The street was finally renamed in February 2002, after a year-long battle between Delanoë and the right-wing mayors of the 1st and 8th arrondissements, Jean-François Legaret and François Lebel. Today, the story of Chevalier Saint-Georges reaches beyond his homeland. Disney's Searchlight Pictures has announced that a new film, titled *Chevalier*, will be released in 2023. And although Disney's involvement can be read critically, depicting Chevalier's life will bring light to another hidden Black story.

Figure 6.4: The Toussaint Louverture Garden. Photograph: Epée Hervé Dingong, 2022

Other unwritten histories include that of François-Dominique Toussaint Louverture, the famous Haitian general and abolitionist and the most prominent leader of the Haitian Revolution. In 2021, a small garden was named after him in the former Square des Amandiers in the 20th arrondissement. The decision to rename the park was voted on by the Paris city council in April 2021 after a similar measure was adopted by the district council. In the renaming ceremony, city hall called Louverture "a great abolitionist and emancipatory figure."[25] However, even though Louverture is one of France's most prominent Black figures and an inscription honoring him was engraved on a wall in the Panthéon in 2009, he is rarely found in the French school curriculum. Writer Lauren Collins explains that, while Louverture and the story of his country's revolution is taught in high schools in some of France's overseas territories, in metropolitan vocational high schools, whose students are more likely to come from working-class and immigrant families, the recently updated curriculum acknowledges the Haitian Revolution as a "singular extension" of the American and French Revolutions and not as the starting point of the global process to abolish enslavement (Collins 2020). Since it is not part of the general high-school curriculum, the typical French student completes their high-school education without hearing much about the revolution or its heroes. This is despite the fact that Louverture was hailed

---

25 Author's translation of: "Grande figure abolitionniste et émancipatrice," "Le jardin Toussaint Louverture inauguré dans le quartier des Amandiers (20ème arrondissement)," Paris Lights Up, May 10, 2021 (https://parislightsup.com/2021/05/10/le-jardin-toussaint-louverture-inaugure-dans-le-quartier-des-amandiers-20eme-arrondissement/)

as "the Black Spartacus" who embodied the ideals of the French Revolution (ibid.). He was also a hero of abolitionist Frederick Douglass, while activist Marcus Garvey asserted that his "brilliancy as a soldier and statesman outshone that of a Cromwell, Napoleon, and Washington" (Hill and Bair 1987). Aimé Césaire believed that Haiti was the place where "negritude stood up for the first time and proclaimed its faith in its humanity" (Césaire 1970), which in turn inspired the modern anticolonial movement all over the world. In spite of all of this, France has not seen him and his fight as indispensable elements of its national narrative but rather as a minor part of it (Collins 2020).

At present, the Fondation pour la Mémoire de l'Esclavage (Foundation for the Memory of Slavery), which was created in 2016, is pushing French authorities to correct these oversights. In a September 2020 report, it asserted that not all French children learn the same history. The report was issued just before the 20th anniversary of the Taubira law, which was marked by national ceremonies. The 2001 law was spearheaded by French deputy Christiane Taubira (born in French Guiana) and designated enslavement as a crime against humanity. It also mandated that school curricula accord these subjects "the substantial place that they merit" (Collins 2020). Following the passage of the law, France updated and revised its textbooks, although, in 2005, the French legislature mandated that schools emphasize the "positive role" of colonialism. However, the center-right president Jacques Chirac eventually gave in to the longstanding demands of campaigners and established a national day to commemorate the end of enslavement after riots in the banlieues (Bennhold 2006). The work to create a day of commemoration had been a long and arduous struggle; it had received widespread public attention in May 1998, the 150th anniversary of the abolition of enslavement and eight years before Chirac's declaration, when more than 40,000 Caribbean, Guyanese, Réunionese, and metropolitan women and men took part in a silent march in tribute to the victims of colonial enslavement. This pulled back the curtain on a taboo subject and led to the passing of the Taubira law. In May 2006, Chirac finally stated that tributes would be paid to abolitionists, including Louverture.

Meanwhile, another 'unknown' Parisian, political pioneer Severiano de Heredia (the first and only Black mayor of Paris, elected in 1879), received recognition when a street was named after him in October 2015. Paris mayor Anne Hidalgo presided over the ceremony for the unveiling of Rue Severiano de Heredia, a new street in the 17th arrondissement. The inauguration paid tribute to Heredia, who was born in Havana, Cuba, as a free Black man in 1836. Heredia came to Paris in 1845 after being adopted by a French woman, Madeleine Godefroy, who was married to his godfather, Don Ignacio Heredia y Campuzano-Polanco. An excellent student, he became a poet and a literary critic, winning the Grand Prize of Honor at the well-known and prestigious Louis-le-Grand high school. In 1870, he officially became a French citizen and, with a growing interest in politics, skillfully and confidently threw himself into the field.

Heredia was the defender of many causes, such as universal education and the separation of church and state. In 1873, he was elected to the municipal council of Paris as a representative for the 17th arrondissement and spent six years in the position before he was elected president. This position is equivalent to a mayorship today, de facto making him the mayor of Paris from 1879 to 1880. Heredia, however, was met with racism from French conservatives and others. One newspaper referred to him as "The Negro of the Elysée" while others called him the "chocolate minister" or worse (Atisu 2019). Heredia died of meningitis in his Paris home on February 9, 1901.

Like previous Black heroes, Heredia was never mentioned in French history books at any level – not at elementary, high school, or university. It took until the 2015 tribute for the mayor of Paris to acknowledge that Heredia had been sidelined. She said that, with the street naming, the city was correcting this forgotten history and "guilty oversight" (Triay 2015). As this and other examples throughout this chapter have shown, the absence of remembrance of Black contributions to France denies the true nature of the relationship between the country and its former colonies or Caribbean *départements*. Instead of extending its motto of *Liberté, égalité, fraternité*, to Black citizens, it contests their national identity, forcing them into invisibility at the periphery of French life.

References

Atisu, Etsey (2019) "Meet the Little-Known Black Mayor of Paris Who Served France Diligently in the 1800s," July 25, https://face2faceafrica.com/article/meet-the-little-known-black-mayor-of-paris-who-served-france-diligently-in-the-1800s

Bennhold, Katrin (2006) "158 Years Later, France Recalls End of Slavery," *New York Times*, May 10, https://www.nytimes.com/2006/05/10/world/europe/10iht-slaves.html

Bouchard, Jennifer Westmoreland (2009) "Negritude" in Eric Martone (ed.), *Encyclopedia of Blacks in European History and Culture. Vol. 2*. Westport CT and London: Greenwood Press.

Césaire, Aimé (1970) *La tragédie du roi Christophe*. Paris: Présence Africaine.

Chadwick, Benjamin (2020) "Confronting Our Racist History: The Statues and Street Names of Paris," Fabric of Paris, June 16, 2020 https://fabricofparis.com/2020/06/16/confronting-our-racist-history-statues-street-names.html

Chaffotte, Thibault (2016) (2016) "Sarcelles inaugure une fresque en mémoire des victimes de l'esclavage," *Le Parisien*, Le Parisien, November 27, https://www.leparisien.fr/val-d-oise-95/sarcelles-95200/sarcelles-inaugure-une-fresque-en-memoire-des-victimes-de-l-esclavage-27-11-2016-6382581.php

Chichizola, Jean (2020) "Une place Claude-Mademba-Sy à Paris pour honorer la mémoire des 'héros d'Afrique'," *Le Figaro*, August 25 https://www.lefigaro.fr/actualite-france/une-place-claude-mademba-sy-a-paris-pour-honorer-la-memoire-des-heros-d-afrique-20200825

Collins, Lauren (2020) "The Haitian Revolution and the Hole in French High-School History," *The New Yorker*, December 3, https://www.newyorker.com/culture/culture-desk/the-haitian-revolution-and-the-hole-in-french-high-school-history

Dussart, Jade (2020) "Taking Down Statues: France Confronts Its Colonial and Slave Trade Past," *Global Voices*, June 27, https://globalvoices.org/2020/06/27/taking-down-statues-france-confronts-its-colonial-and-slave-trade-past/

Enwonwu, Ben (1956) "Problems of the African Artist Today," *Présence Africaine*, 8 (10): 174–8, http://www.jstor.org/stable/24346898

Grollemund, Philippe (2018) *Fiertés de femme noire. Entretiens, mémoires de Paulette Nardal*. Paris: L'Harmattan.

Gueye, Christine H. (2020) "Déboulonner les statues et rebaptiser les rues, la meilleure façon de lutter contre le racism?," Sputnik News, June 19, https://fr.sputniknews.com/20200619/deboulonner-les-statues-et-rebaptiser-les-rues-la-meilleure-facon-de-lutter-contre-le-racisme-1043979224.html

Henley, John (2002) "Parisians Bid Adieu to Street Name Not Desired," *Guardian*, February 4, https://www.theguardian.com/world/2002/feb/05/jon henley

Hill, Robert and Barbara Bair (eds.) (1987) *Marcus Garvey: Life and Lessons*. Berkley: University of California Press.

Koda, Maïté (2013) "23 mai à Sarcelles: Sur les traces de nos ancêtres esclaves," May 23, https://la1ere.francetvinfo.fr/2013/05/23/23-mai-sarcelles-sur-les-traces-de-nos-ancetres-esclaves-36820.html

Lock, Etienne (2013) "The Role of 'Presence Africaine' in Awakening of the Black Diaspora in Europe in 20th Century," March 22, https://ssrn.com/abstract=2236907

Machemer, Theresa (2020) "France Seeks Proposals for Memorial to Victims of Slavery," *Smithsonian Magazine*, June 15, https://www.smithsonianmag.com/smart-news/france-seeks-proposals-paris-memorial-victims-slavery-180975097/

Martirosyan, Lucy (2020) "In France, the Killing of George Floyd Invokes the Memory of Adama Traoré," *The World*, June 8, https://www.pri.org/stories/2020-06-08/france-killing-george-floyd-invokes-memory-adama-traor

Miller, Christopher L. (2010) "The (Revised) Birth of Negritude: Communist Revolution and 'the Immanent Negro' in 1935," *PMLA*, 125 (3): 743–9.

Nye, Malory (2016) "'Discourse on Colonialism' by Aimé Césaire," October 30, https://medium.com/religion-bites/discourse-on-colonialism-by-aime-cesaire-793b291a0987

Phalnikar, Sonia (2021) "Remembering that Napoleon Reinstated Slavery in France," Deutsche Welle, April 5, https://www.dw.com/en/remembering-that-napoleon-reinstated-slavery-in-france/a-57408273

Sprague, Kevin (2018) "From Aimé Césaire to Black Lives Matter: The Ongoing Impact of Negritude," February 23, https://www.international.ucla.edu/asc/Article/188973

Terriennes, Liliane Charrier (2021) "Paulette Nardal, inspiratrice oubliée de la négritude," August 28, https://information.tv5monde.com/terriennes/paulette-nardal-inspiratrice-oubliee-de-la-negritude-419363

Triay, Philippe (2015) "L'hommage de Paris à Severiano de Heredia, maire noir de la capitale et ministre de la République au XIXe siècle," October 5, https://la1ere.francetvinfo.fr/2015/10/05/l-hommage-de-paris-severia

no-de-heredia-maire-noir-de-paris-et-ministre-de-la-republique-au-xi xe-siecle-292827.html

Vergès, Françoise (2020) "Selon Françoise Vergès, la question du déboulonnage des statues racistes et coloniales est une question de JUSTICE MÉMORIELLE," June 16, https://www.facebook.com/watch/?v=609976029621741&t=1

Chapter 7
Black Rome

Kwanza Musi Dos Santos

The first protest against racism in Italy did not take place with the rise of Black Lives Matter (BLM) in June 2020, but rather as a consequence of the homicide of Jerry Essan Masslo, a South African man who had escaped from apartheid in 1988. Harvesting tomatoes for €2 an hour in southern Italy, he had found himself trapped in another racist system where he was forced to work in underpaid, harsh conditions. Protesting against this unjust system, he joined unions and organized strikes, and he became popular after he was interviewed on national television.

On the night of August 24, 1989, a group of four young white Italians, who already had criminal records, entered what the media and the politicians referred to as "the ghetto of Villa Literno" (Capua 2020), where immigrants lived in dire conditions. While they were trying to rob Masslo and his friends, they shot and killed him. A large protest in reaction to the murder took place in Rome in October 1989, creating the first such antiracism action in Italy's history.

Since then, other antiracist protests have taken place following similar incidents, but what was special about June 2020 was that it was the first time when demonstrations happened simultaneously in so many cities in Italy. The rise of the BLM movement brought with it anger toward white people who seemed to have never cared about racism, especially those who had always declared themselves "antiracist" but never allowed Black people to speak for themselves and often minimized the negative impact of micro-aggressions, claiming that Italy is not a racist country and that "Italians are good people"[1] – hence, "they can't be racist." Notions like this seemed to confirm that the USA had a bigger racism problem than Italy.

In fact, when the Malian-born civil rights defender Soumaila Sacko was killed by unknown assailants in southern Italy in 2018, while he was collecting scrap metal from an abandoned factory to build a shack in the tent city of San Ferdinando, only a handful of local newspapers reported on the case and no large protests took place. Yet, when a Black man on the other side of the ocean was brutally killed by the police, people took to the streets in massive numbers. Surely, the pandemic contributed to highlighting that momentum. When Black people in Italy started realizing the potential of this, they became hopeful. The possibility now presented itself to finally start a conversation about racism that was long overdue.

The organizational phase was a challenge, but bringing all the groups together created a meaningful moment. It was important to transform BLM from a US-centered agenda into local, Italian requests. Therefore, after a long discussion, members of Cantiere from Milan and QuestaèRoma from Rome, two historical antiracist organizations, wrote and adopted the following manifesto to support the protests in their respective cities:

> The racist ferocity that we have seen with the killing of George Floyd and the children in the favelas in Brazil is supported by a system of oppression that continually absolves itself, in order to continue acting undisturbed. To oppose it, it is not enough to denounce it, it must be questioned, torn out from its cultural and economic foundations. Racism does not let us breathe.
> #BlackLivesMatter in Italy means tackling Afrophobia.
> #BlackLivesMatter in Italy means to stop identifying the Black body as a foreign body.
> #BlackLivesMatter in Italy means listening and giving a voice to Black and racialized people.
> #BlackLivesMatter in Italy means renouncing one's privileges and questioning a system that allows a few to live on the shoulders of many.
> #BlackLivesMatter in Italy means to stop postponing the reform of the Italian citizenship law.

---

1 In Italian: "italiani brava gente." This is a very popular motto that has always been used and disseminated, but especially during the colonial wars.

> #BlackLivesMatter in Italy means to remember Abba Abdul Guiebre, Jerry Masslo, Idy Diene, Soumaila Sacko, Emmanuel Chidi Namdi, Becky Moses, Jennifer Otioto, Gideon Azeke, Mahamadou Toure, Wilson Kofi Omagbon, Omar Fadera.
> Racism does not let us breathe. It's like dust in the air. It seems invisible, even when it takes your breath away until you choke. If you let the sun in, on the other hand, you can see it: it is everywhere. As long as we shed light, we will have the ability to eliminate it wherever it is. But we must be vigilant, because it is always in the air.[2]

In June 2020, more than 3,000 people gathered in Piazza del Popolo in Rome and knelt down for more than nine minutes, the same length of time that the policeman stood on George Floyd's neck. That long moment was one of the few occasions when Black Italian people felt acknowledged as human beings by the rest of the Italian population, as citizens of the same country, hopeful for equal human rights. However, this moment was not as impactful or as lasting as many wished. Some of the protests were organized by white-led, mainly communist organizations that left out any Black people who did not embrace their ideology. As a result, many Black people went back home afterwards even more frustrated than they had been before. Therefore, the involvement of people belonging to the groups most exposed to discrimination and racism is often instrumental and unequal.

In reaction to the coverage of BLM on social media, people started to compare the case of George Floyd, and many other Black people before him, with the case of Stefano Cucchi – a poor, young white Italian man from the Roman suburbs who was charged with drug dealing and died in a prison hospital after he was brutally beaten up by guards in 2009. His death contributed to the confusion that often happens in Italy when one tries to address the problem of racism: It is often used as an umbrella term for different forms of discrimination, which often leads to "race" being obscured by "class," as if they were mutually exclusive, instead of two separate entities that intersect. This misunderstanding occurs when the concept of white privilege is addressed; working-class white Italians claim that, since they have been living in poverty, they do not have white privilege. But race is always there, even in the working class, so comparing Floyd with Cucchi misses the point.

---

2 Translated from Italian.

Tracing Colonial History

For many young Italians of Color Roma Termini was the main meeting point between 2007 and 2010. Even when the station was not their final destination, they would still pass by to see if there was anything interesting happening. Nowadays, it is no longer a point of reference for youth, but it is still a central location for the African diaspora, tourists, and immigrants from the entire world. In the area surrounding the station, which includes Piazza dei Cinquecento and Piazza Vittorio, one can find currency exchange shops, international restaurants, African hair stylists, and shops that sell international foods. Many people, however, are unaware of the history behind the name "Piazza dei Cinquecento," where the Dogali obelisk, a significant memorial to Italian colonialism and anti-Blackness, once stood. "Cinquecento" (Five Hundred) symbolically referred to the number of Italian soldiers who died in the battle of Dogali, a small city in Eritrea, where the first major Italian defeat on the African continent took place on January 26, 1887, during the first phase of Italian expansion into Eritrea.

Erected to commemorate the Italians who lost their lives on this occasion, the monument is composed of an ancient obelisk that was commissioned by Pharaoh Ramses II and later brought to Rome by Emperor Domitian, who placed it next to other obelisks in the temple of Campo Marzio (in Rome, there are ten obelisks in total). Centuries later, the obelisk was found during archeological research by Rodolfo Lanciani in the area of Santa Maria sopra Minerva. In 1887, a few months after the defeat of Dogali, the architect Francesco Azzurri was commissioned by the government to build a base for it to make a monument and place it in the center of the square. However, his work was heavily criticized, not because it was commemorating colonialism, but because it did not provide the majesty and grandeur that the government had wished for the fallen soldiers. In 1924, the mayor decided to renovate parts of the central station, so the monument was moved to Via delle Terme, where it still stands today, almost hidden and disregarded.

According to historians, the Italian defeat was due to strategic mistakes, an underrated evaluation of the Abyssinian army, and a lack of military preparation.[3] Colonial Lieutenant Colonel Tommaso De Cristoforis

---

3 "Dogali, Dizionario di Storia," *Treccani*, 2010 (https://www.treccani.it/enciclopedia/dogali_%28Dizionario-di-Storia%29/)

in particular minimized the risk of being brutally beaten by an African army, probably due to a sense of race superiority that was at the core of the entire colonial campaign. However, it was not uncommon to find intellectuals sharing skeptical expectations with regard to the decision to start colonial expansion. They knew that the Italian army would not be ready: They had just reunified the nation and they did not have enough motivation or resources to undertake such a mission. And for this reason the government decided to commemorate the death of Italian soldiers in a heroic way to somehow convince the population of the rightness of the Fascists' desire to go to war to build the Italian Empire. Thus, officials ordered the monument to the battle of Dogali to be erected. Some left-wing politicians voiced their opposition, but the general patriotic feeling that was triggered did not allow for the necessary evaluation of the loss and possible abandonment of the colonial mission. Moreover, the Ascari, Eritrean mercenaries who fought for the Italian army and also died in the battle, are not remembered. Many deserted because of the abuses they suffered at the hands of the Italians.

Figure 7.1: The Dogali obelisk was a site of protest, denouncing state violence and proclaiming "Black Lives Matter." Photograph: Kwanza Musi Dos Santos

In addition, in 1936, after the conquest of Addis Ababa, a golden lion was stolen from the emperor, brought to Rome, and placed next to the Dogali obelisk, in order to commemorate the possessions and territories that officially represented the Italian Empire. Today, the lion is no longer there. Thanks to diplomatic negotiations it was finally returned to Haile Selassie, following his first visit to Rome in 1970, after more than 30 years. Despite the presence of these monuments, most Italians ignore the history of colonialism, and those few who do know about it often think that Mussolini initiated the colonial campaign in the Horn of Africa around 1925. In fact, colonialism started decades before, shortly after Italy had become a nation state in 1861.

After Francesco Crispi became minister of the interior in 1877, Italian colonial expansion made a decisive leap. According to the statesman, the bases in Eritrea were the starting points for the creation of a vast dominion over East Africa, where, however, Italy faced not only the resistance of governments and local populations, but also European competition from Great Britain and France. This history has been made increasingly visible in recent years. On June 2, 2020, during the national holiday to celebrate the birth of the Italian Republic in 1946, Rete Donne Migranti e Figlie (Network of Migrant Women and Daughters) organized a flash mob to protest against the idea of a "colonial republic" founded on institutional racism and systemic discrimination. They took impactful pictures in front of the monument to Dogali, holding signs denouncing state violence, while some stood topless with the words "Black Lives Matter" written on their backs. The aim was to shine a spotlight on the symbolic presence and significance of the monument, and also to show how colonial history is still present in Italian society, although the country's colonial past is often denied or disregarded. They also wanted to underline the hypocrisy of celebrating the democracy of a so-called republic while leaving commemorative monuments to colonialism throughout the city.

The following year, on February 6, 2021, Collettivo Tezeta, an interdisciplinary collective that carries out research, cultural, and didactic dissemination activities on Italian colonialism and contemporary immigration, inaugurated its first urban trekking route within Rome's African Quarter. *"Tezeta"* is a word in Tigrinya and Amharic that means memory, or memories that could be nostalgic and melancholy. The "narrative walks," called "Trekking UrbaAfricani," comprise long promenades in the company of Eritrean people, with recorded conversations that offer new names that refer to contemporary Eritrea (Via Agordat, Via Asmara, Via Assab, Via Cheren, Via Dancalia, Via Massaua, Via Senafè, Viale Eritrea). The recollections from past and present Eritrean residents who have chosen to share their stories and their experiences focus on Eritrean history and the ties, legacies, and wounds that have resulted from Italian colonialism. The collection of the first oral testimonies, which were intertwined with historical studies, took place in October, November, and December 2020.

Renaming these streets gives them a new and different meaning, a spokesperson of the organization said in an interview (Peretti 2021). A selection of the collected audio testimonies has subsequently become an integral and fundamental part of the tour, connecting the stages of the route and opening up or resuming historical themes, including colonial urbanism, town planning, and the first peasant revolts in Eritrea. The landscape of Rome's African Quarter serves as an impetus for the witnesses, who, together with the collective and the walkers, draw a map of the neighborhood from these counternarratives.

Supported by ARCS Culture Solidali and Archivio Memorie Migranti as part of the Pinocchio–Culture, Sport, Participation project, a civic and social network working against discrimination and for greater social inclusion, the tours have been popular since their inception, selling out in January and February 2021. The first 13 urban treks brought between 200 and 250 people to the neighborhood. One year later, the collective felt the need to go back to the drawing board to create route number two, which is currently being planned. The aim of the tours is to promote knowledge, (re)discover the connection between Italy and Eritrea, encourage public debate, and discuss the dominant themes in education, which are characterized by languages and attitudes that need to be decolonized.[4]

However, the stories reach beyond colonialism. Some of the interviewees are young immigrants who extend these common accounts well beyond 1947 (the year of the official end of Italian colonial dominance in Eritrea):

> The stories are not all focused on colonialism; we still try to talk about it to touch on this topic, but their stories cannot be limited only to this aspect because otherwise we silence them again, creating a relationship of subordination.[5]

In addition to being able to continue the guided tours, the collective also plans to bring its work to schools, as Italian schoolchildren are taught that

---

4 Website of Collettivo Tezeta at https://resistenzeincirenaica.com/collettivo-tezeta/
5 "Trekking UrbAfricano: un percorso lungo un anno", Febuary 6, 2022 https://resistenzeincirenaica.com/2022/02/06/trekking-urbafricano-un-percorso-lungo-un-anno/

Italy never had colonies and that only England and France did. Meanwhile, ongoing coloniality is experienced in everyday life.

In April 2021, Collettivo Tezeta, TrekUrbano, and QuestaèRoma collaborated to create an anticolonial tour that passed in front of the Dogali monument and finished at the Cinema Impero (Empire), located in the multicultural neighborhood of Torpignattara. Identical cinemas were built in Rome and Asmara in 1937 during the Italian occupation. The name clearly recalls the superiority that the Italian Fascist government sought to suggest to their colonial campaign. The tour also passed the Pilo Albertelli school, located behind Termini station, which Isabella and Giorgio Marincola (to be discussed below) used to attend. The name commemorates the anti-fascist professor who was the head of Partito d'Azione (an anti-fascist resistance party) and who encouraged Marincola to become a member.

Not far from Termini station is the Di Donato school, which is known to be one of the most multicultural schools in Rome. There are more than 15 different nationalities in each class, and, initially, some white Italian parents asked that their children be placed somewhere else, because they thought that such a large number of children with foreign backgrounds might be damaging for them.[6] Moreover, representatives of educational institutions stated that, if classes had such a high percentage of pupils with different mother tongues, it would be more difficult for them to learn Italian. Fortunately, a group of parents, mostly white Italians, created a committee and rejected the allegations. Instead, they started organizing events aimed at valuing cultural diversity. Since then, the school has become a model for many parts of society and for various institutions and now has a waiting list.

Decoding Public Memory

Black knowledge is essential to decoding symbols, memory, and celebratory monuments, which is otherwise a difficult process. On the one hand, there are streets and buildings named after Black historical figures from other countries. Many are in honor of the South African leader Nelson Mandela,

---

6 "SCUOLA/ La lettera: troppi stranieri, ecco perché ho ritirato mio figlio", September 20, 2013 (https://www.ilsussidiario.net/news/educazione/2013/9/20/scuola-la-lettera-troppi-stranieri-ecco-perche-ho-ritirato-mio-figlio/428513/)

such as a library in Rome. On the other hand, there are hardly any streets or markers dedicated to any of the Black Italians who have played a significant role in history. Such figures include: Domenico Mondelli, born Wolde Selassie in Asmara, Eritrea in 1886. He was adopted by an Italian general, hence his name, who brought him to Italy where he attended the military academy. He became a captain, then a highly decorated general during World War One, and he is considered the first Black pilot in European and Italian history. Then there is Alessandro Sinigaglia, the son of a white Italian Jew and Cynthia White, an African American woman who came to Italy and worked as a waitress for a family from Saint Louis. Sinigaglia joined the Communist Party in 1926, which was considered an illegal organization at the time. He went to Spain to participate in the anti-fascist resistance against the dictator Francisco Franco, but was eventually exiled in France. He came back to Italy to help the resistance movement, but in 1944 he was killed by Fascists in an ambush.[7] There is a plaque at the site of his execution in Florence, but no other recognition of his contribution.

Even before 1900, there is evidence of the presence of Black Italians such as St. Benedict, who is considered the protector of the city of Palermo, Sicily. St. Benedict was born in 1524 in San Fratello, a small town west of Messina, and although he was the son of two enslaved Africans, he was granted freedom from birth. However, he still had to provide for himself, so he became a cow breeder. When he was 20 he met a hermit and decided to retire to a friary and lead a humble life, entirely dedicated to prayers and charity. He is remembered as a very good advisor: People would come from all parts of Italy to ask for his help and moral support. After his death, his legend spread even beyond Italian borders; in 1807, he was officially proclaimed a saint by the Holy See, becoming the first Black saint in history.

Another important figure who is often disregarded in Italian history is Alessandro de' Medici, known as Il Moro (the Moor), a pejorative name given to Black people at the time as mentioned in previous chapters. In school books, pupils often read about the Medici, one of the most powerful families ruling the Duchy of Florence during the Renaissance; they financially contributed to the first expeditions to South America in the 15th century. However, the story of Alessandro is very rarely told. He is believed to have been

---

[7] "Donne e Uomini della Resistenza. Alessandro Sinigaglia", July 25, 2010 (https://www.anpi.it/donne-e-uomini/723/alessandro-sinigaglia)

the son of Giulio de' Medici, who became pope, and a Black woman who was serving the family. He grew up in the court of Pope Leo X and became the first Duke of Florence and the first Black regent in Europe in 1532. His portrait can be found in the Uffizi Museum in Florence. His story has become more popular, thanks to a short movie produced by the Black Italian director Daphne Di Cinto in 2021 (Tondo 2021).

At first sight, this lack of memorial symbols could be associated with the fact that the presence of Black Italians is not generally known by the public, but on closer examination it becomes clear that this selective amnesia is part of a systemic denial of the Black presence in Italy. This diminishes the impact of their acts, while symbols commemorating the colonization of Africa can be found everywhere in Rome. For example, similar to the case in Berlin, there is a quarter located in the northeast part of the city commonly known as the "African Quarter" because the streets are all named after former Italian colonies: Viale Libia, Viale Etiopia, Viale Somalia (Libya Avenue, Ethiopia Avenue, Somalia Avenue). However, under the signs indicating the name of these streets, no additional description can be found to explain what happened in those territories and why the streets were dedicated to those specific places.

Another marker of the country's colonial past stood in Piazza di Porta Capena for decades. The *"Stele di Axum"* (Axum obelisk) was stolen from Ethiopia and brought to Rome by Benito Mussolini in 1937, during the Italian occupation of the East African nation. Twenty-seven meters high and weighing about 150 tons, the obelisk can be traced back to a period between the 1st and the 4th century AD. Italy erected the stele to celebrate the 15th anniversary of the March on Rome as a glorification of the then "new Roman empire" (Sarnelli 2016). The Italians had located the obelisk in 1935 and transported it to the port of Massawa, 400 kilometers away from its original location, to load it on a ship bound for Naples. It was an unprecedented two-month undertaking. At the end of World War Two, the obelisk became the source of a diplomatic dispute that divided Italy and Ethiopia. Addis Ababa asked for the return of assets stolen by the Fascist regime, and among the priorities of the treaty signed between the two countries was the repatriation of the obelisk. In 1969, the ministry of foreign affairs decided to send it back to the court of Emperor Haile Selassie, but he never managed to retrieve it, probably due to the high shipping cost. Thirty years later, after Selassie had been deposed, Ethiopia again requested its return. The monument was eventually sent back to Ethiopia in 2005 after long and embarrassing negotiations and has been replaced by a memorial to the victims of the September 11 terrorist attacks (ibid.).

The Fascist tendency to dictate public memory still continues today. In 2018, Virginia Raggi, the first female mayor of Rome, firmly opposed a motion approved by the national parliament to dedicate a street to Giorgio Almirante, one of the main members of the Fascist party. Although Italy has a law that criminalizes acts of Fascist apology or celebration, it is very common for right-wing parties to evoke members of the former Fascist regime, to praise their actions, and to honor their contribution to the nation. Therefore, the approval of this motion should not be so surprising; however, it raised indignation, especially from the Jewish community.

As a consequence, in September 2019, with approval from the council, the mayor renamed three streets that were formerly titled after Fascists: Via Arturo Donaggio became Via Mario Carrara, passing the baton from the biologist who edited the 1938 Fascist "Manifesto of Race" to a pioneer of Italian forensic medicine, who is remembered as one of the very few Italian university professors who refused the oath of allegiance to Fascism. Largo Arturo Donaggio was renamed Largo Nella Mortara, after the only female physicist at the famous Physics Institute in Rome, who was banned from the academic world because she was Jewish. Finally, Via Edoardo Zavattari was changed to Via Enrica Calabresi, in honor of the Italian zoologist and entomologist of Jewish origin who killed herself in order to avoid deportation. However, none of them were subsequently dedicated to Black Italians.

Meanwhile, of the few memorials to Black Italians, one important accomplishment for the antiracist and decolonial Italian movement, can be partly attributed to the rise of BLM. The name of the metro station Amba Aradam-Ipponio (which has been under construction since 2013), was initially taken from a nearby street and refers to a small mountain in Ethiopia where, during Italian colonialism, Fascist soldiers killed 20,000 people using mustard gas, a toxic substance that was forbidden by the Geneva convention. Due to this incident, the name of the street had been questioned for many years, but no concrete answer was given. On the night of June 19, 2020, a group of activists called Rete Restiamo Umani, who are mostly white Italians, went to the nearby Via dell'Amba Aradam and substituted the signs, renaming it after George Floyd and Bilal Ben Messaud.[8] The latter was a 28-year-old Tunisian immigrant who died in Porto Empedocle on May 20, 2020 as he desperately swam across the Mediterranean, trying to reach land. He had escaped from forced confinement on a "quarantine ship" where immigrants were kept by government mandate for two weeks after their arrival to stop Covid-19 transmission.[9]

The same group then went to the city center and threw red paint on the bust of Italian colonialist Antonio Baldissera that stands on the Pincio terrace, where many locals and tourists often go to admire the view. According to the activists, throwing red paint on the bust was done to symbolically reject the celebration of colonial history that is considered glorious for one side but undoubtedly tragic for the other, and, most importantly, to interrupt a history that memorializes white supremacy. A panel was added on the wall with the following quote: "No street can have the name of oppression."[10]

With support from both the BLM movement of Rome and the Association NIBI (Neri Italiani/Black Italians), journalist Massimiliano Coccia launched a petition addressed to the mayor, requesting the official renaming of the metro station Amba Aradam-Ipponio and for it to be dedicated to Giorgio Marincola. Marincola was the son of a white Italian man and a Somalian woman, Aschirò Hassan. Although during Fascism white Italian men were discouraged from legitimately recognizing their children with Black women, Marincola's father accepted his son and, without the consent of their mother, brought him and his sister Isabella to Italy. Marincola should be remembered especially for his courage and loyalty to the resistance movement – the *Partigiani* – that fought against the Nazis during World War Two.[11]

Many organizations and intellectuals signed the petition, including Roberto Saviano, a Neapolitan journalist famous for his courage in denouncing the Mafia and other corrupt systems he investigated. Another important

---

8 "Black Lives Matter a Roma: via Amba Aradam diventa via George Floyd. Vernice rossa su una statua al Pincio," June 19, 2020, (https://www.romatoday.it/cronaca/black-lives-matter-a-roma.html)

9 "Italy anti-racism activists deface statue, alter street name, June 19, 2020 (https://www.reuters.com/article/minneapolis-police-italy-idINKBN23Q274)

10 In the original: "nessuna stazione abbia il nome dell'oppressione."

11 "Italy: Rome to name metro station after ‚black partisan'", August 25, 2020 (https://www.wantedinrome.com/news/italy-rome-to-name-metro-station-after-black-partisan.html)

supporter was the writer Antar Marincola, the son of Isabella and nephew of Giorgio Marincola, who had previously collaborated with Wu Ming to map Italian colonialism.[12] The petition obtained more than 2,000 signatures in only a few days and, although it was initially rejected by the local municipality, the mayor brought the motion to the attention of the city council, which finally approved it on August 4, 2020. Two years earlier, in September 2018, to commemorate his birthday, a plaque dedicated to Giorgio Marincola had been placed in Piazza Enrico Cosenz, in the neighborhood of Casal Bertone, on the building where he used to live in Rome. The celebration was independently organized and promoted by ANPI (Associazione Nazionale Partigiani d'Italia), not by the local municipality. So far, it is the only visible marker in Rome.

Figure 7.2: Plaque honoring Giorgio Marincola, a hero of the World War Two resistance. Photograph: Kwanza Musi Dos Santos

The month after the council's approval of the station's renaming, and just three months after George Floyd's murder, Willy Monteiro Duarte, aged 21, was killed on September 6, 2020, after intervening when a group of four white youngsters beat up his friend in Colleferro, a small town on the outskirts of Rome. It is interesting to note that, while covering the news of his death, the media failed to recognize Duarte as a Black Italian. Many referred to him as the "Cape Verdean" or

---

12 Wu Ming is an anonymous collective of Italian journalists. The map can be found at https://umap.openstreetmap.fr/it/map/viva-zerai_519378#6/41.894/7.998

the "foreigner," although he held Italian citizenship and was born in Rome. The family of two of the white aggressors declared: "[H]e was just an immigrant." (Di Benedetto Montaccini 2020). This happens often, suggesting the idea that a Black person cannot be Italian, for Italians are (only) white.

Two weeks later, protests took place in several Italian cities calling for "Justice for Willy" and reclaiming the BLM motto. For most Black activists, the link with the brutality of George Floyd's murder and racism was undeniable. However, Duarte's family asked that his death not be associated with racism. In a Facebook post, they explained:

> We, the family, would like these demonstrations not to be a political tool to talk about racism, fascism or various parties. As much as we condemn and consider deeply wrong feelings such as racism, Willy was the victim of unwarranted cruelty and ferocity, which has no color or race. And we, the family, think everyone is the same. Nobody has to die like this anymore![13]

In the following months, many initiatives were dedicated to Duarte's memory, including a scholarship at the University of International Studies in Rome for a student from Cape Verde. And, on October 16, 2020, the municipality of Rome accepted a motion presented by many associations to name a little garden after Duarte; this is located in the area of Piazza Vittorio, a neighborhood not far from Roma Termini central railway station.

QuestaèRoma: This Is Rome

Historically, most organizations of immigrants and People of Color in Italy are based on the ethnicity or nationality of their members: for instance, the Association of Cameroonians or the Association of Filipinos, which periodically organize cultural events, parties, and gatherings and sometimes offer support to newcomers from their countries. Unlike France's assimilation system or the UK's multiculturalism, Italy has never had a real integration model that was planned and implemented by the government. Thus, there are no specific areas where populations of color and/or immigrants are deliberately concentrated; however, the industries and commercial hubs of

---

13 Translated from Italian.

northern Italy have attracted many people. In addition, because the current census does not include either race or ethnicity, it is difficult to calculate how many Black people live in Italy. In fact, once they acquire citizenship, Black Italians all fall under the category of "Italian citizens."

QuestaèRoma (This Is Rome) is an association that was founded in May 2013. Its name draws on the romanticized idea of Ancient Rome, as a crossroads between various worlds and cultures. It represents the heterogeneous plurality of the so-called "second generation"[14] – or, as they prefer to call themselves, "Italians of foreign background." In fact, out of the 5 million immigrants currently residing in Italy, half of them – i.e., more than 2 million – are white (for example, from Romania, Albania, and Ukraine). So not every Person of Color has the status of immigrant and not every immigrant (or their child) is a Person of Color. However, during the last ten years, when the media talk about immigrants or immigration, they mostly use images of Black people, even though they represent a minority demographically.[15]

QuestaèRoma started its activity at a time when it seemed likely the reform of the citizenship law would soon be implemented. The main left-wing party had won the elections and had gained a majority of seats in the Italian parliament. Hence, the organization's primary focus was on the social and political citizenship of young people of "foreign background" in order to secure their active and conscious political participation. The current law claims that a child born and raised in Italy by two foreign parents must stay in the country uninterruptedly for 18 years in order to be eligible to request Italian citizenship. They must make the request within a year and pay for it. If a child was not born in Italy, but came to the country at an early age with their foreign parents, they need to prove uninterrupted residence for ten years and present numerous documents, including a clear criminal record from their parents' country of origin (translated into Italian), in order to apply for citizenship. After each request, the minister of the interior, by law, can take up to 36 months to respond. Requests can also be rejected for trivial reasons, without the fee being reimbursed.

Since 2005, activists had been trying to move beyond this concept of citizenship, which is ambiguous. In fact, although the current citizenship law

---

14 Website of Rete G2 at https://www.secondegenerazioni.it/about/
15 "Il vero contributo degli immigrati alla crescita del Pil italiano", June 7, 2013 (https://www.agi.it/fact-checking/immigrati_pil_italia-5648357/news/2019-06-13/)

can be considered the main tool of institutional racism, racist policies and attitudes can be found at many other levels of society too. As a consequence, a Person of Color who, for example, was born Italian, inheriting citizenship from one of their parents, would still have to deal with racial profiling and everyday racism. At the same time, children of white immigrants can also encounter legal difficulties and discrimination because they do not have Italian citizenship, or because their name is racialized. The challenge is to consider the diversity of what it means to be Italian.

To tackle these issues, QuestaèRoma was established by seven young Italian activists and artists of color – some with Italian citizenship, some without. Half of the board is composed of People of African Descent (PAD). The members realized that Rome lacked an organization that did not deal with rights in "silos" – for instance, women dealt only with gender equality, LGBTQA+ people with homophobia, Blacks with racism, and so on. Instead, they strongly believe in the principle of intersectionality – namely, that a single person can be the bearer of multiple characteristics and therefore subject to different social and systemic oppressions that occur at the same time. Furthermore, it is not necessary to be part of a socially marginalized group in order to fight against the discrimination that group experiences, as it is important to combat all injustices even if they do not affect you directly.

At the same time, it is key to avoid paternalism, political exploitation, tokenism, and trivialization. Therefore, QuestaèRoma aims to represent the many young people who need to overcome the obstacles that prevent them from participating in decision-making processes. One of the main objectives of the association is to bring politics closer to young people, and young people closer to politics, since they are often disillusioned or disinterested. Its goal is to create new social and safe spaces, preferably in informal contexts – and also to promote arts and culture as tools of interaction that encourage collectivity and the exchange of experiences between those fighting discrimination, despite their differing legal and family situations.

In 2014, one of the first events organized by QuestaèRoma was a public debate that involved youth leaders of all parties. It was designed to enable them to discuss their ideas about youth policies. The meeting provided a rare opportunity for young people of different backgrounds to have a direct experience of politics and to understand that voting is not the only way to be actively involved. A particular commitment is to education; at a programmatic level, QuestaèRoma is working to increase the number of teachers and other professionals with a "foreign background" and to change the curriculum so that, for example, the history of Italian colonialism is included and the weekly civic education hour, which is compulsory in all schools, is used to increase dialogue.

Figure 7.3: QuestaèRoma's campaign against racism featured a photoshoot featuring People of Color

One year later, QuestaèRoma organized its first protest in solidarity with BLM, in response to what was happening in Ferguson (USA) and created one of the first campaigns against racism, #ItalianoNonèUnColore (Italian Is Not a Color). It included a public call to participate in a photoshoot in Piazza del Popolo that would then generate a traveling exhibition. The images showed the participants with traces of white paint on their faces, captioned with provocative phrases such as "Can I vote now?" and "Can I be respected now?" More than 100 people attended. They felt empowered by the impact they had on passers-by, who were intrigued by seeing such a large gathering of Italians of Color. For some people, it was the first time they had been portrayed by a Black photographer, Carlos Lora Toma Acosta, who enhanced their traits and gave value to their skin color.

In 2020, the prominence of BLM renewed the fight against systemic and structural racism and Afrophobia and led to the creation of a video series called Fading,[16] which was promoted under the hashtag #prendiamolaparola. QuestaèRoma was involved in the series and supported the collective aim to denounce the effects and causes of structural racism in Italy. The materials are now being used to raise awareness and to create workshops promoting antiracism in schools all over the country. Following this campaign, in April 2021 a group of antiracist organizations and independent activists from

---

16 "FADING #prendiamolaparola", April 25, 2021 (https://www.youtube.com/watch?v=vWV-J1lxuX2g&t=3s)

all over Italy sent a public letter to RAI (the national public broadcasting channel), challenging the media's repeated use of racial slurs and Blackface during several TV shows. Under the name of #cambieRAI they conducted a successful mass mailing to all representatives and employees of public television. In the letter, they firmly condemned recent incidents, calling for more respect toward minorities as well as for more representation (Hughes 2021). The following year, the TV channel's division dedicated to social issues, called Rai per il Sociale, launched a call inviting all organizations dealing with antiracism to create a permanent consulting committee. The negotiations on who will participate are still ongoing.

The recently founded organizations and the activities they are creating are putting pressure on officials to address structural racism; at the same time, they are educating the public about the country's history as well as its current treatment of immigrants and People of Color. It is important to note that the changes taking place are thanks to a resistance that will keep expanding into the future.

References

Benedetto Montaccini, Veronica Di (2020) "Omicidio Willy, i familiari degli arrestati: "Era solo un immigrato, non hanno fatto niente di male"", September 8, https://www.tpi.it/cronaca/omicidio-colleferro-willy-familia ri-arrestati-era-solo-un-immigrato-20200908660717/

Cappelli, Rory (2020) "La fermata Amba Aradam della Metro C sarà intitola a Giorgio Marincola," *La Repubblica*, August 1, https://roma.repubblica.it/ cronaca/2020/08/01/news/roma_raggi_la_fermata_amba_aradam_del la_metro_c_sara_intitola_a_giorgio_marincola_-263419893/

Capua, Patrizia di (2020) "30 anni RepNa. Villa Literno, l'incendio del ghetto, La Repubblica, April 6,

Chauffourier, Gustavo Eugenio (1887) "La stazione Termini con il Monumento ai caduti di Dogali" [photograph], Museo di Roma, http://www. museodiroma.it/it/collezioni/percorsi_per_temi/fotografia/la_stazio ne_termini_con_il_monumento_ai_caduti_di_dogali

Chelati Dirar, Uoldelul (2004) "From Warriors to Urban Dwellers," *Cahiers d'Études Africaines* 175: 533–74.

Del Boca, Angelo (2014) *Italiani, brava gente?* Venezia: Neri Pozza..

Falocco, Silvano and Carlo and Carlo Boumis (2022) *Roma Coloniale*. Rome: Le Commari.

Hughes, Rebecca Ann (2021) "The activists calling out racism In Italy's media", eu*observer*, May 17, https://euobserver.com/news/151843

Marincola, Antar Mohamed, Carlo Costa, Lorenzo Teodonio, and Wu Ming 2 (2020) "'Stazione Giorgio Marincola'? Purché il colonialismo non riposi in pace," Giap, June 26, https://www.wumingfoundation.com/giap/2020/06/stazione-giorgio-marincola-purche-il-colonialismo-non-riposi-in-pace/

Negash, Tekeste (1987) *Italian Colonialism in Eritrea 1882–1941: Policies, Praxis and Impact*. Uppsala: Uppsala University and Almqvist & Wiksell.

Peretti, Luca di (2021) "Memorie eritree nel Quartiere Africano", February 27, https://www.dinamopress.it/news/memorie-eritree-nel-quartiere-africano/

Pesarini, Angelica and Camilla Hawthorne (2020) "Black Lives Matter anche da noi?," *Jacobin Italia*, 8: 72–7.

Pesarini, Angelica and Carla Panico (2021) "From Colston to Montanelli: Public Memory and Counter-Monuments in the Era of Black Lives Matter," *From the European South: A Transdisciplinary Journal of Postcolonial Humanities*, 9: 99–113.

Piattelli, Ariela (2018) "Presto saranno rinominate le vie di Roma intitolate a chi aderì al Manifesto della razza," *La Stampa*, January 22, https://www.lastampa.it/politica/2018/01/22/news/raggi-presto-saranno-rinominate-le-vie-di-roma-intitolate-a-chi-aderi-al-manifesto-della-razza-1.33970557

Sarnelli, Laura (2016) "Affective Routes in Postcolonial Italy: Igiaba Scego's Imaginary Mappings," *Roots & Routes*, https://www.roots-routes.org/affective-routes-postcolonial-italy-igiaba-scegos-imaginary-mappings-laura-sarnelli/

Tondo, Lorenzo (2021) "Story of forgotten black Medici ruler is told in new short film," https://www.theguardian.com/film/2021/sep/06/story-of-forgotten-black-medici-ruler-is-told-in-new-short-film

Valeri, Mauro (2016) *Generale nero. Domenico Mondelli: bersagliere, aviatore e ardito*. Rome: Odradek.

Vergès, Françoise (2021) *De la violence coloniale dans l'espace public: Visite du triangle de la Porte Dorée à Paris*. Paris: Shed Publishing.

Chapter 8
Black Warsaw

James Omolo and Natasha A. Kelly

Being a conservative white homogeneous society, Poland addressed the murder of George Floyd with increasing incidents of intolerance toward People of African Descent (PAD) and Persons of Color (PoC). Black Lives Matter (BLM) protests in the streets of major cities such as Warsaw, Krakow, and Poznań highlighted the various manifestations of racism, xenophobia, intolerance, and discrimination at both societal and institutional levels that affect every aspect of Black life in Poland today, including unequal access to education and employment, racial abuse and violence in public places (for example, on public transport), restrictions of movement due to overzealous policing, and hate crimes, among other instances.

The major BLM protests occurred in Warsaw on two different dates. The first BLM event, which was organized by a local non-governmental organization (NGO), Przychodnia Skłot, took place in front of the US embassy on May 31, six days after the incident. The second demonstration took place on June 4 and was organized by No Justice No Peace-Poland.[1] Among the protesters was Bianka Nwolisa, a young girl carrying a sign saying "Stop calling me *Murzyn*." Her actions were part of a larger campaign by Black women in Poland to address racial discrimination (Mecking and Terry 2020). The term has long been used to refer to Black people in Poland and has its roots in the English word "Moor." As argued in Chapters 1 and 4, it is outdated and offensive, but it is also symbolic of the attitude of the white majority society toward Blackness in the country.

---

[1] "Black Lives Matter in Poland", *Detroiter in Poland*, July 29, 2020 (https://v8mile.wordpress.com/2020/07/29/black-lives-matter-in-poland/)

While *"Czarny"* means "Black," "M....n" has a disparaging social connotation. It is used to replace the N-word. As the status of white Poles is often perceived as inferior by other Europeans in the West, using the term for Black people allows them to feel better about themselves, since Black people are considered to be inferior in every aspect. In a widely published scandal in 2014, involving top government officials, central bankers, and ministers, among others, Foreign Minister Radosław Sikorski was reported to have said that the mentality of Poles in general is suffering from *"Murzyńskość"* – a derogatory and racially loaded term to mean thinking "like a Negro." He continued to allege that Poles suffer from a lack of pride and low self-esteem, referring to the Polish–American alliance, which he described as worthless and harmful (Omolo 2017: 77).

In the same year, Janusz Korwin-Mikke, who led Poland's small New Right Congress party during the European parliamentary elections, affirmed that the minimum wage should be "destroyed." He claimed that "four million N*s" lost their jobs in the USA as a result of President John F. Kennedy signing a bill on the minimum wage in 1961. He also asserted that 20 million young Europeans were being treated as "N*s" as a consequence of the minimum wage (Omolo 2017: 78). The list of examples goes on. In 2012, Law and Justice Party (PiS) MP Marek Suski was overheard in parliament referring to Nigerian-born John Godson, then a member of Civic Platform and Poland's first ever Black MP, as "your N*" (ibid.). And in early 2016, Foreign Minister Witold Waszczykowski said on national television that Poland's new government had shed the country's "N* mentality" when it came to relations with the USA (ibid.). These discourses create a particular image of Black people – or, rather, a precise image associated with the term. Even though the term is regarded as contentious, for many it remains a justifiable and uncontroversial depiction of Black people in Poland.

Even though the Black community has been outspoken about the myriad manifestations of racism, their outcry has been muted by unfolding events. A recent exhibition at the Polish State Museum, for example, clearly confirms the insensitivity that Blacks say is part of mainstream culture. A white Danish provocateur, Uwe Max Jensen, was invited to perform during the opening of the exhibition. During the performance he waved a Confederate flag, stripped naked, painted his body black with the help of another artist, and dragged himself on the floor as he repeated the words "I can't breathe!" – not only George Floyd's but also Eric Garner's last words (Gera 2021). But some continue to deny these realities. Polish right-wing politicians and social critics, for example, openly ridiculed BLM, distancing Polish reality from such actions.

Despite the uproar about systemic injustices, most Poles were concerned with the defacing of a statue of Andrzej Tadeusz Bonawentura Kościuszko (1746–1817), a Polish general, recognized as the ultimate freedom fighter in the Russo-Polish War of 1792. From 1776 to 1783, Kościuszko also fought for the USA in the American War of Independence. A statue of him was erected in Washington DC and another one in Warsaw. The letters BLM were written on both statues, an action condemned by Polish President Andrzej Duda and other prominent political leaders, brushing over the potential legitimacy of the protests, or the possible link between their cause and Kościuszko himself. The writing was swiftly removed, and protesters warned not to repeat the offense. The country's BLM movement, however, has not yet recognized that Kościuszko was, in fact, a great ally to the cause. He is considered one of the country's greatest national heroes. Although unequivocally a symbol of Polishness, at the same time he represented the ideals of the Enlightenment and supported the worldwide abolitionist movement (Klajn 2020).

Kościuszko opposed the ideology of racial subjugation and white supremacy. Based on his speeches and correspondence, as well as on his last will, he was an avid abolitionist, condemning enslavement and racial prejudice. In one instance, for example, when he was rewarded with an enslaved African for his military achievements, he immediately set him free. According to experts, Kościuszko not only fought for the rights of white peasants in Poland, but, when dealing with Thomas Jefferson, he insisted on the ransom and liberation of enslaved people in the USA. He was also an advocate for the Jews worldwide (Brzezinska 2017). Kościuszko's legacy carries a clear sociopolitical relevance to the BLM movement, even though this particular aspect of history remains widely unrecognized by many Poles and appears especially overlooked by the nation's current political leaders.

The defacing of the Kościuszko statue, however, did present an opportunity to question the lack of monuments to Afro-Polish historical figures, such as the associate of Kościuszko, Jean Lapierre. Lapierre was Kościuszko's own valet and confidante. As a Black man with an unclear country of origin, he was nicknamed "Domingo," a clue that he may have come from the island of Saint-Domingue in the Caribbean. He immigrated to Poland in 1796, and, with his aptitude for languages and accounting, he became a bookkeeper for a Polish nobleman. He was later at the commander's side as he led a revolt to try to free white serfs enslaved by feudalism. His portrait can be seen at the Polish military museum in Warsaw (Boston 2021).

African Immigration to Warsaw

The history of Africans in Poland is characterized by three types of immigration that play key roles at various stages: education, asylum seeking, and family reunification. Asylum-seeking immigration is minimal and covers very few African countries, such as Somalia, Eritrea, Central African Republic, and Libya. Family reunifications are also small in number due to the many restrictions of the Polish government and the Polish embassies in Africa. The majority of immigration from the African continent came through educational immigration, mostly under the communist regime during a period when the country supported the anticolonial movements in Africa as a part of the Soviet strategy (Pędziwiatr and Balogun 2018). Back then, many African students, mainly men, came to Poland through exchange programs between Poland and socialist African countries.[2] During this time, the incoming African students integrated well with the local population, becoming pioneers of the emerging African community. They lived among Poles, shared houses and apartments with them, even married white Polish women, and established NGOs promoting African culture (Omolo 2017).

As a show of solidarity with some of these African states, the communist leaders of the Polish People's Republic promoted socialism as they embarked on a path to independence. Between July 31 and August 14, 1955, Poland hosted the 5th World Festival of Youth and Students in Warsaw. This event was attended by 30,000 delegates from 114 countries. Among them were 911 delegates from then colonized territories in Africa. The gathering was organized by the anti-imperialist and left-wing World Federation of Democratic Youth, an international youth organization founded in London in 1945 with the aim of uniting youth from the allied West with those of capitalist and socialist nations (McDuffie 2011: 247). For many Poles, it was their first

---

2 In his book *Strangers at the Gate: Black Poland* (2017), James Omolo documents the number of students from different African countries present in Poland between 1976 and 1977, almost 3,000 in total.

contact with Black people and PoC after the destruction of the Second Polish Republic, which had been more multicultural, during World War Two. The festival offered images for Polish press photographs that showed PAD beyond racist stereotypes; these were showcased at the exhibition "Afro PRL," curated by Polish photographer Bartosz Nowicki at the Cultural Institute of Warsaw in 2018 (Greenhill 2021).

However, the presence of Africans at the world festival was limited to a few diplomats or students on scholarships. Back then, students needed to return to their countries of origin upon completing their studies. Official statistics from this period show that the number of African graduates in the country increased steadily from just over 200 in the 1960s to almost 400 in the 1970s, rising to more than 700 during the 1980s (Pędziwiatr and Balogun 2018). It was only those who graduated at the time of the collapse of the Berlin Wall who had the opportunity of seeking a livelihood in Poland and stayed (Omolo 2017).

Despite the small number of Africans who settled in Poland, Black people have become a permanent feature of Polish reality. In large cities, seeing PAD is no longer considered exceptional, although they are by no means a common sight. Contemporary figures such as Professor Killion Munyama, a former member of the Polish parliament who came to Poland during communism as a student, demonstrate the progress made by Africans in the country. Professor Munyama stands out even though he is a Polish citizen. One of the country's African political stars, Munyama has been living in Poland for almost 40 years. He is an economist and academic lecturer who served as a local government councilor in Grodzisk (2002–6) and as regional councilor in the province of Greater Poland (2007–10). He was also a member of parliament from 2011 to 2021, and he sat on several committees, such as public finance and the foreign affairs committee. Munyama resigned in June 2021 to take a job in Brussels as an envoy at the European level on EU–Africa relations.

Still, the political landscape in Poland, as in other countries in Europe, has contributed to the negative image of immigrants, characterizing them as a problem and a risk to Polish culture. This has generated an upswing in attacks on PAD and panic among these distressed communities and groups. Without doubt, the current government – a right-wing conservative Catholic government – legitimizes nationalistic and fascist groups. With the mushrooming of these groups across the country, political discourse and narrative openly embrace and express hate speech and propagate negative, prejudicial, and stereotypical information about PAD and other groups of color. The intolerant discourse is facilitated by the use of social media and a variety of internet sites and portals that fan the flames of hatred and intolerance across all sectors of society (Omolo 2020).

For Mamadou Diouf, a Senegalese journalist and cofounder of the Afryka Another Way foundation,[3] who has lived in Poland since 1983, othering is a part of life for Black people in the country. The use of racist terms is commonplace, he says, describing how the words "bamboo" and "asphalt" are widely used when referring to Blacks. As a young student he recalls that he and others had to take an AIDS test although Polish students did not. And in 2015 he heard talk circulating about viruses and bacteria crossing the Mediterranean in the bodies of refugees (Gutfrański 2019). In 2010, Diouf published a book on Africans in the city, titled *Africa in Warsaw: The History of the African Diaspora on the Vistula River*, in which he highlighted Black war hero August Browne's story (to be discussed later). Today, he publishes a blog about life in Poland for Africans. He says that Poland is now home and that you do not need the permission of locals to feel that way (ibid.).

Meanwhile, data on Black people living in Poland is for the most part unavailable. The only existing information is collected and published by the office of foreign affairs. The primary downside is the fact that data is available based on country of birth, but not on acquired citizenship or naturalization. The population of the African diaspora or PAD living in Poland is therefore tentative. Official statistics are based on Africans living in Poland, but they do not include persons of the second or third generation who were born in Poland. It is estimated that there are between 4,000 and 5,000 Africans in the country. Yet, the size and geographical distribution of the African diaspora and the population of individual areas are also uncertain. The African diaspora is spread across the country, from small villages to big cities. The main areas of residence are the metropolises of Warsaw, Kraków, Poznań, Łódź, and Gdańsk, where there are better job opportunities and earning potential.

Unlike other countries in Europe, Poland does not have a well-structured public housing system. Therefore, a majority of Black people are absorbed in

---

3 "Fundacja „Afryka Inaczej"," *Anna Lindh Foundation Euromed* (https://www.annalindhfoundation.org/members/fundacja-afryka-inaczej)

the private housing sector with no particular area of concentration for the Black community. Similarly, data on the level of education of PAD in Poland does not exist. There is, however, some information on Africans who are registered at education institutions in Poland. African embassies have statistics for their respective citizens who register with them, but unfortunately many Africans do not register at their embassies at all. Most of the students enroll in Polish language schools for one year, after which they join Polish universities. Fields of study vary from journalism, law, economics, and business to social sciences, natural sciences, engineering, medicine, and health sciences, among other subjects.

Churches play a central role in the lives of PAD in Poland. Church communities are among the few Black institutions in the country with robust frameworks. The distribution of PAD in Poland based on denomination is not known precisely; however, in major cities, especially in Warsaw, the Anglican Church, Jehovah's Witnesses, and Seventh-Day Adventists are the main churches providing spiritual connection to Africans. There are also a number of churches led by Africans, such as the Redeemed Christian Church of God and Imago Dei Ministries, among others. These churches are not only a place of worship; they also engage in social and cultural activities that connect them with the local community. In addition to their religious functions, religious leaders provide social, psychological, and moral support in the everyday lives of their members.

Honoring Two Africans for the Warsaw Uprising

Black Poles had not been considered prominent heroes of national history until summer 2020, when Polish and international media picked up and covered the stories of Józef Sam Sandi and August Agboola "Ali" Browne, two Africans who played significant roles in the Warsaw Uprising. Lest we forget, the two memorials honoring these men are not just commemorative sites of their involvement, but also symbols that encourage the Black community to feel a sense of national pride and, thus, that they contribute significantly to Black Polish identity.

The first, a 1.2 meter-high monument, is the brainchild of Jarema Dubiel, the director of the Freedom and Peace Movement Foundation. It was unveiled by the Warsaw mayor Rafał Trzaskowski in August 2019, and commemorates

August Agboola Browne (1895–1976). At the time, Dubiel said the honor was a reminder that Poland has a tradition of granting citizenship and national rights to anyone willing to shed their blood for the country.[4] The tribute to the legendary Black insurgent stands at the intersection of Chmielna and Zlota streets in the Polish capital, where the Nigerian-born jazz musician settled with his family before becoming a soldier in 1944. Its sloping top bears the inscription in both Polish and English:

> In honor of Augustine Agboola Browne. Nom de guerre, Ali, a jazz musician and participant in the Warsaw Uprising of African origin. Poland was the country he chose to live in.

Figure 8.1: A plaque to August Agboola Browne in Warsaw. Photograph: afryka.org

Browne arrived in Warsaw in 1922, after a stay in London and the free city of Danzig, where he had played drums in local clubs. Although his marriage failed, Browne had arranged for his two sons and their mother to seek refuge in England at the outbreak of the war while he remained in Poland to fight for the resistance. His second daughter from his second marriage, his only surviving child in Britain, was born in 1959 and brought up in London, where Browne died in 1976 when she was just 17 (Boston 2020). However, it took until August 2, 2019 for Warsaw city council to commemorate the national

---

4 "Warsaw Rising black insurgent commemorated," August 3, 2019 (https://polandin.com/43789422/warsaw-rising-black-insurgent-commemorated)

hero, as Browne's story lies only in the margins of the 1944 Warsaw Uprising's mainstream narrative.

The Nigerian immigrant became part of the history of Warsaw not only as a talented musician, but also as a participant of the Warsaw Uprising – the largest underground military operation in German-occupied Europe. When Hitler attacked Warsaw in the so-called *Blitzkrieg*, Browne was ready to fight for his host country. When Germany invaded Poland in 1939, he participated in the resistance and five years later he also fought during the Uprising. In exile in London, he enlisted as a member of the "Iwo" Battalion of the Armia Krajowa (Home Army), the largest resistance army at that time. He served in the home army primarily by relaying intelligence. The Uprising resulted in over 300,000 casualties, mostly civilians. Browne survived the war and in the late 1940s embarked on playing music again.

As Dr. Zbigniew Osiński, an archivist at the Warsaw Rising Museum describes, Browne was a charismatic individual who assimilated very well in society (Karski 2015). Recently, his story has gained popularity. And while he is not featured among prominent Polish heroes, his recognition with a plaque and portrait at the museum has made him part of national history. Browne's story is a great inspiration and resonates with the realities of many Black people in the country today.

Figure 8.2: A plaque honoring World War One hero Józef Sam Sandi. Photograph: James Omolo

In the western part of Poland, in the duchy of Warsaw, a second plaque – this time to a Cameroonian insurgent – also reminds us of Black Polish history. It commemorates Józef Sam Sandi and reads:

African, citizen of the Republic of Poland. A soldier of the forming Polish Army fighting for the creation of Polish borders. A boxer, wrestler, 'Iron Man' and a loving father.[5]

Sandi came to Poland with the French army during World War One. As a German prisoner of war, he landed in one of the camps in Greater Poland, from where he was freed by the Poles. Grateful to them, Sandi offered his help in the fight against the common enemy. As a result, the Cameroonian was given a Polish uniform and assigned to one of the units that were to fight the Germans. Since Sandi showed a willingness and had a skill that was not very common at the time – namely, being able to drive a car – he joined the insurgent ranks as a driver (Zaradniak 2018).

From then on, Sandi took an active part in the Greater Poland uprising that broke out in Poznań on December 27, 1918. The *Kurier Poznański* newspaper later described him as an exemplary soldier and patriot who was liked by his colleagues. When the war was over, Sandi left the military and started a civilian life, trying to find happiness in Warsaw. He provided English tutoring to ladies in high society and drove taxis, but neither job brought in the expected earnings – perhaps a Black teacher and taxi driver might have been too unusual at the time. In search of another source of income, Sandi started boxing and, after gaining enough weight, eventually picked up wrestling. In 1929, the Staniewski brothers bought a circus on Ordynacka Street and expanded their repertoire to include wrestling fights, which were soon to become popular. It is there where Sandi found a steady income, as the audience became more attracted to and curious about his race. Thus, his fights started to gather larger crowds over time.

After the Polish–Bolshevik wars, at a time when interracial marriages were unheard of, Sandi married his former language student, the 18-year-old Lucia Wozniak. This led to Lucia's family disinheriting her, as they could not accept their daughter marrying a Black man, despite the fact that Sandi was baptized, had adopted the Polish name Józef as his first name, and was fluent in Polish, English, and French. However, their love bloomed, and their two daughters were born – first Gabrysia and then, four years later, Krys-

---

5 "Sam Sandi (1885-1937)" (https://www.blackpast.org/global-african-history/people-global-african-history/sam-sandi-1885-1937/)

tyna. It was only when Sandi's income increased that Lucia's family eventually accepted him (Neybaur 2019).

After moving to Gniewkowo and ending his employment with the circus, Sandi found a job in one of the restaurants in Poznań in the mid-1930s. He was officially employed as a cloakroom attendant, but it is highly probable that he also acted as a bouncer to ease any disputes between the guests.[6] In 1935, his older daughter, Gabrysia, fell seriously ill and died. Sandi never came to terms with her death. Depressed, he also began to have health problems, and he died unexpectedly on April 29, 1937, while out on the street in Poznań. The cause of death, cerebral hemorrhage, was most likely linked to his past of wrestling and boxing. Today, the descendants of the Black Polish wrestler live in cities in Poland and Germany (Neybaur 2019).

Józef Sam Sandi's funeral took place on May 1, 1937. He was buried in the Górczyński cemetery. Unfortunately, his grave was lost over time. However, in painter Leon Prauziński's engraving, *The Colonial Army*, three insurgents were depicted: the Chinese Zdzisław Chen Defu, the German Paul Krenz, and the Black Pole Sam Sandi. The three insurgents aroused the interest of radio and TV journalists Małgorzata Jańczak and Aleksander Przybylski, who started looking for them one by one. Chen Defu was quickly and easily found, because his Polish path had already been documented. However, with Sam Sandi it was more complicated. The first leads were through an open letter on the internet written by Sandi's great-granddaughter saying that she would be very happy to get information about him. A search of the archives began and Sandi's story slowly unfolded.

After getting approval, the journalists started fundraising for a plaque and managed to raise enough money with the support of the city council. On Saturday, December 22, 2018, a plaque in honor of Józef Sam Sandi, the Black Greater Poland insurgent, was unveiled at the Górczyński cemetery in Poznań. With the support of Filip Suś from the Society of Hipolit Cegielski,[7] Jańczak and Przybylski also hope to install a bench at Powstańców Wielko-

---

6 "Zelazny czlowiek dandys i diabel rogaty." Sam Sandi pokochal Polske i Polke" (https://tvn24.pl/magazyn-tvn24/zelazny-czlowiek-dandys-i-diabel-rogaty-sam-sandi-pokochal-polske-i-polke,151,2656)

7 The Hipolit Cegielski Society grants awards and lays a foundation for the quality of Polish cultural, economic, and social life. (https://www.thc.org.pl/PL-H74/hipolit-cegielski-society---its-concept-and-objective.html)

polskich Street once city hall accepts its design by Rafał Hodyra (Zaradniak 2018).

Organizing Blackness: Where Africans and Poles Meet

PAD have founded and been active in organizations in Poland for decades. Their aim is to secure assistance in socioeconomic areas and preserve their cultural identity in the context of discrimination and marginalization. They face significant forms of racism, from overt micro-aggressions to more insidious examples such as hate crimes and institutional racism. And although racism and discrimination lie squarely within the context of race and phenotypical categorization, especially in derogatory words such as those mentioned above and monkey chants prevalent in everyday life, the social concept of race is hardly present in Poland. Recently, a famous priest, Tadeusz Rydzyk, made a public remark on national television asking Poles not to marry people from other cultures, especially Africans, because they have to preserve the "white race," referring to a biological categorization.[8]

Living in Poland, it becomes obvious that Polish people have little contact with Africans, considering that Africans constitute about 0.001 percent of the entire population. Therefore, little was known about Africa in the past, or about what constituted the stereotypes surrounding the continent and its people. This gave rise to the establishment of NGOs to tackle these issues, including the Afryka Connect Foundation, established in 2012. Its initial goals were to serve as a platform where Africans and Poles can interact and get to know each other and gain knowledge of Africa. It also strives to provide the African community with engaging activities that can integrate them in society. The cultural, economic, and educational gaps between Poland and Africa are bridged, through seminars, workshops, consultancy, and educational exchange programs. And although the foundation is based in the capital, these activities are held across the country. In 2016, it planned to build an African Center in Warsaw, as a vital space for the wellbeing of the Black community in Poland, a space for participating in social activities such as

---

8 "O. Rydzyk odradza słuchaczom zawierania „małżeństw mieszanych"."To są dramaty"" December 11, 2018 (https://wiadomosci.gazeta.pl/wiadomosci/7,114883,24266810,o-rydzyk-odradza-sluchaczom-zawierania-malzenstw-mieszanych-to.html)

after-school programs. However, it failed due to a lack of funds, and so there are still no focal points for Black people to gather, other than a few African restaurants and churches that act as meeting places.

Later, the foundation started prioritizing human rights issues on the premise that integration is only viable when the environment is conducive. The organization has been at the forefront in advocating on behalf of PAD on social and human rights issues both in Poland and at the international level. The objective of Afryka Connect Foundation is social change leading to a concentration on activities related to sustainable development and integration. Empowerment and capacity building have been cornerstones of its activities, especially those focused on racial discrimination and hate crime. The most effective way to make people more aware of socioeconomic issues is to involve them directly and to encourage them to work together.

At the time of writing, Poland is experiencing the highest rate of intolerance in the country's history. Even though far-right groups exhibit the worst forms of hatred, the problem is more deeply rooted. The current administration of the Law and Justice party is aggravating the situation. In early 2015, the government disbanded an official body for combating racism, the Council Against Racial Discrimination and Xenophobia. The Council had been established in 2013 by the former prime minister and former president of the European Council Donald Tusk. This work is now assigned to the adviser on civil society and equal treatment, who holds the mandate to monitor the work of civil society and NGOs and also to advise the government on particular areas of interest where funding should be channeled. This implies that organizations whose activities do not serve the interests of the current administration are likely not to receive funding. Later in the year, the government also disbanded the department of hate crime control in the ministry of the interior, reducing its autonomy and sending a symbolic message to already susceptible minorities that the government is not concerned about their issues. This department was mandated to monitor and supervise police investigations of hate crime. Defunding the department implies that there will no longer be supervision of the police or measures against hate crime.

Consequently, the objectives of Afryka Connect Foundation are implemented against a backdrop of human rights, immigration, education, and international cooperation. Activities range from awareness raising to advocacy initiatives dealing with problems of racism and xenophobia. The foundation is building a broad and inclusive movement against racism, hate crime, and discrimination and is advocating for inclusivity and diversity by facilitating an equitable share for PAD in education, employment, and economic activities in order to ensure their advancement.

Promoting educational exchange between African universities and their Polish counterparts is also an important part of its work. For many years, prior to the outbreak of Covid-19 in 2020, annual African diaspora conferences were organized with the main objective of bringing together Africans and Poles from different sectors to talk about politically relevant topics and to network. Afryka Connect Foundation has also been actively engaged in conducting nationwide roundtable meetings that address racism and hate crimes in Poland. The organization is entirely run by volunteers, and the activities are project based.

In the panoply of PAD organizations, patterns that are regionally, ethnically, and nationally oriented and that relate to origin form the basis of engagement with the local community as well as with other organizations. Over the last decade, a moderate number of African organizations founded by Africans have been established. The majority are based in Warsaw, with a few spread across the country. African diaspora organizations in Poland are categorized based on their aims and objectives, as noted earlier: cultural organizations; development organizations; student associations and professional organizations. Among the most well known are the Foundation for Somalia and Afryka Another Way, both founded in 2007. The latter conducts training for various Polish groups, including government officials and the police. Its founder, Mamadou Diouf, believes that if members know more about Africans and their culture it may help them interact better (Łazarewicz 2010). Other foundations include Harambi, Adulis, and Omenaa. Cultural organizations such as Afryka Connect Foundation constitute the biggest group, with a total of 12. A number of African diaspora groups fiercely connect to their national identity, and they are often set up along geographical lines. However, while national and cultural affiliation play a role in the organizations, PAD do not necessarily rule out interaction with others in their social lives.

Besides cultural organizations, there are also groups whose role is to undertake development initiatives in Africa. There are very few of these – in fact, in Warsaw there are only two that could be classified as partly development oriented: Foundation for Somalia and Omenaa Foundation. However, the majority of African-based development organizations are run by white

Poles. For example, the East–West Africa Economic Foundation (Fundacja Ekonomiczna Polska–Afryka Wschodnia) is run by a white Pole who has been active in the region, engaging in infrastructure development in Kenya and Tanzania. African student associations exist in an informal setting and are often affiliated with other community or country-based organizations. Regrettably, there is no single umbrella African student association that could actively address students' issues. It is also important to note that there are no African-based organizations engaged in politics in Poland. There is a reluctance among PAD to take an active part in the political sphere, partly because the majority do not have Polish citizenship, a prerequisite to voting rights.

Although the PAD population is very small and there are few organizations, the work of documenting Black contributions and histories continues to be pursued. The increased visibility of the Black Polish experience points to opportunities to address long-standing inequalities and to educate both the white majority and the Black community itself. Yet, with Poland's open hostility toward Black people, the task of writing Black Polish history remains challenging.

References

Boston, Nicholas (2020) "August Browne: The Nigerian-Born Man Who Joined the Polish Resistance," October 3, https://www.bbc.com/news/world-africa-54337607

Boston, Nicholas (2021) "How the Defacement of Two Statues Could Lead to Poland's Reckoning with its Black History," June 22, https://www.calvertjournal.com/articles/show/12214/black-lives-matter-europe-african-polish-tadeusz-kociuszko-jean-lapierre-jabonowski-statues

Brzezinska, Kasia (2017) "Tadeusz Kościuszko: A Polish and American Hero," October 12, https://theculturetrip.com/europe/poland/articles/tadeusz-kosciuszko-a-polish-and-american-hero/

Gera, Vanessa (2021) "Polish Art Show Defies 'Cancel Culture' but Some See Racism," August 27, https://apnews.com/article/lifestyle-business-europe-arts-and-entertainment-race-and-ethnicity-5fa1c7ba22916dca671efacf7bd91242

Greenhill, Richard (2021) "Afro-Poland: A Revolutionary Friendship Captured in Rare Photos from 1955–1989," June 30, https://www.calvertjour

nal.com/features/show/10455/poland-africa-rare-photos-race-bartosz-nowicki

Gutfrański, Krzysztof (2019) "Let's Get Beyond the 'Bambomentality,'" https://obieg.u-jazdowski.pl/en/numery/dis-othering/lets-get-beyond-the-bambomentality

Karski, Michal (2015) "August in Poland: Foreign Fighters in the Polish Resistance," August 8, http://www.krakowpost.com/9756/2015/08/august-in-poland-foreign-fighters-in-the-polish-resistance

Klajn, Maryla (2020) "The Surreptitious Nature of General Tadeusz," September 28, https://www.europeanbordercommunities.eu/blog/polishness-and-blacklivesmatter-the-surreptitious-legacy-of-general-tadeusz-ko%C5%9Bciuszko

Łazarewicz, Cezary (2010) "Rozmowa z muzykiem Mamadou Dioufem," October 16, https://www.polityka.pl/tygodnikpolityka/spoleczenstwo/1509188,1,rozmowa-z-muzykiem-mamadou-dioufem.read

McDuffie, Erik S. (2011) *Warszawa: Africa Another Way Foundation. Sojourning for Freedom*. Durham NC: Duke University Press.

Mecking, Olga and Ruth Terry (2020) "#DontCallMeMurzyn: Black Women in Poland Are Powering the Campaign Against a Racial Slur," *Time*, August 7, https://time.com/5874185/poland-racism-women-murzyn/

Neybaur, Joanna (2019) "Warsaw's Hidden History," November 11, https://whu.org.pl/2019/11/11/rodak-w-kolorze-zalobnem-jozef-sandi/

Omolo, James (2017) *Strangers at the Gate: Black Poland*. Warsaw: Cosmodernity Consultants.

Omolo, James (2020) "8 Minutes and 46 Seconds: A Time to Reflect," June 19, https://unicornerorg.wordpress.com/2020/06/19/8-minutes-and-46-seconds-a-time-to-reflect/

Pędziwiatr, Konrad and Bolaji Balogun (2018) "Poland: Sub-Saharan Africans and the Struggle for Acceptance," Minority Rights, September, https://minorityrights.org/trends2018/poland/

Zaradniak, Marek (2018) "Greater Poland Uprising: Jozef Sam Sandi Was a Greater Poland Insurgent from the Middle of Africa," December 17, https://plus.gloswielkopolski.pl/powstanie-wielkopolskie-jozef-sam-sandi-byl-powstancem-wielkopolskim-ze-srodka-afryki/ar/13740090

Authors

Epée Hervé Dingong is an international freelance writer from Paris. After earning his BA in Journalism from Centre de Formation et de Perfectionnement des Journalistes (CFPJ), he went on to become editor of French hip-hop publication *Radikal Magazine* from 1998 to 2005. As a staff and freelance writer he has interviewed artists from all over the world. His work has been published in print and online, in both US and European publications, such as *Juice*, *Tracklist*, *The Source*, *The Source France*, *Musique Info Hebdo*, *Lady Caprice Magazine*, *Avenue*, *Mugshot Magazine*, Daveyd.com, and Euromight.com. He is the author of *Mixtapelogie*, a book about the history and business of mixtapes in the USA.

Kwanza Musi Dos Santos is an Italian and Afro-Brazilian activist. She has a BA in Political Science and International Relations from the University Roma Tre and is currently working on an MA in Cultural Diversity Management at Tilburg University, the Netherlands. She has published an article on cultural diversity in Italy for *Slow News* magazine. In 2013, she cofounded the antiracist association QuestaèRoma, of which she is president. A guest lecturer on Black Italy at the University of Portland and Montclair State University in 2021, she also lectured at the Black Europe Summer School on Black Italy in 2017, 2018, and 2019.

Sibo Rugwiza Kanobana is an assistant professor in cultural studies at The Open University of the Netherlands. He was a founding member of the hip-hop collective Mobassik and released an album in 2006. In 2017–18, Sibo created and performed *The Reign of Afropeanism* together with performance artist Roland Gunst. Between 2009 and 2013 he was a regular contributor to the Afro-Europe blog and since 2018 he has been editor and writer for *Rekto:Verso*, the Belgian magazine on culture, critique, and society. In 2010, Sibo co-wrote the book *De bastaards van onze kolonie. Verzwegen verhalen van belgische metissen*, which addresses the silenced stories of mixed-race children from Belgian Congo forced into adoption. In 2021, he edited *Zwarte Bladzijden. Afro-Belgische reflecties op Vlaamse (pos)koloniale literatuur*, an anthology of essays that discusses Flemish colonial and postcolonial literature from a Black perspective.

Natasha A. Kelly was born in the UK and raised in Germany. She has a PhD in Communication Studies and Sociology from the University of Münster, Germany. A bestselling author and editor of eight books, Natasha acts as curator, artist, filmmaker, and theater director and has held visiting professorships at numerous universities in Germany and the USA. In 2018 she made her film debut at the 10th Berlin Biennale with her award-winning and internationally distributed documentary "Millis Awakening". As a member of the Black Speculative Arts Movement (BSAM), her academic and artistic works include visions of Black futures. Natasha presently is the founding director of Germany's first independent Institute for Black German Arts and Culture.

James Omolo is a Kenyan living in Poland, and a human rights activist on issues affecting People of African Descent. In December 2019, he was awarded a United Nations Fellowship from the United Nations Office of High Commissioner for Human Rights (OHCHR). He has authored four books on race relations in Poland including *Strangers at the gate: Black Poland*. His past publications also include; Chinese foreign policy in Sudan. James previously served as a lecturer at the University of Social Sciences and Humanities (SWPS) in Warsaw. He has also been a guest lecturer on race relations in several universities in Europe, including the University of Applied Sciences in Potsdam, Germany and the University of Vienna, Austria.

Bernardino Tavares is a postdoctoral researcher on the project "Disentangling Postcolonial Encounters in Globalization" (DisPOSEG) at the University of Luxembourg. He is a sociolinguist committed to a postcolonial and ethnographic enquiry lens. Since 2014, he has researched language, inequalities, and mobilities in/between the Global South and Europe. He is a member of the Institut de Plurilinguisme (University of Fribourg), the Institute for Research on Multilingualism (University of Luxembourg), and the Asociación de Estudios Sobre Discurso y Sociedad (EDiSo). He is also the author of numerous papers. With Kasper Juffermans, he coauthored the book chapters "Language and (Im)mobility as a Struggle: Cape Verdean Trajectories into Luxembourg" (2020) and "South–North Trajectories and Language Repertoires" (2017).

Michelle A. Tisdel has worked as a research librarian at the National Library of Norway since 2008. She holds a PhD in Social Anthropology from Harvard University (2006) based on her research on Cuban museums and Afro-Cuban heritage production. Michelle's research interests include cultural policy, heritage production, and discourses of belonging in Norway and Cuba. She coedited the volume *A Literary Anthropology of Migration and Belonging: Routes, Roots, and Rhizomes* (2020). In 2020, she created Lift Every Voice (LEV), a documentation project about antiracism and civil rights in Norway. She served on the committee for cultural heritage preservation of Arts Council Norway (2009–11). She has also been a member of several boards and is currently chairperson of the organization INN – Ethnic Minorities in Norwegian Cultural Life.

Olive Vassell was born and raised in London. She has an MA in International Journalism, and worked at the British Broadcasting Corporation (BBC) and the UK's Channel 4. After holding several positions in the Black press in the UK and the USA, she headed the pioneering Black European news site, Euromight.com (2009-2022). Olive recently launched BBrit Project, which focuses on People of African Descent in the UK. In 2020, she wrote a chapter on the Black British and Irish Press for *The Edinburgh History of the British and Irish Press, Volume 3: Competition and Disruption, 1900-2017*. In 2022, Olive completed a Fulbright specialist assignment at the Namibia University of Science and Technology. She currently heads the Digital Media program at the University of the District of Columbia in Washington, D.C.

Aleida Vieira is a Cape-Verdean based in Luxembourg. She grew up in Portugal, where she started questioning migration and social justice issues. During her academic trajectory in Lisbon, she joined associations focusing on families and youth with migratory backgrounds. In Luxembourg, she continued this focus where she managed, co-organized, and participated as a speaker at many events aiming to empower women and young people. She received her MA in Engineering of Mediation at the University of Luxembourg (Uni.lu) and is a certified family, legal, civil, and commercial mediator. Aleida is interested in languages from a sociolinguistic perspective, (im)migration, resilience building, and interactions among people with distinct backgrounds and positionings. Currently, at the Uni.lu, she is working in a sociolinguistic-ethnographic study on Lusophone migrants' postcolonial interaction in workplaces they share in Luxembourg.

Historical Sciences

Aurora G. Morcillo
(In)visible Acts of Resistance in the Twilight of the Franco Regime
A Historical Narration

January 2022, 332 p., pb., ill.
50,00 € (DE), 978-3-8376-5257-4
E-Book: available as free open access publication
PDF: ISBN 978-3-8394-5257-8

Jesús Muñoz Morcillo, Caroline Y. Robertson-von Trotha (eds.)
Genealogy of Popular Science
From Ancient Ecphrasis to Virtual Reality

2020, 586 p., pb., col. ill.
49,00 € (DE), 978-3-8376-4835-5
E-Book:
PDF: 48,99 € (DE), ISBN 978-3-8394-4835-9

Monika Ankele, Benoît Majerus (eds.)
Material Cultures of Psychiatry

2020, 416 p., pb., col. ill.
40,00 € (DE), 978-3-8376-4788-4
E-Book: available as free open access publication
PDF: ISBN 978-3-8394-4788-8

All print, e-book and open access versions of the titles in our list are available in our online shop www.transcript-publishing.com!

Historical Sciences

Ulrike Brunotte
The Femininity Puzzle
Gender, Orientalism and the »Jewish Other«

September 2022, 236 p., pb., col. ill.
45,00 € (DE), 978-3-8376-5821-7
E-Book:
PDF: 44,99 € (DE), ISBN 978-3-8394-5821-1

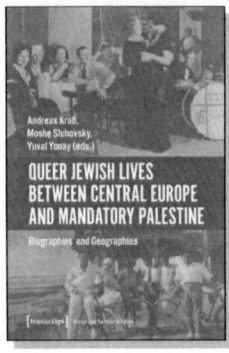

Andreas Kraß, Moshe Sluhovsky, Yuval Yonay (eds.)
Queer Jewish Lives Between Central Europe and Mandatory Palestine
Biographies and Geographies

January 2022, 332 p., pb., ill.
39,99 € (DE), 978-3-8376-5332-8
E-Book:
PDF: 39,99 € (DE), ISBN 978-3-8394-5332-2

Sascha R. Klement
Representations of Global Civility
English Travellers in the Ottoman Empire and the South Pacific, 1636–1863

2021, 270 p., pb.
45,00 € (DE), 978-3-8376-5583-4
E-Book:
PDF: 44,99 € (DE), ISBN 978-3-8394-5583-8

All print, e-book and open access versions of the titles in our list are available in our online shop www.transcript-publishing.com!